Cracking The Matrix

14 Keys to Individual & Global Freedom

Revised Edition

Also by Cate Montana

Unearthing Venus: My Search for the Woman Within

The E Word: Ego, Enlightenment & Other Essentials

Apollo & Me

The Heart of the Matter: A Simple Guide to Discovering Gifts in Strange Wrapping Paper
(co-written with Dr. Darren Weissman)

Ghetto Physics: Redefining the Game
(co-written with William Arntz)

What People Are Saying About

CRACKING THE MATRIX

"*Cracking the Matrix* is a masterpiece revealing the major forces working against us ever reaching the destiny pivotal figures in the history of humanity, such as Jesus of Nazareth or Muhammad, tried to direct us towards attaining. A brilliant analysis of the modern-day issues, Cate Montana's new book is a classic work that will repay seriously pondering its content a hundred-fold."

— **MÍĊEÁL LEDWITH,** L.Ph., L.D., D.D., LL.D.
Author and former advisor to Pope John Paul II

"*Cracking the Matrix* brings the reader face to face with the forces of 'anti-life' – the shadow spell – and then provides a guide on how to break the spell."

— **KINGSLEY L. DENNIS,** author of *Hijacking Reality* and *Healing the Wounded Mind*

"Cate Montana is a compassionate, wise guide who shows us why being in the light requires acknowledging the darkness, without which knowledge our entire culture will remain programmed into a collective blindness."

—**DR. DARREN WEISSMAN,** Developer of The LifeLine Technique® and
Best-selling author of *The Power of Infinite Love & Gratitude*

"Can human beings stand fully in their power while living in idealization and ignorance? Can we thrive while unconsciously under the influence of what can only be called Evil Forces? The answer Cate Montana's latest book presents is a clear "No." *Cracking the Matrix* is a powerful wake-up call, taking evil out of the closet, boldly and factually presenting a case for its very real and chillingly effective presence in our modern-day lives, while giving us simple steps to take to arise out of its hypnotic spell. We ignore the evidence she presents at our peril."

— **SANDIE SEDGBEER,** Host of What is Going Om (OMTimes Radio Network),
founder of The No BS Spiritual Book Club

"The ever-fearless Cate Montana has given us a much needed and timely reminder that we live in a world contested by powers beyond our five senses. In this amazing book she clearly demonstrates the stakes, which have never been higher."

— **JOHN TINTERA,** Publishing Professional

What People Are Saying About

Cracking the Matrix

"*Cracking the Matrix* is magical AND practical, a deep dive into the dark energies that permeate our world. I couldn't put it down!

— **MARLA MARTENSON,** author of *The Magic Seeker*

"*Cracking The Matrix* is a meticulously researched book that explores the dangerous areas where society is heading and the destruction of what makes us human. Not for the faint hearted, but a must read for those who believe there is still hope for humanity."

— **DEBBIE SPECTOR WEISMAN,** author & host of Dream Power Radio podcast & radio shows

"*Cracking the Matrix*, shows us a dark agenda that is more deceptive than any of us could imagine, an agenda that has been going on for longer than any of us have been alive, an agenda to make us feel disempowered and helpless and easily controlled. However, Cate gives us very practical keys to help us break free from these agendas and find peace within simplicity, truth, beauty, and a true understanding of love. Thank you, Cate, for following your own instincts to bring the truth out and free humanity."

— **JEREMY MCDONALD,** author of *Peace Be Still*

"Cate Montana writes like an angel, and the book is full of fascinating and important insights."

— **MITZI PERDUE,** author of *Mark Victor Hansen, RELENTLESS*

Cracking The Matrix

14 Keys to Individual & Global Freedom

Cate Montana

ISBN 979-8-218-09350-1

Cover and interior design by Damian Keenan
Printed and bound in the USA

Cate Montana
Maui, HAWAII
2023

To all who sincerely desire to be free.

Wisdom is knowing how little we know.
— SOCRATES

Contents

CRACKING THE MATRIX

INTRODUCTION

Up until recently, the words "interdimensional forces" weren't even crossword entries in my mind. And about the last thing I ever thought I'd write about is what humanity has termed (rather erroneously, as it turns out) evil itself. I'm a nice person. My friends and clients and neighbors are nice. Even my ex-husbands are nice. My entire career centers around writing uplifting spiritual books and articles about alternative health and consciousness.

On a personal level, evil is nowhere in sight.

But the world in which I live is another matter.

You don't have to be a conspiracy theorist to realize that our so-called modern Western civilization is screwed up beyond hope of genuine repair. Plugging the holes in the dike against the tsunami of corporate and political corruption, greed, global conflict, economic corrosion, pollution, resource depletion, lies, moral decay, sickness and personal despair, is a losing battle.

It's a losing battle not only because things are basically fubar. (A technical engineering term I learned in my network television production days lightyears ago.) But also, because our entire social construct has been built upon a lie.

Several, actually.

Personally, I think our best bet is to have done with the entire decomposing edifice and let it slide into the abyss and start over. Thankfully, breakdown, as appalling as it is to experience, is also the precursor to breakthrough. So, on the one hand, our future is bright!

On the other hand, we still have to get there.

It is in the spirit of getting there that this book presents a radical explanation for Western civilization's current condition. It also presents a pathway through the nightmare, describing the evolution of the kind of consciousness necessary to avoid repeating, out of blind hubris, our past mistakes. It also lights a torch, presenting a powerful vision of what can be built once people remember Who They Really Are—beings of pure love on an eternal journey of evolution and discovery.

Without a doubt, these pages contain heretical information, although not in a religious sense. My friend Míceál Ledwith, former Catholic priest, professor of theology, and advisor to Pope John Paul II, has graciously acknowledged the truth behind my basic explanation, as I know many other religious authorities will. (Although they undoubtedly will reject most of my accompanying religious commentary.) A few spiritual teachers might get onboard. Certainly, the shamans of the world will nod, yawn, and say, "What took you so long to talk about this?"

But as far as the modern, social world is concerned? If there is such a thing as the typical John or Jane Doe on the street, most would probably regard the whole topic of evil, let alone the presence of interdimensional beings on this planet, as superstitious at best, superfluous or even taboo at worst.

It's fine to terrorize children (and adults) in movie theatres with images of devils, demons, wraiths and all sorts of horrific alien creatures on screen. It's all just good fun. But present unseen intelligences with their own agendas interpenetrating this physical reality as fact?

Uh ... no.

Our general love affair with scientific, intellectual rationality—our "seeing is believing" myopia—has blinded us to much of what our global history has to say, as well as much of what is presently going on in the world right before our astonished, dismayed eyes.

We see and yet don't see. We believe the growing devastation is solely caused by us—stupid, greedy, evil, short-sighted, lazy humans. But it is not. Yes, most certainly, humanity has contributed, at various levels to various degrees, to creating the mess we're in. Like pawns on a chessboard, we've allowed ourselves to be moved into position to take the fall. And yet, contrary to popular belief, humanity is not to blame.

Stupid, greedy, blind, lazy, complicit, ignorant, naive, gullible ... yes.

To blame? No.

This staggering truth is not hidden. But it takes an open mind and some digging to get to the supporting facts, and then some willingness to examine them.

I'd like to thank in advance some of the people upon whose research much of the foundation of this book has been built: Paul Levy, Paul Wallis, Zacharia Sitchin, Erich von Däniken, Graham Hancock, David Icke, and many other brave beings pointing stalwart fingers at the obvious unobvious all around us.

I'd also like to thank you, dear reader, for your inquisitiveness and willingness to boldly draw back the curtain to see what's pulling the strings behind the show.

Cate Montana
Maui, Hawaii
April, 2023

PART I

BLINDED

1

A Wakeup Call

The world is currently in the after-throes of a global pandemic. Personal liberty is under attack, democratic nations are becoming more autocratic and totalitarian. Global media censorship is crippling the free flow of scientific and medical debate. Politicians spew Orwellian "double-speak." Nobody knows what's true and what's not. Families, congregations, clubs, towns, states, political parties and nations are violently split asunder.

Why is this happening?

What's really going on?

Why, 2500 years after Gautama Buddha brought lessons of enlightenment and 2000 years after Jesus walked the earth teaching about love and eternal life, is humanity floundering like an elephant in quicksand, sinking fast?

Why, despite thousands of religions and spiritual teachings pointing out that human beings are *non-physical spirit beings*, have we never caught on to the reality of the situation? Why, despite science's corroborating discovery over 100 years ago that matter and pure energy are the same thing, do we still not get it?

We are eternal beings of pure love who have chosen to experience the most miraculous thing in the cosmos: Life in an energy body that is created to *seem* physical, dwelling on a larger energy body called a planet (and a stupendously beautiful planet at that), having all kinds of adventures. But instead of acting like the loving, eternal, creative beings we are, we're trundling around in a daze, believing we're nothing more than walking talking lumps of clay.

We think we're dumb animals that have to be led and whipped into some sort of shape in order to be made presentable to a God that presumably created us as perfect ... but then we obviously screwed *that* up, so here we all are, reaping our just yet terrible desserts.

We've taken this sad, impossibly wrong story and run with it for millennia trying to make up for our awfulness. Now, two decades into the 21st century, despite all our efforts to be good, despite our desire to evolve and change, despite great knowledge and technological know-how and a million self-help books, we seem to be devolving, teetering on the very brink of self-destruction.

Why?

From my introduction, you already know the answer. Humanity is, and has been for some time, in the grip of a powerful, intelligent, interdimensional Force—an all-pervasive, destructive influence that has thrived on this planet, sucking most of humanity into its orbit, much like a black hole swallows everything that comes within its gravitational grasp, including light.

Priests and shamans, psychics and mediums, medicine men and women, witch doctors and televangelists have all been pointing out the existence of this hostile Force for ages. But for the average person growing up in the 20th and 21st centuries, accepting a negative alien Presence on this planet as something that's actually separate and *real* is a difficult thing to do. For most of us, nowadays, evil is nothing more than a concept ... a vague threat associated with sermons from the pulpit and horror movies like *The Exorcist, The Omen, Constantine,* and *Hellboy.* Making what amounts to an enormous existential switch takes some doing.

I only recently awakened to the reality of this hostile Force when a confluence of "coincidences" in the form of global events, books, videos, conversations and interviews collided with spiritual teachings and hundreds of my own face-to-face encounters with these negative interdimensional beings.

When the whole Covid debacle hit in 2020, I was suddenly confronted with a perfect storm of *external* evidence that perfectly matched up with the frightening *internal* encounters I had had with this Force—encounters I had marginalized, trivialized and ignored for far too long. Watching the world's rapid descent into fear-driven madness, standing firm in my own experiential knowledge base, I could no longer maintain the illusion that humanity's spiritual, mental, emotional and societal degeneration was solely of our own doing.

Something else was going on.

The ah ha! was sudden, but it came as a natural result of a lot of little pieces coming together over a long period of time.

So, why haven't human beings, as a whole, seen this Force and dealt with it?

Good question. And the answer is really quite simple, if multilayered. 1) The beings plaguing us are etheric and non-physical. They are most easily seen in the astral realms and when they work *through us.* 2) We have been programmed to believe this degenerate, anti-life Force originates *within us,* so we don't spend any time searching for outside causes of our dilemma. 3) Nobody likes to look at scary stuff except in the movies. And last but not least, 4) these technologically advanced, spiritless beings have created a thought matrix of lies, a mental reality for us to live in that keeps us relatively oblivious and fundamentally cooperative with their agenda.

But the matrix is rapidly unraveling. Ever since the Wachowski brothers (now sisters) delivered the movie *The Matrix* in 1999, pretty much everybody in the world with media access knows the basic plot about humanity being hijacked into a computer simulation. Millions, if not billions, of people can identify the following lines:

> **Morpheus:** The matrix is everywhere. It is all around us. ... It is the world that has been pulled over your eyes to blind you from the truth.
>
> **Neo:** What truth?
>
> **Morpheus:** That you are a slave, Neo. Like everyone else you were born into bondage. Into a prison that you cannot taste or see or touch. A prison for your mind.

Like Neo in the movie, most of us have felt all our lives that something isn't quite right here on planet Earth. Deep down we sense the world is not supposed to be this way—this hurtful, this joyless and nonsensical.

And yet what else is on offer?

The magnetic pull that guides you to go sit quietly in nature. The communal closeness you feel with family and friends. The kindness and concern you feel for people you don't even know. The tenderness and compassion you extend to animals. The awe you feel seeing a dewdrop reflecting the morning light.

None of this is supported.

Nothing of this is encouraged.

Global cultures are somehow perfectly constructed to steer us *away* from expressing our innate goodness and loving nature. Materialism, money, media, porn, drugs, war, politics, poverty, Covid, fame, power, prestige—all of these things seem skillfully and purposefully designed to keep you and me stressed, frightened, and at each other's throats.

Via one program or another, society relentlessly keeps us from discovering and expressing the beauty and unfathomable power that lie within each of us, sending us down a different path than the one our hearts would actually choose if left unmolested. Within the imprisoning web that has been spun, the unique song we were each born to sing is squashed before it can rise to our lips. And we despair that there is so little meaning and love in the world around us.

So, what inhuman Intelligence created this program? How is it getting away with it? Is humanity complicit? How? Are there humans aligned with this Force, deliberately carrying out its agendas? What can we do about it? Is there hope?

Answering those questions is what this book is about. And I'm not going to make you wait for the most import answer of all:

> ***It is inevitable that this vampiric, interdimensional Presence will soon be sent slinking back to whatever anti-life source it sprang from uncounted millennia ago.***

But here's the deal. A necessary part of making that happen is us waking up to this Force's presence and no longer blindly supporting its goals. We must embrace a larger picture of reality and understand all the various players, forces and dynamics involved in life on planet Earth. Most of all, we must remember Who We Really Are and start living from our true nature.

Pure Love

And if a part of you quails at the thought of accepting that an evil Intelligence exists; if part of you is frightened at the prospect of facing evil square on; if you would rather cut and run; if you would rather count rosary beads or call on Jesus or Allah or say a mantra or pull a curtain of white light around yourself and wish it all away; if you would like to believe that nothing like this could possibly exist, I totally understand.

I've been there. With the exception of the rosary beads and calling on Allah, I've done all of that. We've all been doing all those things and ever so much more for thousands of years, desperately trying to figure out what's wrong so we can fix it, and we're *still* sliding into the pit. Unfortunately, none of our old beliefs and actions have gotten us anywhere because they are *all* based upon one simple, erroneous belief that's been relentlessly pressed to us: That it's *us* that is the problem. That it's *us* that need to be fixed.

This is the foundational lie.

This is the core program these non-physical, interdimensional beings have designed and programmed into us. *And, being the powerful creators that we are, by accepting this lie, it is us who make the lie into a reality.*

Get it? Pretty slick, right?

So, what can we do about it?

Well, first and foremost: See the lie.

From personal experience I can tell you there is something deeply, quietly, authentically transformative about turning to face your greatest fear. And let's face it, humanity's greatest unnamed abyssal fear has *always* been the darkness and what it contains.

But here's the thing. Once we face evil it dissolves. Not because we were powerful enough to overcome it. But because once we face evil, we see it for what it is:

Not Us

These beings don't belong on this planet. Evil is not a part of us because it's not frequency specific with Who We Really Are: Spirit beings of pure love.

Love and evil are like oil and water.

It's like two magnets repelling each other.

It's life versus anti-life.

Once we see evil for what it is and stop adopting it as part of us, we finally see ourselves as we truly are and set ourselves free. *That* is when we step into our power. That is the "open sesame" to the long-prophesized New Heaven and New Earth.

Are the times dire? Yes, they are. But we are waking up. People are seeing through the matrix. The ancient Presence among us is losing its grip. Like vampires in the movies, they cannot stand in the light of day. Being seen, they fade away.

So, let's part the shades and throw open the window.

CHAPTER ONE KEY

Stop and remember you are Spirit

I was sitting here trying to come up with a way to begin this journey out of the matrix. Finally, I stopped, closed my eyes and just sat, silent and unthinking. And it hit me, that is exactly the First Key.

- Next time you're faced with a conundrum, a puzzle, a choice ... stop for a moment.
- Don't try to figure things out immediately.
- Take a breath.
- Ask from your spirit nature of pure love: "What's best to do here?"
- Now *listen.*

As citizens of planet Earth, we have been assiduously programmed to believe we are purely physical, and that our only choice is to do things the hard way—to wrack our brains and toil and sweat and strain throughout our lives.

So, rest for a moment and realize that that is not how a beautiful spirit approaches life.

I'm not saying you won't ever have to work again. I'm not saying you'll never write another To Do list or angst over another quadratic equation. I'm just saying *the first step to regaining awareness of your spirit nature is to start acting like a spirit being instead of a spiritual person.* And the way to start doing that is to turn to spirit *first* for answers, then be quiet enough to hear the still small voice within.

It may take a while or no time at all. But the answer will become apparent.

Just pause, remember your true nature, and ask for what you need to come to you. Then let it go.

Don't sit and sweat. Don't tap your toes, impatiently waiting for "it" to arrive. It's not even important that what you ask for shows up. That's not the real point here. The real point is that:

You acted like a spirit being instead of a human being.

This simple shift from immediate mental effort towards easeful deep listening is what triggers a rearrangement of self-identity, which then opens the door for more and more information and grace to flow your way.

The more you do this the more easily and quickly things will happen. And remember, you're asking, not as an inept weak human begging God for something, but as a great spirit turning at last to your own nature, recognizing your own power and infinite resources, opening the door to what needs to come to uplift you and help set you free.

2

My Name is Legion for We Are Many

Until I was 16, my mother dragged me to the local Episcopal church twice a month on Sunday, not because she was all that religious, but because she wanted to make sure she was doing her duty raising a proper God-fearing Christian daughter. At that point I convinced her I'd absorbed all the religion necessary to make me a good person and escaped from church completely.

But by age thirty, recovering from a divorce, drinking too much, overstimulated in a high-stress career in network television production, relatively depressed and completely rudderless, I realized something was deeply missing and that nothing in the outer world could fulfill me. At that point, it seemed the only other logical path to follow lay inward.

For several years I wandered from spiritual teaching to spiritual teaching, exposing myself to a wide variety of messages, most of which blended together talks about angel guides, meditation, chakras,[1] the "Higher Self," and various methods of "realizing God" (consciously uniting with the divine). One teacher, however, stood out from the crowd by casually saying during a retreat one day, "By the way, when you die, for God's sake, whatever you do, don't go to the light."

What? I thought. *Don't go to the light? Everybody goes to the light.*

New Age spirituality was all about the Light with a capital "L." We were beings of Light. The Light was our salvation. Every story of a near-death experience involved people talking about the amazing love, beauty and magnetism of the Light. The Light was where family and friends and your dog went when they died. That's where God resided.

Why not go there?

I'm paraphrasing here, but basically the answer was: Because that light is a false projection and not the light you're looking for, which is *within* you.

Because the beings that created that false light designed it as a trap.

If you go to the light when you die, you will be stripped of your memories—all except your crappiest moments which you will be shown over and over again while these non-physical beings feed on the energy of your sorrow, regret, anger, guilt and shame. When done, they'll cavalierly toss your soul back to Earth to enter another body where they will continuously feed on all the negative emotions experienced during *that* life—negative emotions that they program the conditions on Earth to produce—and then do the stripping/feeding process again at your next death.

And on and on and on.

As the early 20th century British poet and historian Robert Graves described it in his poem "Instructions to the Orphic Adept:"

> So soon as ever your mazed spirit descends
> From daylight into darkness, Man, remember
> What you have suffered here in Samothrace,
> What you have suffered.
> After your passage through Hell's seven floods,
> Whose fumes of Sulphur will have parched your throat,
> The Halls of Judgement shall loom up before you,
> A miracle of jasper and of onyx.
> To the left hand there bubbles a black spring
> Overshadowed with a great white cypress.
> Avoid this spring, which is Forgetfulness;
> Though all the common rout rush down to drink,
> Avoid this spring! [2]

I remember being horrified receiving this teaching. Reincarnation was supposed to be an opportunity for continued learning and growth as a soul, not some vampiric energy recycling system.

But the story didn't stop there.

Apparently, the beings perpetrating this had been on Earth for a very long time, were non-physical yet capable of taking form through us and apparently lived mostly underground. They had achieved a high level of energetic technology by which they constantly beamed negative images and low frequency messages around the world—frequencies designed to foster war, division and turmoil as well as trigger intense emotional pain and suffering in humans. These emotions they used as an energetic food source. Their ultimate agenda was to terraform the planet into a hotter, drier climate and alter our genetics to make our bodies more serviceable for their own use instead of ours.

I didn't know what to think hearing all this. But I trusted and admired the teacher giving the information, so I decided to poke around a little bit. This led to studies on the seamier side of things—ancient aliens, crop circles, cattle mutilations, alien abductions, and subterranean serpent beings preying upon an unsuspecting humanity.

Needless to say, I didn't sleep very well for a couple years doing such reading. Not only was the content frightening, it was disturbing how much of the information actually seemed decently researched. Let's just take the topic of undiscovered subterranean civilizations for example. An idea that initially sounded absurd, I was startled to discover just how extensive and relatively unexplored subterranean systems are on this planet.

The underground city of Derinkuyu in Turkey is believed to have been created around 800 BCE (or much earlier) and was discovered in the 20th century. It is 18 stories deep, fitted with thousands of ventilation shafts and waterways supplying air and water to rooms at each level of the site. Capable of housing over 20,000 people it is connected to another underground city miles away called Kaymakli.[3] There are all sorts of legends about subterranean passageways connecting the Giza pyramids to temples in Luxor. An ancient unknown civilization referred to as the Gizeh people is reputed to exist over 500 feet below the surface of the Giza Plateau.[4]

Some tunnels are said to connect Giza to other underground cities in Eastern Europe and the Balkans. In the small village of Casal Paula in Malta, in 1902 workmen discovered a series of underground rooms now called The Maltese Caves. Legends say they contain passages connected to rooms as far away as the Catacombs of Rome.[5]

The village of Liyobaa located in the province of Zapoteca in Mexico contains temples, several of which are subterranean, one of which is referred to as The Cavern of Death. Sealed off by the Mexican government, it is said to connect to miles of subterranean chambers. In South America an ancient system of underground cities is believed to extend throughout the Andes mountain range of Peru all the way to Lima and down to the Chilean border.[6]

Several underground cities are rumored to be located in or near the Himalayan mountains, including an underground system of caves near the Tibetan capital of Lhasa.

America is no stranger to rumors of subterranean civilizations either.

In 1885, the *New York Times* apparently ran a story about an ancient underground city found by coal miners in Moberly, Missouri.[7] There are all sorts of reports of alien beings, reptilian and otherwise, inhabiting underground cities below the Superstition Mountains east of Phoenix.[8] Vast underground complexes have been reported in California, Pennsylvania, Arizona, Arkansas and Utah. And, of course, in the Grand Canyon region, Hopi legends refer to ancient ancestors who lived underground, uncomfortably close to an even deeper underground complex inhabited by a lizard race.[9]

It was all definitely food for thought.

But strangely, as macabre as some of the material got, there was never any talk about evil per se. That, it seemed, was a topic best relegated to religion. About the only reference to evil that I ever ran across in my early years of spiritual study was the book *The People of the Lie* by the psychiatrist M. Scott Peck, Ph.D. In it he talked about the nature of evil and how it reveals itself through people. From what I recall, his foundational opinion was that it manifests as a conscious desire to inflict pain on others in order to receive pleasure from witnessing their suffering.

As a psychiatrist, he didn't spend a lot of time placing evil in any sort of spiritual context, and I somehow failed to associate his insights with the possible presence of an advanced race of underground beings and their energetic cannibalism. I just filed the information away and never really thought about any of it again.

Until now.

The Great Deceiver, the Slanderer, the Tempter, the Evil One, the Angel of the Bottomless Pit, the Father of Lies, the Great Enemy. These are just a few common descriptors of the presence I'm talking about.

For the ancient Greeks it was the Archons—the rulers of Earth who were malevolent, sadistic beings controlling the thoughts, feelings and actions of humans. For Christians it's Satan or the devil, Belial or Beelzebub. For the Hebrews it's Abaddon. In Islam it's Iblis or AshShaytān. Buddhism teaches that we are not inherently evil, but that we create evil because Mara—the demon who tempted Siddartha and who is "the personification of the forces antagonistic to enlightenment" is whispering in our ear.

The Gnostic text *Pistis Sophia* calls the antimimon pneuma (evil principle) an illness that has attached itself to humankind. Because it does not have a physical form, this illness uses us as vehicles to manifest *its* desire, creating a physical reality to *its* liking. The Apocryphon of John calls it a "counterfeiting spirit" that numbs and toughens human hearts, closing us down, making us small and twisted like itself, with the intention of eventually creating a prison-like reality that it can rule over forever.

For the Hawaiian kahunas the presence of an evil malevolent force destructive to mankind is called the 'e'epa. For the Cree tribes in America the evil whisperer is wetiko. To the Algonquin tribes it's windingo, a hunger-driven cannibal. For Chinese and Tibetan Buddhists, it's the hungry ghosts of insatiable desire whipping us along the trail to self-destruction.

According to the book *Wetiko*, by Paul Levy, Swiss psychiatrist Carl Jung called this deceiving force "antimimos, the imitator and evil principle" and equated it with the Antichrist. The Russian mystic philosopher George Gurdjieff called it "the machine." Sri Aurobindo, an Indian philosopher and guru, termed it the Hostile Forces.[10] Hollywood portrays these entities as vampires. Modern-day philosophers and science fiction writers often refer to these Forces as the mind parasites.

Most of the time, these entities take form *through* us in some sort of parasitic way, the worst cases of which show up as total possession.

Traits in common that it evidences through us are deception, sadism, perversion, and an insatiable hunger for power and twisted emotions and an overindulgence in food, sex, drugs—any and all substances available to mankind which this Force feeds on through us—none of which can ever fill the aching black emptiness of its ghastly void-like existence. Another common characteristic is that these beings are imitators. People possessed by these demons can imitate what love looks and acts like, although they do not know or feel love.

As ugly and concrete as the *effects* these beings have, their actual presence is almost impossible to pinpoint and describe. This Hostile Force is the ultimate shapeshifter. I've actually read whole books about the Archons/wetiko and at the end still didn't understand exactly what they are. As non-physical and interdimensional, this Force most commonly shows up in what is known as the astral levels of existence—forms that correspond in some spiritual traditions with the human emotional body, the highly sensitive non-physical "sheath" that lies closest to the physical body in vibratory frequency.

Small. Large. Winged. Wingless. Fanged. Horned. Toothless. Appearances vary wildly. It's like this evil Force worms its way inside and learns what scares us most and that's how it shows up. I've seen some of these beings in the astral realms taking the amorphous shape of a human body with a crocodile head (similar to figures carved on ancient Egyptian temple walls) and snakes with quasi-reptilian humanoid heads.

No matter what their appearance, the inescapable nature of these thought forms weaving between non-physicality and the physical world is to prod, goad and prick humans into doing despicable acts so that they descend into debauchery and supply the powerful emotional energy these beings rely on for sustenance, both via the victims they pursue and their victims' victims—as in situations where they have managed to drive a person to rape, mutilation (of self and others), torture and grotesque murders.

It's like this Force has no life of its own sufficient to call it "causal." And yet its effects are profound to the point they are its most defining characteristic.

An invisible, non-living Force that drains all that is lively and lovely away, the Archons suck the light out of a person's eyes and all warmth out of the human heart. They feed on the life force, subconscious fears and insecurities and any powerful emotion. They twist goodness, pervert beauty, debase sexuality, crush hope and corrupt creativity while voraciously asserting more influence, power and control over their victims, eating away at their spirit.

And yet these Beings easily slip away from sight and defy all concrete description. In keeping with its chimerical nature, I vary the name of this presence throughout this book, most often calling it the evil Force, the hidden Force, the anti-life Force, the Archons, wetiko, 'e'epa and mind parasites. My favorite epithet, however, is the anti-life Force, because that's what it most seems to be.

I could also call it the anti-love Force, because the life force and the force called "love" are one and the same. But since there is so much superficial programming around the word "love," I won't use that term. Just please keep it in mind.

How have Westerners overlooked the fact that hundreds of geographically dispersed cultures over thousands of years have created the same "myth" of horrific ephemeral tormenters? Why has such a ubiquitous evil presence written about with such authority by some of the greatest minds the world has ever known been consigned to mere myth in most peoples' minds?

How has such a powerful Force been reduced to a horror movie plot device?

Two things. First off, surprisingly, the Old Testament Bible has nothing to say about "the devil" or some overarching evil Force. The word is never used. There are a few references to an "adversary" (the proper translation of the word "satan" in Hebrew), many of which are in a political context. We have a snake in the Garden of Eden playing the role of tempter. And there a few references to demons stirring things up occasionally. That's it.

There is no Old Testament support for this overarching presence.

In the New Testament, however, references to "satan" begin to proliferate—mostly in the context of evil tendencies within mankind. In Judaism as well, "satan" is not an actual being, but rather a metaphor for our evil inclinations, the "yetzer hara" in every person. Same thing in Islam.

The New Testament introduces evil as a human characteristic, not something external.

By the time the New Testament was officially adopted at the Synod of Hippo in 393 AD, there was a lot of stuff about original sin. The basic concept of inherent evil in man was introduced by a repentant Augustine of Hippo (354-430 AD). Despite the fact that his mother was a devout Christian, Augustine spent much of his early life as a sexual reprobate and atheist. Ignoring his mother's tears and lamentations over his fallen state, Augustine continued his life of sin until he was introduced to the religious philosophy known as Manichaeism.

Manichaeism, as set forth by the Babylonian prophet Mani (216 AD), outlines the struggle between a good, spiritual world of light and an evil material world of darkness where every person is born into sin merely by the fact of being physical. Mani arrived at this view because he was coached into it by what he called his "other self"—an invisible "spirit" that talked to him.

Spirit? Or Archon?

We'll never know. But the fact that the concept of original sin—the single most insidious and corrosive idea that has ever been introduced to humanity—was proposed by some disembodied "voice" is indeed suspect. And the fact that a guilt-ridden Augustine picked up the concept and ran with it as a way to explain and excuse his own sinful youth is suspect as well.

The whole setup reeks of Archon influence.

Unfortunately, Augustine was a brilliant scholar and thinker who heavily influenced Catholic creed for centuries—so much so that he was granted saint status by Pope Boniface VIII in 1298. His mother, Monica, was given much of the credit for his turnaround later in life, sainted and proclaimed the Patron Saint of Mothers.

Augustine's argument that mankind is inherently evil has been indelibly stamped upon Christianity, Judaism, Islam and the psyche of much of humanity ever since—successfully turning away attention from any *external* Force of evil and placing it inwards.

Our entry into what is referred to as the "Age of Reason" in the 18th century was the icing on the cake. The elevation of science and logic guaranteed a carte blanche dismissal of stories about an evil Presence as superstitious nonsense. Any person or culture who believed in such things was labeled "primitive" at best.

If there was any explanation given for the hundreds of cultures around the world that came up with eerily similar descriptions of invisible demons, it was that these primitive peoples must have externalized their own malevolence, giving it a variety of shapes and names so that they didn't have to take responsibility for it.

In other words, it was all simply a common psychological projection.

Really?

Never mind most of the "primitive" cultures supposedly doing this fancy projecting were talking about evil spirits long before anybody ever heard of original sin. Never mind native tribespeople living so close to the land most likely had few deeply twisted psychological issues to even project. (That's *our* gig!)

Early peoples who talked about this Presence lived grounded in nature. They were incredibly sensitive to elemental forces. They could sense and see elemental beings. As English author/philosopher Kingsley Dennis writes in his excellent essay "Changes in Humanity's Spiritual Make-up:"

> "Until the time of ancient Greece, the living human body was determined and maintained by the immediate environment. Human beings were intimately bound up with the space immediately around them. ... [Today] people perceive the world around them, in so far as it is perceptible to the senses, in quite a different way from the ancient Greeks, for example. The Greeks also saw colours and heard sounds; but they still saw spiritual entities through the colours. ... Modern people think thoughts. The Greeks did not think thoughts in the same degree; they saw the thoughts which came to them out of the world they perceived

> around them. This created an intimate relationship to the world. It also created an intense feeling of being connected with an environment which had spiritual qualities."[11]

Not only were non-physical beings clearly perceived by the general populace, the priestesses and shamans of the ancient civilizations blatantly dealt with these interdimensional creatures in ceremonies and in their healing work all the time.

They still do.

I have lived and worked with traditional Peruvian shamans raised deep in the Amazon jungle who were trained since childhood to perform ayahuasca and other types of serious healing ceremonies. And they *all* talk about dealing with these Forces and entities. They all talk about how omnipresent these being are and how modern man is clueless about its own possession by these entities. They worry about New Age "wannabe shamans" trying to heal people in ceremonies when few can even perceive these interdimensional beings and even fewer know how to command and clear them out of peoples' energy fields.

The Archons—these ancient bedeviling energy beings—are just a fact of life to indigenous shamans. But us "modern" folk? Without psychic perception, we're basically blind as bats.

The physical human eye can detect wavelengths roughly between 380 to 700 nanometers in length. These are the wavelengths that constitute the visible light spectrum. Some animals can see into the infrared range (>700 nanometers) or ultraviolet range (<380 nanometers). But compared to the *infinite range of possible wavelengths* that might be perceived in the universe—down to the level of the Planck Scale and up to the size of our universe—the visible light portion of this universe's electromagnetic spectrum amounts to about zero percent.[12]

Despite the fact that our physical senses are capable of perceiving next to nothing of what's going on around us in the universe, hundreds of years of materially-based scientific study have convinced us that we know what's going on. That we own "the truth" about life and all of existence. Science and logic arrogantly propose that we're highly advanced and on top of the game.

And yet nothing could be further from the truth.

Society is deteriorating and the world is being destroyed before our very eyes. We're being marched, roughshod, in a direction almost nobody wants to go. Since Covid, the world has descended into madness.

And we think we've got a handle on "reality" and all it contains?

How could such a warped perception possibly arise unless our individual and collective minds had been hypnotized into some kind of slumber?

And if we are asleep, lost in a matrix of some diabolical design, what are the consequences if we do nothing and refuse to wake up? Paul Levy and Larry Dossey, M.D. authors of the most excellent book *Wetiko: Healing the Mind Virus That Plagues Our World* have this to say:

> "If we don't use the divine gift of our creative imagination in the service of life, these adversarial mental forces will use our imagination for (and against) us, with deadly consequences. Once it "puts us on," fooling us into buying into its version of who we are, it can then piggyback onto and plug into our intrinsic creativity. In this, it coopts our creative imagination to serve its malevolent, inhumane, and soulless agenda.
>
> In essence, when we are under the thrall of wetiko, the creative spirit within us—the very function that connects us to something beyond ourselves—becomes malnourished and impoverished. We then can't even imagine things being any other way, let alone being able to actively imagine a way out of our dilemma. This points to the profound importance for each of us to intimately connect with the creative spirit living within us as a way of abolishing wetiko's spiritual death sentence. These deceivers of the mind continually encourage us to indulge in our lower, more base impulses, offering us every justification imaginable for doing so. To the extent we are not awake, the 'e'epa/wetiko virus knows our mind better than we do. With the 'e'epa/wetiko virus, it is as if an alien, metaphysical "other" is subliminally insinuating its own thought-forms and beliefs into our own mind, which if identified with, compel us to act against our own best interests.

To recognize them is to see through their deception, which is their worst nightmare as they are rendered impotent once they are seen. Recognizing—and then dealing with—their covert psychological operations within our minds is the first stage of a transformational process. This process potentially leads us to cross an event horizon within our minds through which we enter a new world in which nothing is ever the same. Recognizing who and what the 'e'epa are, helps us to more easily recognize who we are, and our potential for spiritual evolution then becomes practically limitless."

Years ago, I wrote a novel called *Apollo & Me.* As the themes unfolded, the idea that evil is a distinct anti-life intelligence was seriously pressed to me. I reluctantly wrote about spiritless beings posing as gods that fed upon the fear and worship of primitive peoples they ruled over, moving from planet to planet over the course of billions of years.

A moveable feast, as it were.

I wrote that it was this malevolent Force and not God talking to Moses. That it was this anti-life Force that introduced the concept of original sin, whispering in the ears of early prophets (and guilt-ridden wannabee saints), pushing the lie that *we* are the problem, that *humans* are the evil ones.

I look back now and marvel at how spot on the plot was.

But back in 2015 it was just a story idea that wouldn't go away ... a subconscious voice waving a flag saying "Hey, look at this!" Back then, my spiritual and social programming wouldn't let me see or contemplate any of it as actually *real.*

Even if I'd seen all the pieces I'm finally putting together here, I couldn't have written about it the way I am now because I would have been too frightened to do so. Why? Because up until recently I was too deeply under the spell of these mind parasites to be able to expose them—aside from writing a fictional story—for fear that something bad would happen to me if I did.

This, of course, is the reason most people don't address the topic of evil: *They're afraid.* And rightfully so if you're still stuck believing evil is a part of you. It is this one terribly effective lie that keeps humanity cowed with a jackboot across our necks. We haven't realized evil has no power in and of itself. Haven't understood that the only power evil has is the power *we* give it.

And we give it lots of power. Bucket loads. Tons.

Buying the story that *we* are evil not only do human beings end up afraid of the dark, we end up frightened of *ourselves*. My dear, long-dead mother was one of the sweetest, most obedient souls I've ever known. She got a college degree, married into her socio-economic bracket, raised her family, took care of her aging parents, went to church, paid her taxes and never said an unkind word about anyone. And she *hated* herself. She was terrified to look within herself lest she be forced to see the wickedness she was certain resided there. The palest hint of the occult—even telling ghost stories around the campfire—traumatized her.

That's how much power she unconsciously gave the Archons.

That's how much power billions of people unconsciously give this anti-life Force every day. Because believing this Force is part of us and thus too powerful to withstand *is* terrifying. And our terror drives our focus *away* from paying attention to it.

Which means we stay stuck.

We never cross the "event horizon" and never gain entrance to the new world in which nothing is ever the same.

I will state it boldly: When I turned and faced this presence and realized my innate purity, I crossed the event horizon.

And nothing is the same.

Collectively, if humanity doesn't turn and do the same thing—if we don't step out of our hypnotic trance—we won't see our goodness. We won't rise to our potential. We won't create a world that is the most beautiful place possible for ourselves and all the rest of the amazing creatures populating this planet.

We will stay frightened and controllable.

Which is just what this Force intends.

CHAPTER TWO KEY

Examine your thoughts about evil and understand it is not you

PART I

- Give yourself a nice chunk of time and go sit somewhere in nature to contemplate. Turn off your phone. Now, what is evil to you? What were you taught about it? How does it show up for you?

Do textbook images from your religious upbringing come up? Does evil seem far away and insubstantial? Does it bring to mind images of worldly life?

- If you find yourself coming to the conclusion that "Evil isn't so bad. What's the big deal?" you're not looking at the reality of evil. You're thinking in terms of bad versus good.

It's hard not to confuse being bad with being evil these days when religion has condemned people to eternal hellfire for not believing in Scripture or for having sex before marriage, calling such acts "evil." This kind of programming confuses people about what evil is—which is a major reason it continues.

Evil is not about being a bad person who lies or cheats or steals—somebody who occasionally kicks the dog or beats their wife or slut shames their daughter in public.

- To get a handle on what evil is, contemplate a few things that go on *all the time* on this planet and reassess.
  - Imagine the ritual group rape of a five-year-old child and imagine the parents both facilitating and participating
  - Imagine horrific torture for the fun of it
  - Ritual cannibalism

    - The deliberate use of starvation to eliminate millions of people
    - Military forces raping little girls, women and old women to humiliate and control a population
- Imagine these things and briefly *feel* into them. *Feel* the ghastly horror of such things.

I know it's extremely unpleasant, but feeling is the key. If we are numb and unfeeling as a population—and we are fast being driven in that direction—anything can be perpetrated upon us.

Now, here comes the hard part.

PART II

- Do you have fantasies, sexual and otherwise, that include pain, abuse, and degradation? This includes gang rape fantasies, enslavement fantasies, torture during sex etc.

I'm not talking about enjoying the sense of sexual domination, which about 65 percent of women and 53 percent of men admit to. I'm not talking about fantasizing multiple sex partners and a little bondage play. I'm talking deliberate pain, degradation and abuse and getting off on it.

If your answer is "Yes," or a quavering "Maybe," understand that *this is not part of who you really are*. These types of acts and the imagery of such acts have been programmed into us in a deliberate campaign to defile the Life Force and the very act of creation itself.

These types of fantasies lower our electromagnetic frequency—they dim our light. And as our frequency lowers, it opens the door for penetration and overshadowing by the Archons because they operate at a lower frequency than we do. *This is one way they get in.*

I speak about this from experience.

When I was five years old, I started having nightmares about torture chambers. What I believed were dreams became more and more real until I didn't know what they were. But the images of writhing bloody bodies and the screams horrified me. The worst "dream" was of me standing on a slave block in some city during Roman times. I was pregnant and a soldier stepped up to the block with a short sword and slit my belly open. I died in a pool of blood trying to save my baby, clutching it to my breasts as the bearded soldier laughed at me.

I had seen no movies or books about torture, Roman culture, short swords, or slavery. There was absolutely no logical reason images like this were in my head. Where did they come from? Back then I had no idea.

The torture images persisted through puberty and soon became linked to self-pleasure. By the time I was in my twenties I couldn't have an orgasm without fantasizing about being raped.

I was deeply ashamed of this and never told anyone.

Eventually, I determined that if the price of an orgasm was those images, I would do without, thank you. It took me *years*, but I eventually trained myself to experience pleasure as a result of pleasure, not as a result of pain and humiliation and I broke the association and broke free of the images and dreams.

I wrote about this in my first book, *Unearthing Venus,* and had a lot of conversations in group talks and on radio shows, mostly with women, where this subject came up. And the number of other women who shared this fantasy of pain, humiliation and degradation was shocking. None of us had a clue where these fantasies came from. The most common suggestions were "past life memories" and media programming.

All of us felt intense shame and blamed ourselves.

No one suggested evil interdimensional influences.

Only now do I finally understand where those images came from. My family was deeply dysfunctional and abuse ran in my female ancestral line. The psychic door to the Archons had been opened long before I was even born.

As a deeply sensitive child, I was easy pickings.

Having walked a short way down this path, I am beyond saddened to see countless millions being seduced by anti-life Forces into porn addiction—all of it deliberately loveless and most of it violent.

Humanity is being programmed to debase sexuality and degrade themselves and others as part of the overall agenda to 1) endlessly feed off one of the most powerful energy sources in the universe, the human orgasm, and 2) dehumanize humanity and separate us from our true nature.

I'll get into some of the other ways the Archons get to us later on.

For now, the vital thing is for you to realize this Force is no joke. It's important to begin to see how it might be showing up in your life and in the lives of others around you. Most of all, it's crucial to understand just how much *not you* these mind parasites really are.

3

A Contemporary Presence

There are many global influences keeping the wool pulled over our eyes, keeping us blind to the Archons' presence among us. I'll get into some of the religious and spiritual programming in the next chapter. In the meantime, I'd like to briefly talk about the modern-day satanic movement.

Currently, in the US, more people believe in Satan—56 percent—than believe in God.[13] Satanism is the nation's fastest growing religion and some sources believe that as many as one in ten people—men, women and children of all walks of life—are practicing Satanists.

Personal empowerment is the main reason people give for joining this most ancient of cults. As one news source reports, during these shaky times, vast numbers of people are feeling helpless. Following Lucifer, the original rebel angel, makes them feel more powerful and in control.[14] After all, look at the state of the world and what four thousand years of obeying God has brought us.

In a sort of religious-rebound, the surface level of this movement is closely akin to Wicca, with groups like the Global Order of Satanism touting the importance of individual autonomy, respect for other life forms, science, justice over the rule of law, and the importance of embodying emotions like empathy and compassion. Practitioners favor Goth attire and newspapers run articles about them, calling it the "new cool trend."

This is the most benign and superficial expression of satanism. As with most religious cults, there are other layers and levels of initiation. The outer layer and most favorable face serves to misdirect and obfuscate the agendas of the real forces running the show.

Several friends of mine are professional psychologists. Over the years they've talked about what lies underneath the black leather, inverted crosses and eyeshadow, admitting to me that the number of satanic abuse victims they work with is "shocking." Back in the day I never gave it much thought because what was I ever going to do with information like that?

And yet way back in 1994, the International Journal of Clinical and Experimental Hypnosis (IJCEH), the leading voice in hypnosis for researchers and clinicians in psychiatry, psychology, social work and medical specialties, published a study titled "Satanism, ritual abuse, and multiple personality disorder: a socio-historical perspective."[15] The study stated that from the mid-1980s to 1994, a growing number of mental health professionals were reporting that between 25 and 50 percent of their patients in treatment for multiple personality disorder (MPD), now termed Dissociative Identity Disorder (DID), have recovered early childhood memories of ritual torture, incestuous rape, sexual debauchery, sacrificial murder, infanticide, and cannibalism perpetrated by members of clandestine satanic cults.

Based upon 2020 mental health statistics, roughly one and a half percent of the general US population 18 and older have been diagnosed with MPD/DID. Which means roughly 3,870,000 people in the US were diagnosed and treated for MPD/DID.[16] The actual number of people who have gone undiagnosed is unknown.

If we use the percentage figures from the 1994 study, the calculated number of MPD/DID patients reporting satanic ritual abuse should run somewhere between 967,500 and 1,935,000 people. Given the fact that the actual number of cases of MPD/DID could be double the figure of those diagnosed, the number of people suffering from the ramifications of ritual rape, torture and other abuses in the name of Satan in the United States could be as high as four million people or more.

Please remember this figure is based upon a percentage of patients in a study done 28 years ago. Satanism and satanic ritual abuse were barely being whispered about back then. Today we have the Dallas-based corporation Match.com releasing a web ad called a "Match Made in Hell," about Satan dating a girl called 2020. As funny as the concept is, it's also disturbing. Opening the Super Bowl LV halftime show, Canadian singer Abel Makkonen Tesfaye, better known as The Weeknd, portrays Satan's fall from heaven accompanied by a choir of red-eyed fallen angels dressed as church choir members rising out of a pit. Toward the end of the show Tesfaye is surrounded by zombie-men dressed in red with jockstraps over their faces instead of bandages.

Hello?

In the name of being modern and hip, the satanic presence on this planet is becoming more and more brazenly utilized and displayed. Cult-busters point to subtle messaging everywhere—from Google's Chrome browser logo to the Vodafone logo to the Monster Energy Drink logo flaunting 666 the "number of the beast."

Check out the pictures online yourself.

The Chrome and Vodafone logos are obvious once you see it. The Monster Drink logo (those puke-green monster claw marks always looked sinister to me) is the least obvious. Apparently, each minim of the letter M looks like the Hebrew letter vav (ו), or 6. Put three of those together and you get vav vav vav, ווו, or 666. (A minim is a short, vertical stroke used in handwriting.)

Frankly, even suggesting that Google and Vodafone might be promoting satanic imagery makes me cringe. It isn't possible. It's conspiracy nuts seeing the boogieman in even the most innocuous things because that's what they're looking for. And even if the 666 image is there (which it clearly is in both cases) maybe it's accidental. Maybe the graphic artists just didn't notice.

This is where my mind instantly goes. Is it true? *Nah, it couldn't be.*

Is it *possible*?

Well, yes, I guess. Subliminal messaging in marketing and advertising is a teachable art that's been known and utilized to effectively manipulate the subconscious of consumers for over 70 years. So, yes, I suppose it is possible. But why is this being done? For what reason?

This is a normal person's response to this kind of stuff.

This is *my* response.

Even sitting here, writing about an anti-life Force run amok on my planet trying to enslave all of humanity, I still can't wrap my mind around a reality where this kind of high-level infiltration and manipulation is present in my daily life.

Even when it's obvious—as in Super Bowl obvious—none of this is obvious because most of us aren't wired for this kind of bizarre crap. We don't see the symbols and patterns, not just because we're not educated to look for them, but because we're plain, old-fashioned decent people trying to get along in life, doing the best we can and none of this stuff is part of our reality.

Plus, when dealing with Satanism, again, there's always the fear factor.

I once had a music teacher who told me he realized his next-door neighbors were into Satanism. His cats kept disappearing. (He found one expertly disemboweled in the neighbor's garbage can.) He often heard weird noises coming from their house, and the family's kids were strange. He described them as "frightened zombie children." When I asked him why he didn't report them to the police he just looked at me like I was crazy.

"What?" he said. "And call down that kind of bad juju on my head? No way!"

It's this primal, gut-shaking, mind-numbing, hand-shaking, sweat-inducing fear that keeps our faces turned away from this Presence among us. And the Archons—this windingo/'e'epa/wetiko/antimimos/devil force—use that fear to control us. Plus, remember, fear is one of the base emotions the Archons feed on. What better way to keep the general public uneasy, on-edge and fearful than subliminally bombarding us with scary symbolism on seemingly innocuous products sitting on the grocery store and refrigerator shelves and on our computer screens, subconsciously triggering us over and over again.

Can you spell "diabolical?"

This hidden Force also depends upon our innocence and goodness to remain hidden. When rumors of what was going on at Auschwitz and other Nazi death camps first started to circulate during World War II, it took a while for people to believe what was happening because it was too inhumane to be possible. The same is true with modern sex trafficking of babies, infanticide, cannibalism and satanic ritual abuse of children.

Who would do such things?

And if such abuse were happening, surely, we'd know about it?

Thing is, we do know about it.

Famous bands like Pink Floyd write lyrics like: "You lock the door and throw away the key. There's someone in my head, but it's not me." Black metal bands from around the world like Oath, Deicide and Mayhem belt out tunes with lyrics straight from the black mass:

> "In the name of Satan, the ruler of Earth
> Open wide the gates of Hell
> And come forth from the abyss
> By these names: Satan, Leviathan,
> Belial, Lucifer
> I will kiss the goat …"

Hollywood psychic Sloane Bella talks about Lady Gaga's pact with the devil and Justin Bieber and Brittany Spears' nervous breakdowns and fall from superstar status being the result of refusing to participate in baby-slaying satanic rituals.[17]

We hear rumors about Queen Elizabeth drinking the blood of children and dismiss it automatically. (You think I have trouble believing Google is pushing Satanism? Queen Elizabeth (RIP) summoning Baphomet is definitely NOT in my wheelhouse.) And yet … gassing Jews, flaying them and using their skin to make lampshades and book covers wasn't possible either.[18] It's a painful truth that even the wildest of wild conspiracy theories usually ends up having a grain of truth behind it.

Even when Satan and his zombies show up in the Superbowl halftime, we just shrug and label it "weird entertainment." It might be tasteless, but "You know those Hollywood types." By the fourth quarter the lurid images are already forgotten. *And when we do see or hear about it, we're educated to identify and label evil as something else.*

Let me tell you a personal story that shows you what I mean.

When I stepped onto the spiritual path back in the 1980s, I left a lucrative and exciting career in network television and a good husband to retreat to the wilderness by myself. For three years I lived in an isolated one-room cabin with no indoor plumbing up in the mountains of North Georgia. My only companions on the journey were two dogs, a cat and a white Lippizan stallion named Golly Gee.

I had no training in meditation, but I was desperately in search of "something more." And so, meditate I did. I mean, how hard could it be? You just close your eyes and look within. Right?

Yeah, right.

I won't get into the disaster zone that was my mind. Suffice it to say that the first six months meditating were hell. But I kept looking within several hours a day and a couple hours every night, asking the simple question, "Who am I?"

Eventually I had a breakthrough.

During one morning's meditation, I fell into an ocean of peace and "rightness" where life made total sense and I was just where I needed to be. I knew the sweetness of that moment would last forever. It didn't, of course. But I was encouraged to keep going.

Soon, the intense, untrained meditation work unleashed powerful, normally quiescent energies residing at the base of my spine, and "kundalini energy" was let loose. Which meant I was suddenly aware of a whole bunch of psychic forces I was oblivious to before.

Now, every time I meditated or simply lay down to sleep at night, waves of energy coursed through my body—hissing, rolling waves that I could hear as well as feel—waves that grew in amplitude until they lifted "me" right out of my body.

A nightly experience both terrifying and exhilarating, I had no idea what was happening to me or what it all meant. Sometimes my spirit body floated gently up through the ceiling and out into the night. Sometimes I shot out of my body and hurtled through the cosmos at tremendous speeds. Sometimes part of my spirit body got stuck and I'd lie there, physical legs inert under the covers while my spirit legs thrashed overhead like I was madly peddling an invisible, upside-down bicycle.

But it wasn't the out-of-body-experiences (known as OOBEs)

that bothered me. It was the eerie phenomenon that often came with them. As the waves of energy bathed me, I heard voices and strange laughter far away. Sometimes I could feel what were clearly hands on my body, pulling and tugging. Balls of light would flash around the room. As I kept meditating, the phenomenon became more intense and I started sleeping with the lights on. Even then I could still see the lights whizzing about and hear the distant, insane laughter.

This went on and on until one night I was pulled out of my body and thrown into an experience that drove me to call my former academic advisor at the University of West Georgia and ask him for references to a good psychiatrist in Atlanta. (I'd studied for a Master's Degree in Psychology while still working in television. I graduated the year before I left the world to go meditate in the cabin and had stayed in touch with a few professors.)

He sent me three names and I picked the one that attracted me most, called and made an appointment. At $175 an hour (and this was in 1987!) I was grateful the doctor's initial consultation was free. Unnerved by the thickly padded door between his plush office and the waiting room and the barred windows hidden behind heavy damask drapes, I tentatively lay down on the leather sofa.

At the good doctor's prompting, I cut loose.

For almost an hour I spilled my guts, talking about my meditations and visions until I finally got to the episode that had scared me so badly. "I felt hands on my legs, pulling me out of my body. Then suddenly I was yanked out and hurled into this disgusting graveyard." Pausing for breath, I glanced across the small space between me and the doctor. Legs negligently crossed, writing on a leather note pad, he listened impassively. "Uh-huh," he said. "Then what happened?"

"Well, as I tiptoed around a big slimy crypt, this huge monster appeared from around the corner, all dripping fangs and bloody claws and red eyes. I was so terrified, I couldn't even scream. But as the Beast lurched up to me this enormous blast of love suddenly swelled up inside and I looked at the Beast and felt only love and stepped forward to hug it. But it screamed and ran away. Then I found myself back in my body in bed, wide awake."

"Hmmm." He tapped his pad thoughtfully with his pen. "I think that's enough for a first session."

I sat up, nervously pushing a few strands of hair behind my ears. At the time it had been the most shockingly real experience. But telling the story to a psychiatrist made it sound more like an encounter with an unintegrated part of my own psyche than an actual monster.

"So," I ventured, not really wanting to know. "What do you think?"

He didn't answer. Instead, he got up and went to his big polished desk. There he jotted some notes and then pulled out his appointment book. Again, the pen tapped gently. It was a gold Waterford. "I'd like to see you three times a week initially. Then, after six months or so, let's reevaluate and take it from there."

Three times a week?

Christ, he thinks I'm a schizophrenic. I couldn't possibly afford it and told him so. But he didn't bat an eye. "How much can you afford?" he asked.

Wishing I'd never walked into his office, I threw out a figure I knew he wouldn't accept.

"Um, maybe $25 an hour?"

"Fine," he said, flipping pages. "How about 2 p.m. next Monday?"

~

The doctor was a respected psychiatric professional. He was trained to interpret phenomena such as I was experiencing as aberrant. He was trained to see evil forces as unresolved projections from within the individual pointing to issues that needed to be integrated. He had been efficiently educated (programmed) to see only one reality: Mental illness. And there was not a shred of doubt in his mind that his view of reality and his interpretation of my experiences were correct.

Forget the actual experience. It wasn't valid *because such an experience isn't possible.* Forget me. I was seeing things and thus my perceptions weren't to be trusted.

I was delusional. I was sick. I needed help.

Talk about disempowering.

I'm not saying there aren't plenty of mentally ill people in the world.

I'm not saying schizophrenia and hallucinations don't exist. I'm saying mental illness isn't the only answer to phenomena like I experienced—phenomena that millions of people experience every day but are told are basically "nothing" or worse.

Don't worry. It was just an Oedipal dream. Go back to sleep …

Walking out of the doctor's office that day, I felt depressed, hopeless and helpless. It was a cold rainy day in February, and I remember sitting in my car, despondently watching the rain wash down my windshield as I cried. But after a while something stirred in me—a small voice from deep down inside that said "No."

I straightened from my slump at the wheel.

Dammit! I know I'm mentally stable. And I know what I experienced was real!

I wiped my eyes, started the car and drove to the mall and went shopping. Then I had a margarita and some nachos and another margarita. Feeling much better, I drove to my chiropractor ex-husband's house and told him the whole story. He promptly told me I was crazy for even going to a shrink in the first place. Then he gave me a phone number for a spiritually-oriented psychologist he knew.

I called her.

Her first visit was not $175 and it wasn't free. She listened to the same story and said, "Huh. You've obviously cracked open your psychic centers and astral energy is becoming available."

I hadn't even heard of astral energy.

"It's normal," she said. "Unusual, but normal. It's actually a sign that you're evolving. Congratulations! Frankly, I'm more concerned about your issues with your step-father."

Huh. Go figure.

I worked with her once a week for six months, got a good handle on here-to-fore unacknowledged trauma sustained around childhood emotional abuse and that was that. So, what would have happened if instead of trusting my inner voice and what I *knew* to be true—that I had literally come face-to-face with some sort of evil Beast in some sort of hellish, low-vibration astral hinterland—I'd believed the doctor instead?

What if I'd kept that Monday appointment?

I might still be in therapy to this day.

~

The fanged Beast adventure was the first *major* encounter I had with obviously evil forces. The second major encounter, which occurred while I was wide awake, didn't happen until almost 20 years later.

Looking back now, I can easily see why I underwent such a harrowing experience.

Going into my three-year retreat in the woods, I was psychologically, emotionally and spiritually immature and completely unprepared for the intense amount of introspection I was doing. Despite a graduate degree in psychology, I was untrained, and diving deep into my psyche without supervision was a precarious proposition at best. And I'd already been molested by these mind parasites as a child and young woman.

I can hear the dinner bell now, ringing through the interdimensional realms.

Snack time boys!

Psychically exposed and raw from all the meditation, it was a simple matter for the Archons to enter and prey upon my fears. Plus, it's kind of a rule of thumb that the more intense a human's desire and efforts towards the light are, the more intensely evil rushes in to try to stop the process of awakening.

My longing for a "new awakened me" was intense.

Which is why these forces attacked me with such a vengeance.

I continued to have bad dreams and mildly weird experiences for a while. But the immense lightning bolt of love that channeled through me that night made me keenly aware of the enormous power of the essence of Who I Really Am: A being of pure Love with a capital "L." This powerful embodiment apparently served as a sort of "Archon repellent" during the initial years of my continued spiritual pursuits.

Plus, frankly, I slammed the door on any more psychic awakenings.

Eventually, as my consciousness elevated, so did my energetic field, and I moved out of "frequency feeding range." I was not totally immune to their influence. When I was exhausted and under a lot of stress or when I was engaging in healing practices that directly involved these

Forces, I was sometimes assaulted—usually at night when I was sleeping.

It rarely happened. And when it did, I knew what to do about it.

Remember the scene in *The Fellowship of the Ring,* where Gandalf is facing the demon Balrog, standing on the narrow stone bridge over the yawning chasm down in the mines of Moria? Fearlessly he brings down his staff upon the rock and roars, "You shall not pass!"

Actually, what I would do was more of a firm, "No! You have no right to trespass into my mental and physical field. Get out!" And then I would consciously bring up love and *feel* love and emanate it.

And that would take care of *that.*

When I started writing this book, I actually congratulated myself on being relatively impervious to these Forces. Holy Moses. What a truth it is that, "You don't know what you don't know."

~

When interdimensional attacks occur, they usually happen in that in-between state between waking and sleeping when we're most open and vulnerable. Which means the experiences themselves are hazy—dreamlike occurrences that are … well, dreamlike.

Which means they don't seem quite real.

Which means they stay inconsequential—like some annoying psychic mosquito that intrudes occasionally, only to be batted away. *Nothing to really worry or think about.*

Prior to finishing this book, not only were these invasions surreal, I was so focused on seeing these beings as an *external* threat, it never once occurred to me that I might already be influenced *internally.*

There's an old spiritual joke about how people so often teach best that which they need to learn about the most. Such has been the case with me. I wrote the first draft of this book, completely oblivious to the fact that I was being energetically messed with by these beings. I write about retrieving traumatized parts of "me," and how I finally faced these entities in several healing sessions with a practitioner in the "Afterword" section of this book.

It wasn't until I was wide awake, clearly dealing with these interdimensional beings in the presence of another person who also saw/sensed them that they became *real.* I point this out because it's so important for understanding how this presence flies under the radar of consciousness so easily. Dealing with them can so often seem like a hazy, insubstantial dream. *Nothing to worry about ... go back to sleep ...*

It's like the scene in the *Wizard of Oz* where Dorothy and her friends finally see the Emerald City in the distance and they excitedly dash across a field of flowers. Meanwhile, the Wicked Witch of the West is in her lair, hypnotically crooning, "And now my beauties, something with poison in it, I think. With poison in it. But attractive to the eye and soothing to the smell." She cackles and caresses her crystal ball. "Poppies. Poppies. Poppies will put them to sleep."

Quickly, the opiate effects of the poppies slow Dorothy's step. Lion, Dorothy, Scarecrow and finally Tin Man stumble and fall, dazed, to the ground. Eyelids drooping, they curl up and go to sleep.

The perfect metaphor for our world today.

People, everywhere, asleep in a field of red poppies.

A few see what's behind the curtain. But, like me just a year ago, it's all so bizarre—so like a fantasy—they do nothing about it. They're drowsy. And if they do something, few listen because it's all just a dream.

Awake but still asleep. That's what it's been like.

And now?

I feel like Neo when he's just been pulled out of the matrix. He sits there, gripping the sides of his slimy glass cocoon, staring in shock out at the field of billions of humans that are being harvested by the machines. Like Neo, the entire fabric of reality has changed right before my eyes.

And what do you do with that?

In the dream, I always thought "awakening" would involve the music of the spheres and angels singing as I floated away on a cloud of bliss into the arms of nirvana. So much for that fairy tale!

Apparently, waking out of the matrix is the first concrete step.

True, this particular awakening isn't pretty. But it must happen. For what remains hidden controls our lives. What is not acknowledged cannot heal. And that which is not seen cannot be dealt with and transcended.

CHAPTER THREE KEY

Trust your feelings, your heart & your body

PART I

Unlike our minds, the body does not lie. It accurately informs us, moment-to-moment, exactly what's what.

Stopping and turning to spirit first for answers is Step #1 on the path to knowing Who You Really Are. Taking a hard look at evil and beginning to acknowledge that evil is *not* who you really are is STEP #2.

- Paying close attention to your feelings and beginning to trust your body's subtle prompts and *following* those prompts is STEP #3.

So many people, myself included, talk about wanting to get divine guidance. Then we wait around hoping to hear a voice, or see a burning bush, or have an angel materialize in our kitchen, or have some amazing dream. But the body is equally divine and much more direct and MUCH more trustworthy in its guidance.

The body is pure energy. It is spirit.

As such, it registers *everything* and acts as the most exquisite, subtle, spiritual messenger system.

Let's say your dog ran away. You search for weeks to no avail. And then, as you're headed to Kinkos, miles from your house on the other side of the expressway, you have the sudden inexplicable *feeling* to slow down and stop at a fish market. You don't need fish. You don't even like fish. But you stop and go inside and sure enough, somebody's posted a picture of your dog with a FOUND! message on top and a telephone number.

Or you interview someone for an accounting job. They're the perfect candidate. But "something"—a feeling—says "Nope." A year later you hear that same person embezzled funds from the company that ended up hiring them.

We are guided every moment of every day from inside.

Our subtle intuitive feelings whisper "Go this way!" Our hearts prompt us to say "Yes!'" Our gut shouts, "No! Don't go there!" Trusting the messages from within is an enormous key to self-empowerment and actualizing Who You Really Are.

After all, Jesus didn't say "The kingdom of heaven lies above your head." He didn't say it lies in a book or in some religious leader or government official somewhere. He said it lies within us.

And if the kingdom of heaven lies within us, so do the keys to the front gate.

PART II

Counter to *all* the spiritual training I received for 40 years, I have learned that my safe place, my awake place, is my body.

Down and in versus up and out.

Pretty much everything in the matrix is inverted. (Like the pentagram.) I'll talk more about this in the next chapter and about how religion and spirituality have been perverted and twisted to serve this anti-life Force.

In the meantime, I highly recommend getting grounded into your body.

There are plenty of what's called "somatic exercises" on the web. Check them out and explore. But one of the simplest things you can do is simply sit with your bare feet on the floor, get comfortable, and get in touch with your body.

Starting at your feet, simply notice how your body feels—feet, ankles, calves, knees, thighs ... and on up, step-by-step, body part by body part.

Breathe calmly and normally as you do this.

The slower you go and the longer you take becoming deeply aware of your entire body, the more in-tune and grounded you'll feel.

4

Blinded by the Light

Anthropologists tell us the devil is an unsubstantiated myth no rational human being could ever believe in. Behaviorism maintains that belief in the devil is simply a conditioned response from continued exposure to superstitious ideas promulgated by religion. Logical positivism asserts that metaphysical and subjective arguments not based on observable objective consensus data are meaningless.

In other words, subjective reports from individuals like me who have perceived otherwise non-observable "other-worldly" beings are worthless. And then, of course, psychiatry tells us any sort of perceived influence or encounter with an evil force is imaginary and hallucinatory.

The only real advocates for the reality of the devil anymore are the Abrahamic traditionalists. But even in religious circles there is never any urging to actually account for and investigate the nature and origins of this anti-life Force. What's to investigate? Everybody knows the story. Satan/Lucifer was once an angel who, in his overweening pride, challenged God who then tossed the angel overboard to Earth to do his worst and reign forever over Hell.

Mystery solved.

The religious take on evil is simplistic in the extreme. The devil is amongst us. He's trying to get us to do bad things. Turn away from the devil and accept Jesus/Allah/Jehovah into your heart and become good and go to heaven. In other words, here's the problem, here's the solution, don't think about anything else and don't ask any questions.

The other way the Abrahamic religions keep the Archons' presence hidden is by intermingling accounts of the presence of evil with a ton of easily rejected stories, such as a snake in a garden tempting a woman to eat an apple; one man and one woman populating the entire world without committing generations of incest; and a loving God testing His most faithful follower by asking him to slit his son's throat as proof of his Godly love and obedience.

I don't mean to demean people's beliefs, but interpreted literally, the Bible presents such a stream of easily-dismissed nonsense that by sheer association rational people end up inoculated against any and all talk about Satan/Shaitan/wetiko/'e'epa and interdimensional forces.

Unfortunately, also by association, they are inoculated against any "silly talk" about being God's child and a spiritual being.

Rational people adopt other kinds of stories—like science proving that life happened by accident and that we're all just a bunch of physical bodies milling around trying to make the best of it. Consciousness, love, compassion and everything else "somehow" arise out of the three pounds of grey matter sitting on top of our shoulders. Nothing else is reasonably possible.

So, shoo!

Go away with your preposterous talk about spirits and evil forces.

Once we think we know what's what—once we believe we know what's real and true, we stop asking questions. We stop looking around for other possible explanations for why life on Earth is such a crap deal and why we can't seem to really change.

No questions = invisibility.

Not only do traditional religions help keep this anti-life Force hidden, they have been deeply infiltrated by this Force. Most of the teachings of mainstream religions have ended up designed to actively promote the Archons' agenda of ultimately possessing and enslaving humanity. Especially culpable in this area are the highly authoritarian Abrahamic religions born out of the Middle East.

Christianity, Judaism and Islam wield enormous psychological control over their followers because they are fear-based—threatening eternal damnation and torture if one fails to follow the rules. They deliberately foster enormous amounts of shame and guilt in followers by teaching that all human beings are born corrupted and require redemption which only obedience to God (and the priests) can supply.

The toxic teaching that human beings are inherently bad to the bone forces little children and adults to adopt and internalize feelings of being evil and inadequate. Any sense of the personal self as being good and decent or wise is labeled as pride—a horrible sin first committed by Lucifer that is punishable by eternal damnation if not corrected. Only God is good and wise. We can only attain these qualities from Him if He deems us worthy by being obedient and slavishly humble, chronically begging forgiveness for the sin of being born as God created us.

Is this messed up or what?

Of course, original sin is a completely irrational idea.

Anyone who has ever looked into the eyes of a baby for more than five seconds knows that it's just plain *wrong*. But tiny children exposed to such insanity can't help but be scarred by it. Some of us swallow it whole cloth and end up despising ourselves and all of humanity our entire lives. Some of us end up wracked with subconscious guilt, playing it out through low self-esteem issues, addictions and self-mutilation that only a massive amount of therapy can heal. There is now a name for the terrible psychological and emotional trauma inflicted by Archon-influenced religion: Religious Trauma Syndrome (RTS).[19] Uncounted millions of people worldwide currently suffer from RTS, and billions of people around the world have needlessly suffered RTS over the past two millennia or more.

The epigenetic impact of this is incalculable.

Epigenetics is the study of how events cause emotional impacts that affect biochemical changes that affect the way our genes work. Our emotions literally imprint our DNA, impacting generations far beyond us and the originating event/influence. As we inherit our ancestors' Emotional DNA patterns, we end up living our lives unconsciously mirroring how our predecessors lived theirs.[20] For example, studies show that the grand-children of Holocaust survivors experience higher levels of anxiety and more relational difficulties under stress than their non-Jewish peers.[21]

Epigenetics is the scientific explanation behind the old Biblical saying "The sins of the fathers shall be visited upon their sons."

They are. And their daughters, too.

All the people on this planet—every single one us—are literally a cumulative dumping ground of ancestral emotions, the most powerful of which are shame, guilt, remorse, humiliation, self-hatred, dishonor, disgrace and mortification—all the emotions that arise around the concept of sin and the belief that we are terrible, rotten people. These deeply corrosive emotions have been passed down from adults to their children for over a hundred generations.

And we wonder why we all struggle with self-esteem issues?

Hello?

Maybe I've lived an incredibly sheltered life, but personally I haven't met anybody who was so "sin-full" that they deserved to suffer eternal damnation. I mean, how many people have *you* met who deserve eternal hellfire?

I don't care how awful your ex is, nobody deserves that.

I've traveled from England through Europe into Russia and Turkey. I've spent months in the Amazon jungles of Peru and Ecuador in South America, lived for years in Central America and briefly lived in South Africa and India. And the people in all the places I lived were generally decent and kind.

Everywhere in the world—even in LA, London and New York—everybody I've ever met pretty much wants the same thing: To be left alone to do what makes them happy, find a mate, raise their kids to be healthy and happy, contribute to their community as much as they can and feel fulfilled by living a loving, productive life.

That's it.

Sure, there are assholes you meet along the way. And I'm not saying there aren't criminals and horrifyingly bad and cruel people in the world. I'm not saying there aren't evil people possessed and run by the Archons, doing their bidding. Obviously, there are or I wouldn't be writing this. But it's shocking how disproportionate the impact these "bad apples" have in the world. It only takes one power-mad sociopath to influence and destroy the lives, livelihoods and ecosystems of entire nations. Which is, I think, a testimony to the genuine gentleness of humanity as a whole.

So, why were destructive religious teachings such as original sin put in place?

Well ... what emotions are most tasty to the anti-life Force?

What emotions make us most vulnerable, most miserable and thus easiest to control?

Unfortunately, the world of New Age spirituality doesn't come off any better than most traditional religions when it comes to aiding and abetting evil forces and their agendas.

If I had to sum up the most dangerous spiritual notion in a single book title, it would have to be Peter McWilliams' 1988 *You Can't Afford the Luxury of a Negative Thought.* I remember seeing the book in the stores when it first came out and my first thought was: *Well, I guess that means I'm screwed.* The premise is unrealistic and sets up an impossible expectation which defeats most people right from the start.

No human being can go through life without a negative thought. And yet once a self-help idea as enticing and marketable as the ideal of A Better Life Through Total Positivity is birthed, it's hard to stop its momentum—especially with so many self-help gurus and spiritual teachers pushing the agenda.

But what a setup.

On top of knowing going in that I don't stand a chance of accomplishing this "zero negativity" feat—now I'm terrified of having the negative thoughts that I do have, adding fear to the mix of existing negativity. Which exponentially ramps up the power my negative thoughts have over me.

Is it a good idea to be aware of negative thoughts when they crop up? Yes. Is it a good idea not to let them fester and dominate your thinking? Of course. But look at the cycle of self-judgment and fear that flows from thinking "I can't have a negative thought."

I can't have a negative thought. Wow, my hair looks like crap. Oh God! Oh no! I had a negative thought! I knew I couldn't do it. Oh my God! There's another one! Shit. This is impossible! Oh no! Another one!

What a circus.

I can't tell you how deeply this whole negative view of negativity affected me and all my friends. We were terrified of our negative thoughts and emotions. What monsters would they create? What diseases in the body would they unleash? What misfortunes and accidents would befall us?

To cancel them out (we couldn't get rid of them), we plastered positive affirmations on refrigerators and bathroom mirrors. Chanted positive affirmations before bed. Listened to positive affirmations while we slept. Bought and read more books about positivity. Paid for more classes and workshops.

Caught in the midst of this cult of mandatory optimism, when painful situations arose—losing a spouse, losing a job, losing faith, losing a pet—instead of close friends being there to support each other during rough times, people would listen to your story then unsympathetically ask, "Gee, how did you create *that*?" And we would ransack our minds for the negative thoughts that must have triggered our misfortune. And when we inevitably found them, we brutally blamed ourselves for being spiritual failures. How else could the cancer have arrived? Why else would the car have broken down when it did? No wonder the cat got eaten by coyotes.

We did our best not to admit the pain we were suffering, including the guilt we piled onto ourselves over creating negative experiences with our negative thoughts. We coached ourselves back to positivity by thinking things like, *When one door closes, another opens. Look on the bright side.*

Not being able to have a single negative thought eventually meant anger became inadmissible. Normal human emotions like sorrow, grief, despair, and remorse became taboo and we battled them endlessly. Or we tried to meditate them away. Or we stuffed them into a closet and simply refused to admit they existed. And what a relief that was! The emotional repression and issue avoidance in the name of being spiritual worked wonders.

And thus, spiritual bypassing was born.

Did we see what was happening to us, living in the Cult of Positivity? No. How could we? We were all so grimly focused upon being good, so obsessed with happy thoughts, that we actually began to believe we were winning the battle and approaching enlightenment—at least I thought I was. And yet all I was doing was bypassing genuine growth and authenticity, desperately trying to get out of the painful experience of being human by getting "out there" —out of my body, out of my emotions, out of reality—to some "higher place" where all was bliss and light.

I lived in this dysfunctional spiritual dreamscape for decades.

Many of my friends still do.

There are other spiritual teachings that are equally damaging, steering people away from reality and the ability to be effective in their lives and the lives of others—teachings that ultimately blind people of good heart to actual evil in the world around them.

For example, the anthropomorphic belief that Earth is a school.

The very first "spiritual" explanation I received for why life is the way it is, the school model holds that as souls we are all on a steep learning curve to figure out how physical bodies work and how life in general is supposed to be lived on planet Earth. In this model, reincarnation is a given. How else could a non-physical being possibly manage to figure out physicality? A single lifetime couldn't do the job. One saber tooth tiger sauntering into your cave or a bus coming from the right instead of the left and WHAM!

Lesson over.

In the school model, everything that happens is okay because it's a lesson all the participants agreed to experience ahead of time. Cancer, betrayal, financial ruin, adultery, satanic ritual abuse—it's all there to help us grow.

Of course, with any luck, *all* life experiences—the painful ones and the sweet—teach us stuff and hopefully make us better people in the end. But this whole "life's a school" philosophy has a terrible downside to it because it automatically enables us to brush off ghastly situations and downright evil occurrences with a quick shrug and a label.

If rape, genocide and starvation are lessons we deliberately choose to go through, we stop seeing these things as dysfunctional occurrences that need to be dealt with at an individual, communal and global level.

We can completely dodge responsibility.

And then there's the whole cult of Love.

The relentless focus on goodness started by Abrahamic religions has resulted in New Age spiritualism obsessively pushing the theme of love to such heights that in the minds of millions is now instilled the concept that "everything is love." And it makes sense. God is love and God is everything and everything comes from God, so Q.E.D. everything is love, right?

Which means evil comes from God and must really be love too. Right?

Talk about a mind job.

If evil is birthed from the One Source called love, then it is redeemable. It means that evil really, deep down, isn't evil. It's twisted love. And if something's been twisted, it can be untwisted. Like maybe Lucifer is redeemable and can go back to heaven and make up with dear ol' Dad. (Hey, wait a minute. Isn't there a TV show about that?)

Personally, I bypassed the subject of evil by imagining love as being a kind of "God particle" that constituted everything from cotton candy to chopped liver. I figured if love could be both cotton candy and chopped liver then certainly it could be both good and evil. And that was as far as I took the subject.

I never contemplated ritual torture and rape like I asked you to do at the end of chapter two. Of course not! My eyes were firmly fixed on the Light.

I hadn't yet met a friend of mine who was raised by deeply spiritual parents who, by day, were devoted members of the Saint Germain Foundation, worshipping at the violet flame of the I AM teachings, wearing the proper "spiritual colors" associated with the different days of the week.

Parents who, by night, became completely different people.

It took two decades of healing work for her to uncover memories of satanic ritual abuse … of being stripped, tied up and bent over a rocking horse by her father as he whispered in her ear before she was ritually group raped at age five, "Close your eyes darling, and go to the Light."

And that wasn't the worst of what she endured.

Few raised in a culture steeped in the Abrahamic religious traditions haven't wrestled at some point in their lives with the puzzling question of why "bad things happen to good people." How unspeakable acts like my friend went through could possibly occur if God is the loving God that He's made out to be.

If "everything is love," how could this possibly happen?

I get into a discussion and explanation of this later in the book. For now, I will simply say that I have finally solved this conundrum (at least for myself!) by realizing that evil is not love. It is a different Force altogether. It comes from a different source. Its existence and purpose are precisely 180 degrees out of phase to the universe of love/life we dwell in.

Evil has *nothing* to do with a "fallen angel"—which is just more Archon propaganda espousing the idea that love can be twisted into something else and that we can "fall" in consciousness as well and become what this anti-life Force is.

Convincing us of this is this Force's major agenda. And twisting and confusing us about what "love" actually is, is a huge part of that plan.

A million sermons talk about love as sacrifice. The suffering and death of Jesus is elevated far above his love and example of the eternal life of spirit. Popular songs croon about how love hurts. How we are betrayed by love. How we are the victims and fools of love. A billion ads and songs and TV shows and stories try to convince us that sex is love.

Spirituality tries to convince us that even evil is love.

Deeply programmed, lacking an expansive, multidimensional understanding of what this outrageous, powerful, omnipresent force called "love" actually is, I—and everybody I know—inevitably came to understand love in a less than complete way. And then the program of mandatory positivity came along, and love ended up being trivialized to the point where I had to be sweet and nice and "loving" all the time to everybody—even when I didn't want to be.

And thus love became hypocrisy.

And yet humanity is love made real.

Humanity is love expressing itself.

Human beings are living, breathing temples of love.

Which is why this anti-life Force is doing its damnedest to destroy this understanding by erasing our true nature and the true nature of love and the true way love acts from view.

For pity's sake, over 8,000 children die of starvation *every day* around the world—an agonizing process that's unimaginable. But secure in our belief that "Everything is love and serves a purpose in Earth school" we can shrug off the ghastliness of starving children without a second thought.

The Eastern concept of karma allows us to pass beggars on the street with a clear conscience, assured that they've obviously brought the situation down upon themselves. Sex-trafficking children is common around the world, including in the US. Three-month old infants have been discovered in sex-trafficking sting operations. And while it's hard to imagine anyone saying in the face of such an abomination, "Well, it must be the baby's karma," that's basically where this kind of thinking takes us.

Another spiritual belief we can depend on to keep us from facing the true horror and grotesqueness of evil doings is: "This is all an illusion."

This advanced spiritual insight is inevitably played out at a superficial level by people because almost nobody in the world aside from a few advanced avatars and a handful of theoretical physicists actually "get" the illusory nature of "physical" reality. If we did, we wouldn't even be having this discussion. Sure, we can read about quantum physics and adopt a belief that physicality is an illusion.

But we don't *experience* it as truth.

In the highest, must illumined possible state of consciousness—the state of mind where the great avatars like Buddha and Jesus dwell—I suspect it becomes incredibly obvious that this entire Earth realm we're playing in is not the real world at all. (Imagine you've spent 40 years wearing a VR headset playing Ocular Rift and then suddenly your mother calls you for dinner or the phone rings "outside" the game. Talk about a shock and a paradigm shift!) As the famous Austrian theoretical physicist Erwin Schrödinger put it, "What we observe as material bodies and forces are nothing but shapes and variations in the structure of space. Particles are just *schaumkommen* (appearances)."

Great. So, the world's an illusion.

Go tell that to the sex-trafficked baby.

Which is exactly why the whole "It's all an illusion" philosophy is so profoundly problematic. Unless you're a fully enlightened being, it's just a philosophy. And if you are an enlightened being, it simply doesn't matter. Imagine Jesus or Buddha standing around while a baby is being raped, smiling and reassuring everyone by saying, "Now, now, don't worry about it. It's all just an illusion."

I don't think so.

A fully enlightened being knows that while ultimately duality and physicality are illusions, while in the illusion what happens in the illusion is NOT an illusion. The baby's agony and terror are real because they are experienced.

Illusion doesn't necessarily translate as "not real."

And there are levels of illusion. There's more than one matrix.

The foundational matrix (if you want to call it that) securing the appearance of physical reality so spirits such as ourselves can interact with what is apparently matter (remember $E=MC^2$), is a positive creation and an extension and expression of life/love.

The overlaying matrix the Archons have set in place is a highly destructive, anti-life, mental "reality" being projected onto the world that has been deliberately held in place with a lot of ongoing assistance from various individuals, blood lines and duplicitous organizations over millennia of time.

Seeing through this dark spider's web of the mind that has convinced us we're separate from life and separate from each other is paramount. And seeing this matrix means seeing the means and methods by which it is being perpetrated.

There are many beautiful and uplifting teachings in both religion and spirituality. What I have tried to point out in this chapter is that most of these teachings have been infiltrated and, in many cases, deliberately twisted in order to misdirect and mislead us.

It was a great shock for me to realize that the overarching message of mainstream society, religion and spirituality is all the same: You are not enough. You are deficient and fundamentally flawed. You need to struggle to be ___________ . (Fill in the blank. Thinner, richer, sexier, purer, more positive, more loving, kinder, etc.)

And yet the fundamental truth is: We are beings of pure love.

That's our essential nature. It doesn't get any better than that. Right? So, what's going on?

What's going on is we can be—and have been—convinced we're something we're not. (Bad, wrong, evil, defective, etc.) We have been guided to fruitlessly spend lifetimes trying to correct an illusion, chasing our tails down an endless rabbit hole of "self-improvement."

Yikes!

Ever wonder why, after a zillion hours of meditation, a thousand self-help books and years of expensive retreats and seminars, you're still on the spiritual hamster wheel seeking attainment? Perfection? Enlightenment? God? This is basically why.

We are beings of pure love.

We can't become what we already are.

The body is pure energy, matching the frequency of pure love. It never lies. It houses and guides us faithfully. But we are relentlessly pointed away from the body. Away from nature. Away from our inner flame. Away from self-love and self-trust. Constantly being fed the message: "You haven't got it. Look up there! Look over there! Follow this teaching! Go after that!"

We're relentlessly directed up and out. Up and out. Up and out.

And yet the real journey is down and in. The real goal is embodied love. The real reward is totally being here on Earth, being Who We Really Are, reveling in the seamless meld of mind, body, spirit and emotions. The living, breathing spirit made flesh, having the experience of LIFE!

Millions of tired, disillusioned seekers are standing on the brink of this realization. They stand on the edge of realizing they've been manipulated and that things are not at all as they've been taught to believe.

Is revising (or preferably throwing out) vast amounts of religious/spiritual concepts in this process of discovery a comfortable thing to do?

Absolutely not.

But my, oh my, are the results ever worth it.

CHAPTER FOUR KEY

Recognize beliefs and systems that negate who you really are

KEY#4 is the practice of recognizing systems of thought and belief that keep you stuck in the matrix, thinking you're something you're not.

Any organization or system of thought grounded in the premise that you are less than a perfect expression of the divine already is part of this anti-life Force's program of propaganda.

"But wait!" you cry. "That's pretty much everything! That's my government. That's my church. That's my psychiatrist. My doctor. My teachers. That's the news on TV every night, every advertisement I see and every song I sing along to! It's every philosophy I've ever believed in and pretty much every book, newspaper and magazine I've ever read!"

Yes. You're right. Every single system on the planet has been infiltrated and basically designed to deliver the message: "You are bad. Life sucks. It's all your fault." It's rarely stated so blatantly. But that's the basic premise.

And yet any child will tell you life is *amazing*. That flowers are beautiful, that bees can sting, that you get wet when it rains, that puddles are awesome to jump in, and it's nice to have shelter and warm cookies and milk and somebody to hug and love you at the end of the day.

That's what's real. The rest is basically Bantha poodo. (Thanks to *Star Wars* nerds, I now know that Bantha poodoo is what Bantha's *eat*, not what comes out the other end. Um ... speaking of what we eat, I talk about media messaging in a chapter later on.)

Yes, I'm going for a little humor here. But seriously—kids have the right take on life. Jesus says it plainly in Mathew 18:3: "Verily I say unto you, except ye be converted and become as little children, ye shall not enter into the kingdom of heaven."

"But wait!" you cry. "I'm not pure as a little child! I'm not perfect! I used to pinch my baby sister to make her cry. I cheated on my math exams in college. I had sex with someone else's wife/husband/partner. These aren't things that a *good* person does."

The best I can say to that is, you are Who You Really Are no matter what you do. Being an ax murderer doesn't suddenly change your status as a spirit being of pure love. *It does, however, reveal the extreme degree to which your true nature has become distorted.*

Once you get untwisted and back into alignment with life and knowing Who You Really Are, the ax murderer dissolves into nothing. Is this "untwisting" easy? Hell no. Is there a point of no return for some people? Frankly, I don't know. What I do know is that the twisting part isn't easy either.

As beings of pure love, we're pretty tough. There have been many scientific experiments conducted by the US government using all sorts of mental and emotional programming, including the use of drugs and torture, to see what it takes to get a regular human being to go apeshit and act against basic decency. It can be done. But it takes a LOT.

In general, humans on this planet have been subject to thousands of years of mental and emotional torment and twisting. The fact that so many billions of us are decent people speaks volumes for our innate goodness of heart. So does the fact that so many of us take self-improvement courses and dive into religious and spiritual practices in order to become better, nicer, kinder human beings.

Just try to keep in mind that you don't have to *become* anything ... the journey is down and into the body, into the place of *feelings*—into the inner chamber where your pure heart flame already resides.

So, how do you dissolve the layers of illusion to realign with pure love? As best as I've been able to figure out:

- Hold in mind and heart the sincere and passionate desire to know Who You Really Are.
- Passion and sincerity are the key.
- In the morning when you wake up, ask life every day: "Show me who/what I really am. Show me what love really is."

- Hold the thought lightly for as long as feels right—max 30 seconds—and then let it go. Don't dwell on it.
- Go about your day. Do your best to stay "tuned in" to where your heart/gut connection wants to take you.
- Do the same thing before you go to sleep at night.
- Be patient and trust life to bring you your desire. *Life itself wants this unveiling!*
- Know that you cannot be led astray. If your deepest most passionate desire is to know who/what you really are, *everything* you attract and are attracted to is part of the unveiling.

5

THE C-WORD & PERCEPTION

Many moons ago a dear friend from England told me a highly revealing story. His family lineage was linked to the royal family and historically heavily involved in British royal doings. He was extremely smart, and when he was preparing to take his Oxbridge exams to get into university to study history, his family hired a tutor.

But this "tutor" started off his studies in a very peculiar way.

"From now on you will forget everything you've been taught," the man said. "You will forget everything you've been taught because everything you've been taught up until now is parrot feed for the masses. Essentially, none of it is true. Especially not the history you're so fond of believing in.

"You are being groomed, and this is your first step. From now on you accept nothing at face value. If you want to know something you dig for it—and not in normal bibliographies and research sources. Learn to think for yourself. Learn to go outside the box.

"*That* is what I am here to teach you."

My friend said at that point he became essentially paralyzed. (He was only 16 at the time.) His family had hired a man to tell him nothing he believed was true, that the whole world had been hoodwinked, and that it was up to him to figure his own path through what had suddenly become a very strange and sinister reality indeed.

He stayed emotionally/mentally traumatized for about six months and then he made a choice—and it wasn't to be "groomed." He broke from family tradition, didn't go to university and went his own way. Which is how I met him in the US many years later.

I tell this story to try to soften this book's approach to the "C" word and make addressing alternative realities—which is what we're talking about—perhaps a bit more real and approachable. As Shakespeare put it in his play *Hamlet:* "There are more things in heaven and earth, Horatio, than are dreamt of in your philosophy."

Truer words have never been spoken.

But before we get into a discussion about conspiracies, first let's briefly look at some statistics and social trends.

Over 25 percent of Americans now suffer from a diagnosable mental health disorder.[22] That's one out of every four people. Over 78 percent of Americans over 55 suffer from at least one chronic physical health condition.[23] Over 60.2 percent of Americans aged 12 years or older currently abuse alcohol, drugs and/or tobacco.[24] Suicide rates have risen over 30 percent since 2008.[25] In the 1970s one child in 10,000 was diagnosed with autism.[26] In 2004 it was one child in 150. Today it's one child in 44.[27] Researchers at MIT predict that soon one out of two children will be born autistic.[28]

This is not a pretty picture.

On the economic side of things, over 41 percent of Americans are classified as low-income and over 64 percent of Americans live from paycheck to paycheck.[29] For Millennials the figure is over 70 percent. But take heart, most of us will always have food to put on the table, especially if we begin to harvest and eat insects—the hot new "save the planet" food the media and celebrities are beginning to push. Along with a growing social trend normalizing cannibalism.

No. I am not kidding.

The future of food, apparently, is synthetic meat, recycled sewage,[30] bugs and, if things get really bad, eating each other.

In February 2021, *Time* magazine ran an article titled, "They're Healthy. They're Sustainable. So Why Don't Humans Eat More Bugs?"[31] Angelina Jolie promotes eating tarantulas and apparently feeds them to her children. Nicole Kidman eats live worms.[32] The *New York Times* lists recent TV shows and movies featuring cannibalism in a romanticized light, saying "We've never looked so delicious—to one another."[33]

In December 2020, steak grown from human cells was featured as "art" at the Design Museum in London, UK.[34] And a company called BiteLabs apparently grows meat from celebrity tissue samples, turning them into salami.[35]

Please, excuse my French, but WTF?

The World Economic Forum (WEF) is deeply entrenched in promoting this inspiring vision of the future of food, as are many other global elitist organizations and the billionaires who fund them.[36]

Right, like Bill Gates and Larry Page will ever end up eating worms.

Never mind the *hundreds* of ecologically sound organic methods for raising food sufficient to healthily sustain the 9.6 billion people estimated to be living on the planet by 2050 and the studies that prove it.[37] Never mind the exciting future for regenerative farming and positive agriculture on a global scale.[38] (All of which focus on eliminating commercial chemical fertilizers, pesticides and insecticides.)

Forget all that.

Let's introduce "food" that is 100 percent guaranteed to make us sicker, more depleted, more depressed and degenerate than we already are. Let's promote drinking sewage, ingesting bugs, synthetic food, and our neighbors as the "cure" for the diseases of poverty, hunger, dysfunction, climate change and other self-created problems that plague our world. After all, it's *our* fault we're in this position. All us nasty individual self-centered human beings.

This is the price we all (well, most of us) must pay to set things right.

At least that's the story we're being sold.

I started this chapter on conspiracies with the above information because I wanted to set the stage properly for introducing the "C" word.

Humanity is sick and getting sicker.

If the above statistics and trends don't make that clear, I don't know what will.

It would seem impossible to get people to agree to such disgusting suggestions as eating worms, let alone align with the morally reprehensible idea of eating human flesh. But get enough celebrities behind it, get *The New York Times* to write about it, make it art, make it cool, make it about saving the planet, bang on about the advantages of eating bugs on CNN long enough, create food shortages, make sure meat and poultry and fish prices skyrocket along with inflation and then start selling ground locust patties at the grocery store and put them on sale ... and most people will eventually buy it.

It might take global famine to get us gnawing on each other. But if you've read any headlines about predicted food shortages in the last six months, that's well in the works too.

The next step is to label people who point to studies showing that eating bugs and drinking reclaimed sewage aren't the best answers to solving global hunger and climate change *science deniers.* If somebody dares claim that normalizing eating each other is part of a diabolical plan to keep us sick, depressed, guilty, pliable (and scared), label them a *conspiracy theorist.*

Which brings us to another cloaking device keeping the Archon mind parasites and their agendas hidden from the world:

Demonize anything that can expose evil by tarring that thing with the conspiracy label.

The fact that the Archons are 1) non-physical and 2) have successfully implemented their divisive agendas for thousands of years means there are human beings and human-run organizations that are onboard with this anti-life program promulgating the deliberate degradation and enslavement of humanity. Humans in high places (such as my friend) have been recruited to work as a "front" for this Force, handling operations and the physical implementation of the Archons' agendas since the very start.

But any whisper of such a thing is swiftly dealt with by calling it a conspiracy. And yet so many "crazy conspiracies" over the years have been revealed as true, you'd think we'd catch on to the ploy. For example, the US government running massive mind control experiments through American universities and hospitals for decades, and the CIA kidnapping men out of brothels and flophouses, dosing them with LSD and torturing them to see how far they could be pushed past their mental and moral limits.

Impossible? Nope. Welcome to the US government's program MK-Ultra, exposed via the Freedom of Information Act in 1977 and subsequently investigated in formal Senate hearings.[39] Additional documentation on the program was released in 2001.

And what's the big deal about conspiracies anyhow?

Conspiracies are as old as civilization itself.

Let me ask you, did you ever hang out with a bunch of friends as a teenager and buy cigarettes illegally? Booze? Pot? Something harder? Congratulations. You've officially been part of a conspiracy, which is defined by Merriam-Webster as: An agreement to perform together an illegal, wrongful, or subversive action.

Anybody who pays their tax accountant to cook the books is part of a conspiracy. Anybody who has an affair on their husband or wife is part of a conspiracy. Conspiracies are a dime a dozen, constantly playing out in the bedroom and the boardroom, in the Senate and on the stage. Factions—whether political, economic, educational, scientific, religious or individual—are always trying to secretly one up and control other factions.

The key word here being "secretly."

Of course, the bigger the agenda and the more people involved, the greater the vulnerability and thus the less likely absolute secrecy can be maintained. Which means that smear tactics and disinformation programs must be frequently and effectively deployed. Is it surprising that secret organizations running the Archons' global agenda might use media programming to subvert public knowledge of their actions?

Is it surprising that "educated people" might be trained to have a negative kneejerk reaction to the "C" word? Doesn't it make good sense to set those kinds of defense mechanisms up?

Once upon a time, I was one of those well-educated, well-trained kneejerk sceptics. If anybody had told me (which someone eventually did) about the existence of a secret elite cabal with global mischief on its mind, I would have laughed in their face. (Which I did.) But then one thing led to another and I ended up reading the 500-page, highly annotated book *The Unseen Hand: An Introduction to the Conspiratorial View of History* by Ralph Epperson.

That one book, published in 1985, was so well researched and comprehensive that it effectively destroyed my sense of normal reality, obliterating the rock-solid American Republican View bequeathed to me by my family. I then went on to read other books that imploded my economic and social understanding, including *The Creature from Jekyll Island: A Second Look at the Federal Reserve.* (The current 2010 reprint is #2 in economic policy and development and #3 in money and monetary policy on Amazon.)

Back in the 1980s, my conspiratorial knowledge was limited to economics, and I tried to share what I was learning with my WASP family living in one of the wealthiest areas of America outside Washington D.C. Yeah, right. *That* wasn't happening. I tried to share information with my professional friends in network television. (You'd think people in communications would be interested in learning about stuff to communicate. But nope.) And my spiritual friends couldn't have cared less about the history of the central banking system either.

Graciously I was informed by one and all that information belying the social status quo and mainstream media messaging was a "conspiracy" and that conspiracies were for fruit cakes. Friends forgave my gullibility, chalking it up to a temporary glitch in my operating system. My parents—well, my parents had yet to forgive me for voting Democratic. God knows what they thought about my rants about the Rockefeller and Rothchild empires.

Never mind the large amount of openly-available proof. Forget the fact that every mainstream magazine in America has, at one time or another, published in-depth articles about secret societies and their not-so-secret agendas. (Or at least the agendas the secret societies wished to have known.) Everybody I knew was part of the "impossible" crowd.

"An economic conspiracy is impossible to prove," people said. And when I handed Joe or Janet or Harry a book saying, "Here's the proof. Just check the documentation in the highlighted sections between pages 272 to 312," they refused to look at the information because it was "obviously incorrect," so why bother checking it out?

If they actually looked at it, then where would they be? In the same fruitcake boat as me. And that was unacceptable. Best to resort to scornful ridicule followed by a conciliatory invitation to have drinks somewhere and move on with the status quo and personal comfort zones safely intact.

Other common feedback lines were: "People just aren't smart enough to perpetrate the kinds of things you're talking about." Or "Humans just aren't patient enough to plot for thousands of years to gain control of the world." Or "It's absolutely impossible to keep something like a global agenda for totalitarian economic control a secret."

The other excuse people used was, "I know what's going on. I keep abreast of the news. I read *The New York Times* and *The Washington Post*. If something like this were happening, I'd know about it. I'd see the signs."

Sigh. The signs are all around us.

We just don't see them.

The average human brain receives approximately 11-million bits of information per second about the world around it.[40] Because we literally can't handle that amount of input without going insane, a sensory gating system installs itself early on in our baby brain's development, filtering that enormous amount of data down to an average of 60 bits per second.[41] *Sixty bits per second.* That's all it takes for a human being to get a college degree, have a conversation or fly the space shuttle. Obviously, with an intact sensory gating system, seeing the Big Picture is a difficult task.

Then there's the odd way the human brain deals with what little data does make it into conscious awareness. Human beings perceive, and thus think, in terms of duality. We perceptually function in terms of differences and either/or. It's how our brains are wired to discern reality.

One way to get a visual handle on how we organize what we call reality is a figure-ground study created in 1915 by Danish psychologist Edgar Rubin called the Rubins-vase.[42]

The drawing depicts two images with a common border, in this case identical facial profiles facing one another that create another image of a white vase in between. It doesn't matter which image you see first. Quickly, the other view asserts itself, back and forth, back and forth.

Either this *or* that

This kind of limited perceptual brain function is why millions of sensitive, caring individuals can turn a blind eye to genocide, ritual rape and God knows what else going on in this world, all the while considering themselves to be highly aware, compassionate people. They've been taught "this is just how life is" and they believe it. Similarly, people have been taught "Conspiracies are bullshit." And once this is the reality they accept—just like being caught in the perception of the white vase—it's difficult to embrace another view.

And then there is inattentional blindness.

I know, for an absolute fact, that it's not just deeply-guarded, subversive plots that we miss. People miss the most blatantly obvious, in-your-face things everyday. Let me tell you how I discovered this.

I was sitting in a room with 62 other people when Marilyn Schlitz, Ph.D., researcher, social anthropologist and senior scientist at the California Pacific Medical Center, gave a talk on something called inattentional blindness and selective attention.

During the talk she played a video of six people in a large office hallway rapidly passing a volleyball around the group. Three people wore white shirts and three people wore black shirts. All of us attending the lecture were instructed to count the number of times the ball was passed between the people wearing the white shirts.

About 20 seconds into the video, I lost count and gave up the exercise. To my amazement, a big guy in a gorilla suit suddenly materialized out of nowhere, standing in the center of the circle of people passing the ball. He faced the camera, beat his chest, then turned and walked off while the ball exercise was still in motion.

"How many of you saw something unusual in this video?" Schlitz asked a minute later when the clip finished. One other woman and I raised our hands. The 61 other people saw nothing out of the ordinary. When she ran the same video again, telling us to simply watch the video and not count ball passes, there the gorilla was, clear as day to everyone.

Audience reactions ranged from stunned to indignant to outraged. A couple people accused Schlitz of playing two different videos to trick them. But who needs somebody to trick us when we already trick ourselves?

The whole point of the exercise was to show people how much information humans constantly miss—ENORMOUS things like a freaking GORILLA standing directly in front of a camera in a small hallway. Which begs the question: If I can miss seeing a six-foot gorilla standing the equivalent of ten feet away in plain sight, what else am I not seeing?

CHAPTER FIVE KEY

Be open to different realities and start doing independent research

Nothing is keeping you from seeing this anti-life Force and its effects except for the fact that—just like the experiment with inattentional blindness—*we've been told to put our attention elsewhere.*

We're dealing with a mental matrix that says: "*This* is what's real. Anything else is absurd. Pay attention to *this* and *this* and *this*." Pay attention to inflation and the situation in Ukraine. Pay attention to your bills. Your student loans. Pay attention to the Kardashians and Johnny Depp's courtroom drama. Pay attention to your phone. Yes, that's right, your phone. Clutch it like your life depends on it. Don't let it out of your sight. Place all your attention onto that little screen every moment you possibly can and listen and watch and believe every little thing it has to say. Every piece of "news," every "fact," every carefully crafted headline, meme, op ed piece, video and speech and *believe believe believe* ...

Yeah, no. Don't believe.

I will warn you: Key #5 will take time and effort. But if you're up to the task, here are some steps to take:

- Question everything. (Including everything in this book!)
- Unhook from mainstream media.
- Start investigating "unapproved" sources of news. (Check out resources at the end.)
- Listen to alternative voices on the web in different genres like medicine and health (two different things), politics, etc.
- With any national or global issue, *follow the vested interests*.

I subscribe to *The Washington Post* and *The London Times* electronically to keep tabs on world headlines and what the global elites want people to believe.

I don't watch mainstream news. I do not watch television. (I do watch some shows and movies on Netflix.) I do not listen to the radio when I'm driving.

I turn off the router to my computer at night and keep all electrical devices out of my bedroom. I carry my cell phone in my purse and never on my body. I never hold the phone to my ear (I use the speaker function), and I turn it off at night and leave it in another room.

I'll talk in more depth about why to avoid mainstream media in chapter eight. The short version is this: All the legacy media sources of news are owned by the same global conglomerates that also own the industries profiting from the positive (or negative) news spin around various issues and thus cannot be trusted.

Is doing all this easy? Relatively, still, yes. Is it time consuming? Absolutely. Are people going to love you for thinking independently? Nope. Will such an investigation put you on a government Black List somewhere in the bowels of the CIA or NSA or some other government agency? Quite possibly.

Will such a path be satisfying? Maybe.

Frankly, I wouldn't label any of the research I've done for this book "satisfying." Most of it has horrified me almost beyond words and pissed me off. But by heaven it's made me wake up and get sovereign in a hurry.

And THAT is satisfying.

MIRROR EXERCISE

If you have issues with conspiracies and evil being real, what happens when you finally see that *you're* not even real the way you think you are? I was introduced to the following mirror exercise about 25 years ago and it freaked me out. But it sure taught me one thing: *The body is not really physical and it's definitely not who I am.*

- Looking in the mirror everyday to check our appearance—our hair, our tie, our makeup—is misleading. We unconsciously think "Yep, that's me!" over and over. It isn't until you sit down and *look*—preferably spending *30 minutes to an hour* at this exercise—that you begin to realize that your face is malleable. A light show that flickers and changes, now mirroring *this*, now mirroring *that*.
- Sit down quietly *in a dim room* with no distractions. Sit up close to a large mirror. (A couple feet away.) Late evening/ dusk is the perfect time. Or use a candle at night, placing it between you and the mirror.
- Gaze steadily into your eyes. Really look deeply and don't look away.
- Keep blinking to a minimum
- Do this for 30 to 60 minutes.

After a few minutes what do you see? What feelings come up? Does looking in a mirror like this, really looking at what you think is you, make you uncomfortable? Fill you with disquiet? If so, why?

6

Human Complicity and the Shadow

It's clear there are plenty of evil doings in the world. But how do the Archon/mind parasites gain a foothold into our psyches in the first place?

A more perfect image encapsulating the moment our basically loving human nature is hijacked by "something else" in order to shove us in the direction of our less-evolved, survival-based nature could not be found than that of the little devil with horns and a forked tail sitting on one shoulder whispering in our ear while an angel sits on the other shoulder trying to talk us into doing the "good" thing instead.

Which brings us around to the issue of "the shadow."

Frankly, I think one of the major reasons humans are susceptible to the influence of this anti-life Force is because the first five minutes of life on Earth make it abundantly clear that *bodies can be hurt.* We all have a fear-based side of us that responds to life in a survival-based fashion because we perceive ourselves as walking around in unprotected skin suits that can be easily damaged. Plus, our physical eyes and senses give us the 24/7 message that we are separate from each other and separate from the world and thus alone.

And *that* is scary too.

As a result of our innate but subconscious fear, as we grow up, we often act in negative, self-protective ways, attacking others and lashing out. As adults, we throw ourselves into acquiring as much information, money and possessions as possible to protect ourselves against loss and suffering and any sort of perceived deprivation. Living in this unconsciously fearful state, we are naturally suspicious of anything that is not like us. The fear of the "other" arises, stimulated by a different skin color, language or belief system—and with that fear come judgment and reprisals against the other for self-protection—often in a pre-emptive way.

How much of this is the natural effect of living in physical bodies that give us the inescapable (although ultimately erroneous) message of separation and vulnerability is impossible to say. Fear and self-protection and the violence and acquisitiveness that go with them are just part of our early developmental nature. It's not evil. It's simply a survival program that, with any luck, we incrementally overcome and evolve beyond as we psychologically mature and begin to get in touch with the reality of Who We Really Are, which is spirit/consciousness.

But until we get in touch with our true spiritual nature and realize the truth that we are not separate from each other and only different from one another in superficial physical ways, we are unconsciously run by fear and survival-based programs. Programs that can be leveraged in the direction of ever-greater self-interest, self-importance and self-destruction.

The great 20th century psychoanalyst Carl Jung termed our less attractive darker urges the personal shadow. According to Jung, the shadow is instinctive and irrational and composed of hidden "unacceptable" elements in each individual's personality.

Shadow material runs the gamut from small guilts to near possession.

For example, we're taught in church not to be selfish, but we always take the biggest slice of cake we can find on the tray. We're taught it's a sin to steal, but secretly snatch candy off the shelves at the grocery store and stash it away in our pockets. We're taught not to lust, but can't help but ogle the neighbor's wife the way she dresses. (Or rather doesn't dress.) We gossip about a friend's husband or the boss's secretary. We're jealous of our brother's Mercedes, our sister's income, our landlady's wardrobe and our best friend's hair and flair.

We read the tabloids and are filled with envy over other peoples' perfect lives—their wealth and health, their seamless faces and Botox-plumped lips and hips. We watch *Keeping Up with the Kardashians* and *Selling Sunset* and sink into a pool of black thoughts, ashamed of our lives, wishing we were someone else.

We fear spiders and the dark, heights, fire, water, snakes, the outdoors and paranoically wish we could be hermetically sealed away from germs. We secretly judge others even though we're not supposed to, and feel smug when we think we're ahead of others in the game morally, economically and socially. We feel superior if we weigh less. We look away from suffering and need and wish we had more for ourselves instead—more money, more sex appeal, a bigger house, a better car and on and on.

Then maybe I'll be safe.

Then maybe I'll be loved.

Then maybe I'll be worthy of love.

These are some of the unconscious thoughts behind all this. And it's these subconscious fears and insecurities that open the door for the mind parasites to enter and fan the already existing dark flames. Hatred leads to violence. Self-hatred leads to cruelty. Fear leads to paranoia, aggression and attack. Jealousy leads to stalking and other weird aberrations. Lusts explode out of control.

Because most people prefer not to see unpleasant truths about themselves, subliminal Archonic influences are able to trigger and augment all the shadow material safely tucked out of sight in the unconscious, steadily increasing the darkness within. And as the internal pressures and desires to actualize the shadow build, the external self-image—the person we *think* we are—puffs itself up, trying to create an ever-more convincing case for its righteousness.

Think televangelists Tammy Faye and Jim Bakker.

It's the split between unacknowledged internal shadow issues and the ego—the public persona that has an image to uphold—that's at the root of stories you hear about people like a former neighbor of mine who was a pillar of the community and a self-righteous deacon at the local Presbyterian Church.

I always thought his children were a little weird. Especially his daughter who, at age ten, was abnormally high-strung and anxious. And then one day his wife packed up the kids and left and the bombshell dropped. Her husband had been sexually abusing his little girl and possibly his son as well.

Mic drop.

But this is far from an unusual tale. In fact, it's a cliché. The more righteous the self-image, the further from reality we are. The further from the reality of Who We Really Are, the easier it is for the mind parasites to have their way with us, urging us into ever greater self-inflation, pride, indignation, outrage, cruelty and abuse. Try rewatching the film *American Beauty* sometime. (Ironic that it stars Kevin Spacey.)

For most people, the shadow stays unconscious their entire lives.

Uncovering "the dark side" usually only happens when we're driven to it by spiritual evolution or by catastrophic circumstances, such as a life-threatening illness that ends up prompting us to introspection in order to find answers to our sudden misery.

As Jung himself expressed it: "The shadow is a moral problem that challenges the whole ego-personality, for no one can become conscious of the shadow without considerable moral effort. To become conscious of it involves recognizing the dark aspects of the personality as present and real. This act is the essential condition for any kind of self-knowledge, and it therefore, as a rule, meets with considerable resistance. Indeed, self-knowledge as a psychotherapeutic measure frequently requires much painstaking work extending over a long period."[43]

Spiritually, Jung's shadow goes far beyond Sigmund Freud's earlier psychoanalytic theory of personality in which the id is the part of the personality that works to satisfy basic urges, needs, and desires—mostly sexual—operating solely out of the pleasure principle. But both men came to the same conclusion that humans, when faced with the darkest, most primitive aspects of themselves, usually try to excuse it all away. We project our own shadows onto others and make our issues *their* issues. We use metaphors to describe these shadows, calling them our inner demons. Or we label them the desire body or the pain body. Or we say we're "wrestling with the devil."

Discovering, embracing and going beyond our not-so-pleasant shadows is the nature of personal evolution. It is always part of the psychoanalytic process and is the very foundation of the spiritual journey.

In spiritual circles, this process includes an even deeper examination of what constitutes the "self." With any luck, this scrupulous self-investigation eventually brings the student to the realization that his/her entire personality structure is not really who s/he is at all. Rather, it is a fictitious persona—an imaginary identity—that spontaneously arises in the brain as a result of physical stimuli and external information. A false identity that then becomes the ego vehicle through which they operate in life.

The deeper truth waiting to be uncovered is that our true nature is non-physical.

The deeper truth is that we are pure consciousness and an energy called "love" that is infinite and eternal. And again, the "love" I'm referring to has nothing to do with our romantic notions of love. Rather it is the fierce and awesome force of life itself that is totally unaligned with the superficial, the sentimental, or the foolish.

This deep evolutionary process is sometimes mythically referred to as a "descent to the underworld" and pretty much always referred to as the "dark night of the soul." (Of course, why it's called the dark night of the soul when what this describes is really the "dark night of the ego," I don't know.) Anyway, it's called that because getting stripped of normal human identity is a difficult process to even imagine let alone actually experience. The end result might be extraordinary. But getting there is difficult in the extreme.

But back to the shadow.

What I'm trying to say here is: Shadow material is normal.

We all have crap we think and do that we hope nobody ever finds out about. There probably isn't a parent alive who, at some exhausted, overwrought point in time, hasn't visualized throwing their precious offspring out a window. I can't imagine anybody having made it through life without wanting to slap or throttle somebody or—lying sleepless in bed at 2 a.m. facing the most important corporate sales presentation of their life the next morning—thought about punting the next-door neighbor's yowling dog to the moon. It's just a normal part of life.

Certainly, our shadow elements should not be confused with pathology. They have nothing to do with evil *unless* they aren't consciously addressed.

> ***If shadow issues aren't consciously dealt with, they may well become material for the Archons to manipulate.***

As far as the anti-life Force on our planet is concerned, the unaddressed shadow aspects of the typical human being are the perfect snack food. Our unhappy, irrational, selfish, impulsive shadow material is the equivalent of the much-vaunted "prima materia" sought by alchemists in their quest to create the Philosopher's Stone[44]— the starting material required to shape the Magnum Opus—the Great Work of turning lead into gold, which is a metaphor for the ascension of the physical human into the realization of her or his spirit nature.

Of course, in the case of the Archons, their desired outcome is the farthest thing possible from the creation of the Philosopher's Stone and entry into the brilliant light of eternal life, wisdom and purity sought by the alchemist.

> ***Instead of beauty, this hidden Force uses our worst impulses against us to create a foul and misshapen version of a human being, rather like Tolkien's vision of the Uruk-hai.***

There is much dark "prima materia" for an intelligent malevolent force to work with in humans. The longer we, as a species, remain ignorant of our shadow, the longer we remain prey to evil influences urging us towards our lowest common denominator.

"Go ahead," come the whispers. "Eat more, drink more, do some drugs, watch some porn. Why not? Everybody does it. You know you want to.

"Go ahead. Build that condo project that will destroy the last ecosystem supporting the manatees. Sell the pharmaceutical product that has life-threatening side effects.

"What are you waiting for?

"Get in the game while it lasts and get yours!"

That's the mindset. And in case you're still not sure how the shadow works and how the Archons utilize it, let me give you a personal example.

For the past hour, I've been wrestling against an urge to drive to the store and buy a pint of Ben & Jerry's Phish Food ice cream. The urge is physical—literally an ache of sugar-driven desire. The voices in my head are saying things like, "You can start your diet tomorrow. It's Friday. You just finished that article and made your deadline. Go ahead. It's just one pint. You deserve it."

It's not that eating a pint of ice cream is bad.

It's not bad. It's not good. In and of itself, eating a pint of ice cream is a neutral thing.

However, going into the Covid lockdowns two years ago, I was ten pounds overweight. Now, I'm 30 pounds overweight. My body feels like a boat anchor and, living in Hawaii as I do, I spend a certain amount of time each week in a bathing suit out in public. Not only do I feel like crap, the bathing suit situation is not doing my self-esteem any good.

Yes, I know. I shouldn't allow myself to be affected by shallow things like the casual opinions of strangers. But I'd be lying if I said it didn't affect me. And no, I'm not going to add guilt over being vain to the pile of issues I'm building here. (More shadow!) My point is, 1) I'm wrestling with a habit and 2) a voice in my head is urging me to go in a direction contrary to my physical health, my emotional wellbeing and my own overarching desire to feel great on every level.

Can you spell a-n-t-i-l-i-f-e influence?

It's a moment of choice we all know well: Self-empowerment versus self-sabotage.

Angel or demon.

Again, I want to reiterate, there's no right or wrong to either choice. The issue is *Who do I want to be?* How do I want to feel? Who is at the helm of my life? Me? Or the voices in my head and my body's cravings?

To make matters worse, the religious associations and implications in this scenario are inescapable because the brain works via association. I think *Am I going to rise to the occasion or fall prey to habit?* Instantly, my brain's neurons fire a closely associated religious thought pattern: *Am I going to be a good girl or a bad girl?*

Next my brain fires another set of neuron patterns associated with all the times I've been a bad girl. It fires subconscious memories of church and sermons about temptation and the devil. And now guilt comes into the picture and I'm in a wrestling match.

Fortunately for me, this wrestling match is happening while I'm alone, sitting here writing about consciousness and freedom of choice. I'm not sitting in front of the TV being influenced by commercials for The Cheesecake Factory. I'm not hanging out with friends (who have their own shadows to placate) saying supportive things like, "Oh, go on! It's not heroin. It's just ice cream!"

So, let's go a little deeper.

Habits, healthy and otherwise, are hard-wired.

Every habit is literally its own neurological network in the brain. The more we engage in a habit, the more that particular network of neurons fires, becoming ever more deeply entrenched in the brain. Which means the habit just gets easier and easier to express.

"Feel good" actions like eating and drinking, doing drugs and watching porn trigger the release of "feel good" neurotransmitters in the brain like serotonin and dopamine. This is why we want to indulge in these actions as often as possible. We not only get hooked on the immediate physical sense gratification, we also get hooked on our body's own biochemical responses to those substances and actions.

It's a double physiological whammy right from the start.

Shadow material also drives our physical habits and cravings.

In my case, this shadow material takes the form of self-sabotage which in turn is driven by shadow issues of insecurity and self-hatred. So where do *those* issues come from?

The science of epigenetics proves that our emotions imprint our DNA, which is then passed down to our descendants. So, let's take a look at my epigenetic heritage.

I've already mentioned that my mother was filled with self-hatred and self-judgment. She was also deeply insecure and had an addictive personality which showed up as alcoholism and a heavy cigarette habit. Not to blame my mom or anything, but I don't have to look any further back than one generation to see where I've literally inherited some of my shadow issues along with matching self-destructive habits.

Now ... add to this genetic inheritance all the emotional traumas, big and small, that we pick up over the course of our lifetime.

All the little hurts and neglect, the disappointments, the lies, the perceived mistakes and the false conclusions we've come to exacerbate our shadow material. Nearly forgotten memories ... like my fourth-grade teacher Mrs. Barton's consistently cruel ridicule of me and my thoughts in class. Or my step-father's ugly comments about my body. Or the priest's words about sin. Or the sexual prejudice of my first boss who promoted less-deserving men with less experience instead of me. Or the epigenetic programming of fifty generations of women before me in my WASP family line feeling guilt about their sexuality.

It's a veritable buffet of issues for the Archons to work with!

On top of all this unconscious material add the relentless images of death, addiction, perverted sex, misery and small-mindedness that the mainstream media bombards us with day in and day out. Now, on top of *that,* add advanced brainwashing technologies buried in the earth pumping out negative frequencies designed to drive us towards violence and our lowest possible potential.

And I wonder why there's this voice in my head that says, "Oh, for God's sake, go get the damn ice cream and eat it. You're nothing and you'll never amount to anything, so let yourself go. Who cares?"

This is what I mean when I say the cards are stacked against us.

How can we possibly evolve beyond our more primitive fear-based physical natures if our primal fears and emotional lacks keep getting whipped up over and over again? How can we see our shadows? How can we evolve beyond perpetually acting them out when there are so many negative forces keeping us from doing so?

How?

Let us count the ways!

CHAPTER SIX KEY

Deal with your shadow and negative forces

STEP 1: Address and clear negative interference in your own energy field

One of the most powerful things you can do is a personal clearing of your own energy field. The following is an energetic clearing that Robin Duda, healing practitioner and founder of Sustainable Love Transformation & Training Center in Santa Fe, has supplied.[45]

This invocation uses words, voice, and movement to help clear and energize body, soul and personal will, uniting them. In this process you will be calling on your Multidimensional Self to more firmly embody on Earth and more deeply connect with love as your Source, thus supporting freedom and personal intentions.

Working with body movement and the voice together connects you to the awareness of positive, pleasurable sensations—sensations that are instinctual when you move in dance, ceremony, and celebration, alone or with others.

This clearing addresses that which is not loving or serving you at this time—including mental, emotional, physical and spiritual influences that have controlled or limited your own light and/or authenticity.

The purpose is to help you firmly claim this life in your body, empower you to feel your own power and truth, and enable you to bring all of your gifts into form to serve love and take your next evolutionary steps in life.

Your Multidimensional Self reveals itself through a wide range of manifestations—different colors, images, frequencies, strange sensations, heart opening, unexplained promptings and attractions. Your Multidimensional Self has many gifts, and is evolving right along with your human body.

Soul Alchemy Empowerment Process

You can start off either laying down or sitting.

- Connect with your breath and your body sensations, opening up to an awareness of your inner landscape.
- Take a few minutes to ground into your body and connect.
- Place your attention on your heart center and focus on anything you are grateful for. This will help your heart open and allow you to sense that opening through loving sensations.

Now, stand up.

- Reach your arms above your head about shoulder width apart. From the awareness of your heart, feel the fullness of your chest and say out loud:
    - *"From the power of One Love that I am, I invoke my multi-dimensional soul and my Source in my body. I welcome all that I am to come home in present time."*
- Move your body any way that opens and releases tension. Shake, jiggle, jump, circle your arms ... whatever is spontaneous and energizing. Do this as long as you feel you should. This builds up your energy body.
- Now, speak with clarity and strength:
    - *"I call forth the power of love from this Earth and Source-Spirit to unite in my body in my heart. I claim my right to my Sovereign Self. Love is my greatest power."*

Repeat as many times as you feel moved to do so while directing your awareness inward as you speak. *Your voice is your will choosing and claiming your heart's desire.*

- Now, say out loud:
    - "I release all projections from family, work, lovers, friends, clients, (etc.) that are in my field."
- With your breath and movement, push out anything that is intruding into you energetically.
- When you feel clear, next say:
    - *"I release all mind control from media, technology,*

educational systems, political systems (etc.) that are suppressing my own thoughts and inspirations."

- With your breath and movement, push these energies out through the top of your head and clap around your body while you keep moving.
- When you feel clear, say aloud:
    - *"I bless free all interdimensional energies that are not mine that are attached to my denied fear or emotions. I bless any one else's emotions that I have taken on and I send them back to their own source."*
    - *"I release all entities and forces from known and unknown sources wishing me harm. I release everything that is not loving for me and send them back to their own source."*
    - *"I release any forms of control over my will of love and my power!"*

- When you feel clear, give thanks to Earth and your Multidimensional Self and feel the love and your own soul's essence filling you up.
- Take your time and feel the love. Bask in feeling connected to life and aligned with the Life Force that is you.

I do this basic clearing everyday.

STEP 2: Acknowledge your shadow material

We all have perceived faults and flaws we keep hidden out of shame and guilt and pride.

It helps considerably to stop weighing yourself down with judgment and guilt over having shadow material. That just overlays existing issues with more issues, making healing more difficult.

STEP 3: Don't create the conditions where negative forces can enter in the first place

This is a toughie—at least it has been for me. But here goes: Stop drinking alcohol (or at least cut way back). And definitely stop doing drugs—including marijuana. Mind-altering substances, including prescription pharmaceuticals for depression and anxiety, throw open the door for dark energetic influences to penetrate you psychically, emotionally, mentally and physically.

I'm not being a goodie-two-shoes here. My parents were alcoholics and I started drinking at age sixteen. I've also done a lot of different drugs and plant medicines over the course of my life. In my teens and twenties, I was just stupid and into recreational use. From my thirties onwards I occasionally used medicinal plants as an aide to "waking up." So, I haven't got anything against any of these things. But having worked with a few genuine shamans (not the dime-a-dozen New Age wannabees), I know how dangerous it is for most people to use plant medicines for spiritual insight without true professional guidance and oversight to ensure that they do not come under the influence of dark entities in the process.

And then there's alcohol.

A friend of mine from my early spirituality days was extremely psychic. He told me several times that if I could actually *see* the entities hanging around outside and inside the bars and see what was hanging onto the people drinking, that I'd never go inside another bar or ever drink again.

I believed him. But it didn't change my drinking habits.

Booze was my drug of choice.

I stopped every once and awhile—sometimes for years at a stretch—usually because some spiritual teacher advised it. But then I always started back again. I'm currently disengaging my love affair with alcohol for the umpteenth time—not because I think I "should" or because "It's bad for me." Not even because it opens a doorway for the Archons to enter.

I've quit regular use of all substances because *I want something different. And I can't get to different by doing same.*

Coming clear, I can finally see the possibility of something new. I can *feel* a new life filled with love and excitement and creativity building inside and around me.

So, if you're drinking a lot or using drugs every day, I suggest you ask yourself, "Why?"

I did it because I was bored and tapped out at the end of the day, mentally exhausted and overwhelmed by everything happening in the world. Finally, all it did was make me go numb. And then numb was fine too. A human being can only bear so much.

But feeling numb and distracted is no longer okay with me.

There's light, not just at the end of a long tunnel, but a light shining right here inside my heart. I can feel it. My mind and body and whole being are quivering with possibility. It's a new frequency. A new way. A new day. An honest-to-God, down-to-earth action vibe setting into motion.

The fact that you're reading this book says you've also reached the "get real and get going" part of your life journey. So, yay you!

The ugly old reality is on its way out. Rapidly.

It doesn't look like it, I know. But it is.

When I switched careers from television production to writing for a living, I worked in construction as a framing carpenter, building houses for a few years to make ends meet. I also did a lot of renovation work.

It wasn't lost on me that renovative construction was a lot like the descent to the underworld and the dark night of the soul. There was destruction and a lot of swinging of sledgehammers. There was horrific noise and choking dust. There was unbelievable mess and chaos. There was even blood when I failed to engage prybar and claw hammer correctly or didn't carefully watch my step.

But once the walls were down and the detritus cleared away there was room for a clean fresh start. There was spaciousness and opportunity and room for creativity and imagination. There was a clear platform upon which a whole new structure could be built. And what joy lay in the building!

This is where we are today.

As citizens of Earth, we know the old house we built isn't serviceable anymore.

Millions of people work daily creating new plans and blueprints.

Malcontents and revolutionaries do their best to destroy old constructs. Visionaries speak of their visions. Social architects make the translations. Millions pray for and support change. The permits have already been issued and stamped in our souls.

The wrecking crews are hard at work.

The Old Heaven and Earth are being razed to the ground as it was always foretold.

We are in the midst of the dust and chaos and blood of destruction.

But our future ... Oh! Our future is bright indeed.

7

The God Spell

I started this book because I wanted to expose the presence of an anti-life Force on this planet and how religions, spirituality, and social systems support evil in many ways. I also wanted to shine a light on the astonishing fragility of the modern picture of reality most humans live by.

What I didn't realize at first is that this book is also about exposing the many reasons why we *can't* see what's right in front of our noses despite the thinness of the veil obscuring an astonishingly different reality than the one generally accepted.

So far we've looked at 1) Archon-twisted religious programming that keeps us too filled with shame to expect anything better than misery; 2) spiritual philosophies that erase evil from existence altogether; 3) the demonization and marginalization of viewpoints and information that differ from the accepted social narrative; 4) inattentional blindness and other perceptual limitations; and 5) the presence of a fear-based, easily manipulated shadow side of our nature that reliably provides an explanation for evil doings on the planet.

Now we're going to look at a real biggie:

God

No. God is not reaching out and preventing us from seeing what's going on—at least not in the form of direct interference. But indirectly? Wow. The number of different ways our thoughts and beliefs about God basically put a sack over our heads with no eye holes is pretty incredible.

Let's start with "It's God's will."

For thousands of years, this has been the Western world's go to explanation for everything from the death of a child to volcanic eruptions to the Black Death to the Divine Right of Kings. Things are the way they are because God wishes it so—and who are we to argue with that no matter how bad things get? And if things are bad, it's obviously punishment from God for our wrongdoings. Even people who profess not to believe in religious teachings talk about such things as fate and not being able to outrun one's destiny.

So how did this slavish, "Do with me as you will" orientation come about?

Stay tuned!

~

There are currently over 4200 religions on this planet roughly categorizable into the five main religions: Christianity, Islam, Hinduism, Buddhism and Judaism. Within Christianity alone there are over 30,000 individual sects and denominations with differing beliefs and Biblical interpretations.

All these thousands of different religions and sects sport differing names and faces and interpretations of language and events. But when you start looking at some of the common details surrounding the nature of God and how humanity got its start on this planet, the stories start taking on an eerie similarity and a ... dare I say, extraterrestrial flavor.

Christians and Jews all know from Genesis that God found the earth "without form and void, and darkness was upon the face of the deep." From that state He separated out the heavens from the earth, created light and life in the oceans and on the earth, including humanity. After that, God comes and goes from heaven to Earth and back again as He pleases, issuing orders, favoring and uplifting some people while threatening and destroying others.

In Exodus 19:18 God arrives thus: "Mount Sinai was covered with smoke, because the Lord descended on it in fire. The smoke billowed up from it like smoke from a furnace, and the whole mountain trembled violently."

Um ... why does God arrive as if He's descending in a rocket ship?

Can't He just "arrive?"

Other creation stories from around the world agree that "in the beginning" the Earth was in a condition of darkness and flood conditions.

But wait a minute … in all these accounts the Earth is already present and accounted for. It may be in bad shape. But it clearly already exists. Which gives us a completely different view of "creation."

Whether the "beginnings" being recounted were before or after the Biblical great flood is a matter of some debate. Many world religions tell stories of Earth's god-assisted rehabilitation after a great disaster had befallen the planet. In some accounts it was following a global war. In many accounts, it is "the gods" who assisted Earth after a catastrophic natural event—perhaps a meteor strike.

The concept of "gods" being responsible for Earth's creation seems quaintly primitive to the Western mind. We might not know the actual source of our belief in a singular God—supposedly it was God's conversation and covenant with Abraham after the great flood, an event Bible scholars place somewhere around 2400 BC—but that doesn't matter. We just *know* that there's only "One God, the Father Almighty, Maker of heaven and earth."

Certainly, that's what I was raised to believe.

And yet, over 32 percent of the world's population are polytheistic.[46] By far and away the vast majority of traditions—Hinduism, Buddhism and all tribal religions, whether South American, Polynesian, Native American, African, Australian, Asian and Inuit—refer to gods, plural, not a singular god being involved in Earth's creation and/or rehabilitation.

And the same is true of the Bible.

Throughout the Old Testament, the Hebrew word "Elohim" is the word for "God." A word that is most often translated as "the Lord" and sometimes as Yahweh. But here's the rub. Elohim is *a plural noun* in Hebrew. Eloah is the singular form meaning God. Elohim actually translates as gods or "the gods." In some secondary instances it can also be translated as meaning a singular female or male deity. But "gods" is the most common translation.

Bible scholars have puzzled endlessly over how strange it is that the plural noun form would be chosen as the way to name God. Obviously, the original writers meant "God." So why didn't they use the singular form, Eloah? Why did they describe God as Elohim—the gods—over

2600 times throughout the Old Testament? And why is the translation of the word Elohim so erratic?

When God is commanding something or doing something powerful and God-like, the translation appears as "God" or "the Lord" or Yahweh. When Elohim appears in an obviously plural context it is sometimes translated as "false gods" and "demons." Other times the proper translation "gods" remains.

And what about the actual story of Abraham receiving God's covenant in Genesis 18—the passage which many scholars use to solidify the whole "one God" story in the first place? Here is how the King James Bible version tells it:

> And the LORD appeared unto him in the plains of Mamre: and he sat in the tent door in the heat of the day;
>
> 2 And he lift up his eyes and looked, and, lo, three men stood by him: and when he saw them, he ran to meet them from the tent door, and bowed himself toward the ground
>
> 3 And said, My LORD, if now I have found favour in thy sight, pass not away, I pray thee, from thy servant:
>
> 4 Let a little water, I pray you, be fetched, and wash your feet, and rest yourselves under the tree:
>
> 5 And I will fetch a morsel of bread, and comfort ye your hearts; after that ye shall pass on: for therefore are ye come to your servant. And they said, So do, as thou hast said.
>
> 6 And Abraham hastened into the tent unto Sarah, and said, Make ready quickly three measures of fine meal, knead it, and make cakes upon the hearth.

Scholars interpret Genesis 18 as Abraham meeting God and two angels. But the story itself clearly states Abraham met three men whom he instantly recognizes as "The Lord." Surely, the plural translation of Elohim, "the gods," would be far more appropriate here?

But then it would render the scene quite differently—and not in favor of monotheism. The proper translation would have Abraham being visited by three men that he clearly recognizes as being members of the Elohim—the gods—and thus he treats them with the respect they are due.

So where do we get God and two angels?

By the sixth century BCE the concept of monotheism introduced via Abraham and supported by Moses had solidified into the truth. Which means any earlier editions of stories referring to the gods—or "the Powerful Ones" as Biblical scholar and former Anglican Archdeacon Paul Wallis translates the word Elohim—would have to be drastically modified.

It would never do to have three men meeting Abraham. If the Lord was there, then obviously it had to be two angels accompanying Him.

What else?

Wallis, author of *The Scars of Eden,* makes an interesting case, not just for the plural translation of Elohim as "the Powerful Ones," but also for the obvious presence of spacefaring beings involved in the terraforming of planet Earth and the genetic manipulation and rescue of all sorts of species—including humanity—after a vast disaster had befallen the planet.

He sources Plato (429 BCE - 348 BCE) as being one of the earliest and most profoundly respectable historians to talk about this presence in his books *Phaedo, Timaeus and Critias*, referring to these beings as "children of God." According to Wallis, Plato wrote that these beings modified our ancestors and gave us the capacity for higher intelligence. They lived on "islands in the sky" above the earth, which Plato described as a globe with "surprisingly swirly patterns of blue, white, green and gold."

Wallis points out that over the centuries, venerable Church fathers who supported Plato's references to these children of God and their interaction with early humans in their writings were rather dramatically taken out of the picture. For example, Marcion of Sinope (85 AD – 160 AD) and Origen of Alexandria (185 AD – 253 AD), both enormously respected theologians and prolific writers, were against the deluge of newly edited Bible stories making theological changes, including the deletion of this extraterrestrial presence from history. They suffered dreadfully for their adherence to earlier translations. Marcion was excommunicated and Origen was condemned as a heretic, imprisoned and tortured to death.[47]

The Catholic Church continued its cruel suppression of any message not following the new party line of monotheism. Eventually the Protestant missionaries joined the game, ruthlessly stamping out primitive superstitious "heresies" wherever they found them—in Africa and China, Russia, South America and the continent of North America, the Pacific islands and India. Between the Catholics and the Protestants, thousands upon thousands of precious manuscripts and scrolls, carvings and statues proclaiming a different version of early human history were destroyed. Shamans and priests and storytellers speaking of ancient extraterrestrial teachers were slaughtered. The library at Alexandria was burned to ashes.

And yet despite all this, in the East, to this day Buddhism and Hinduism casually support an extraterrestrial presence on this planet and in the heavens. In the Buddhist view, the universe is created and destroyed, not by God, but by fire, wind and water in a series of endless cycles called "Great Periods" (cycles with Buddhas) and "voids" (cycles without Buddhas). Buddhism accepts the existence of millions of other inhabited worlds, each with a Buddha of its own. Chapter 23 of the Lotus Sutra titled "Gadgadasvara" tells the story of a student who asks his master for permission to visit Earth and listen to the sermon of Sakyamuni, the terrestrial Buddha. His master agrees and lets him travel to Earth, but not before warning him not to form a low opinion of humans and the planet.

Even the *Quran*, the fount of Islamic monotheistic philosophy, makes a vague reference to other inhabited worlds. In verse 42:29 we read the following: "Among His signs is the creation of the heavens and the earth, and the 'dabbah' (creatures) He has spread in them."

And then there's always the Mormon Church which is quite clear about not only God's unearthly origins but humanity's as well. Joseph Smith taught that God and Adam and Eve came from a planet called Kolob, which was God's original home.

Erich von Däniken's *Chariots of the Gods* published in 1968 is the father of all ancient aliens books. I read it when I was 16, the year it came out, and remember the original paperback sitting on my nightstand next to my bed. (An original copy is now worth $499 on Amazon.) I devoured the information and found it fascinating. But then what's one funky book about aliens compared to 16 years of religious, social and educational programming?

And yet von Däniken's research in *Chariots* and one of his other books, *The Gods Never Left Us*, is honest and compelling. I've re-read both and paraphrased a few references he cites as well as a few stories I've pulled off the web supporting the ancient alien reality. If you're intrigued, I highly recommend all of his work.

Here goes:

The origin story of the Republic of Kiribati, an independent island nation in the central Pacific Ocean, centers around the god Nareau who flew "alone and sleeping through space." Upon awakening from slumber, he saw Te Bomatemaki—a planet with abundant atmosphere below. "Four times he circumnavigated the world he had found, from north to south, east to west, and he was alone." Nareau lands upon Te Bomatemaki, mixes earth and water and creates animals and plants and humans and then flies away, never to be seen again.[48]

In the islands of New Hebrides, also in the Pacific Ocean, the God Barakulkul arrives with five of his brothers from the heavens and takes charge of things. The Inuit in Alaska report that their ancestors arrived in "flying houses." The Tungus, a tribe in Siberia, say the first "divine couple" arrived on Earth from heaven in "a silver gondola."

In ancient Egypt, Nun was depicted as the infinite ocean of space from which the god Osiris arrived in a "golden ship." The Finnish refer to a "flame bird," which brought wisdom from heaven. The Tatoosh natives on the NW coast of California report a "thunder bird" which descended from the heavens and instructed their ancestors. Of course, the godly Thunderbird and Feathered Serpent are also part of the religions of the Maya and Aztecs and many other indigenous cultures in the Americas—great gods that arrived from the heavens in thundering flying machines with great knowledge about everything from writing and mathematics to agriculture and architecture—knowledge which they imparted to humans.

The Kogi Indians in Colombia say that heavenly teachers created the first humans, educating them and showing them how to live properly. In 1,600 BCE Hammurabi, who was "born in heaven," became the King of Babylon. He bequeathed humankind a comprehensive body of law, the Code of Hammurabi, which many believe formed the foundation of the Ten Commandments.

Kiev, the capital of Ukraine, was the landing site of the god Perun who "descended from heaven in a pillar of fire" and drove around the earth in his heavenly chariot.

The Bantu peoples in South Africa remember the heavenly god Nzame who descended to Earth to investigate the planet and fell in love with the human woman Mboja. The Dogon tribe in the Republic of Mali speak of their heavenly teacher Nomo who arrived from the constellation Sirius.

The Yamaschi, a Japanese tribe, were taught by demigods who commuted from the heavens to earth and back again. The Pawnee tribe in the central United States says humans were created by stellar beings who visited frequently, arriving "with fire and smoke." In Tierra del Fuego at the southern tip of South America, Kenos came to Earth to bring civilization, then flew back to heaven, never to return.

References to "heavenly cities" and "heavenly realms" and "heavenly places"—as cited in Ephesians in the Bible—abound. In ancient Sumer, the sky god An ruled Earth from a city above the clouds. A "heavenly city" was also inhabited by the King of Salem, a priest of the supreme God of the Jews.

The Tibetan king and "son of heaven," Gesar, lived in a flying city that "shone in the firmament and possessed roofs of heavenly iron which resisted every lightning bolt." Gesar and many other gods arrive from space in much the same way the Biblical God arrived upon Mt. Sinai as outlined in Exodus: "Heaven resounded, the earth shook, and there was the roaring of dragons."[49]

King Al Hadhad, father of the Queen of Sheba, lived in "a flying palace made of metal and towers." In the ancient book Drona Parva from the Indian Mahabharata, cities in the heavens "which gleamed like crystals," are described in detail. In West Africa, Abasi created all living things, but he did not create the human beings because "They lived aloft with Abasi in his heavenly city." Chinese lore is filled with references to the nine heavens where the supreme heavenly god resided and the original emperors were transported to and from earth upon fire-breathing dragons.

Fire-breathing dragons.

It's stunning how including the presence of spacefaring intelligences makes instant sense out of so much primitive myth carved on temple walls and stelae, written in scrolls and manuscripts the world over.

The Latvian people had a king Dievs who lived on his flying steed, only descending to earth at harvest time. The Hawaiian god Lono left Earth in a "cloud ship," promising to return in the distant future. In the Pyramid Texts of Unas from the Third Dynasty, the Pharaoh flies in a "heavenly barque." One of the texts says: "A stairway to heaven has been set up for me so that I can ascend to heaven ... and I climbed up on the smoke of the large vessel. I fly high as a bird and light as a beetle on the empty throne of your barque, oh Re. And I am permitted to sit on your seat and thunder across heaven, oh Re. I am permitted to lift off the land in your barque."[50]

King Solomon gave his lover, the Queen of Sheba, a flying chariot made in accordance to the specs given him by God which flew through the air—a chariot in which "without sweat and exhaustion we covered a distance of three months in one day."

The Drona Parva clearly describes large space ships in the heavens and smaller craft, which we would today recognize as shuttlecraft. It also describes terrible "heavenly weapons" which burn everything with "concentrated heat rays" activated by the eyes of the pilot.

In a tomb at Palenque, a carving of Pakal (see illustration on the following page), the second to last ruler of the Mayans, clearly shows him controlling a complicated machine with flames and smoke shooting out the back. (It totally reminds me of the 74-Z speeder bike used by Scout Troopers of the Galactic Empire to chase rebels on the Endor moon in the movie *Return of the Jedi*.) Many other Mayan carvings show similar highly mechanical devices with drivers perched within.

All of the material cited here and a ton more is available in von Däniken's books and on the Internet. Another prolific author, Zacharia Sitchin, a journalist and economist from Azerbaijan, wrote a famous

12-book series about the coming of the Annunaki—a race of gods who genetically modified the human race to use as slave labor in their earthly mining operations.

And then there is the highly popular 150-episode *Ancient Aliens* TV series. And the mind-stretching investigative work done by people like Dr. Robert Schoch, Graham Hancock and David Icke. The information is well researched, mostly verifiable and comprehensive. Frankly, it is jaw dropping looking at history through the ancient alien lens. So much comes so clear so fast.

And yet people listen. They nod their heads and …

Nothing changes.

In an interview with Dateline NBC in 1996, former Apollo 14 astronaut Ed Mitchell stated there were alien bodies at Roswell and that the government had covered it up. In 2008, he claimed on a radio show that many thousands of UFOs seen over the years were alien visitors from other planets. "I happen to have been privileged enough to be in on the fact that we've been visited on this planet and the UFO phenomena is real," he said.

And nothing happened.

In December 2020, Haim Eshed, former Brigadier General and head of Israel's Defense Ministry's space directorate, told Israel's *Yediot Aharonot* newspaper that Earth governments have been in contact with extraterrestrials from a "Galactic Federation" and that "The Unidentified

Flying Objects have asked not to publish that they are here, humanity is not ready yet."

Eshed said cooperation agreements had been signed and that an underground base on Mars had been built where both American astronauts and alien representatives work and dwell. "There is an agreement between the US government and the aliens. They signed a contract with us to do experiments here."

Eshed also said that President Donald Trump was ready to go public with the news, but was asked not to in order to prevent "mass hysteria." The news story was covered by several major US publications, including *Newsweek*.[51] Granted, the *Newsweek* article was extremely skeptical, making no reference to Eshed's excellent credibility as a source. Even so, the article raised a bit of a ruckus on social media. And then …

Nothing happened.

How is it possible that humanity is so dull and complacent that it's fundamentally non-reactive to mainstream reports from credible sources about the presence of extraterrestrial beings on planet Earth?

Presumptive narrative

This goes hand in hand with the tactic of ridicule (as in labeling something a conspiracy). The presumptive narrative is what we think is going on because we've been programmed by schools and the media to think that's what's going on. Anything outside the box of what we're repeatedly told is marginalized.

For 80 years we've been officially informed that UFOs are swamp gas or weather balloons or mirages etc. and that aliens don't exist. It would take something like the President of the United States announcing alien contact in a national press conference to make a dent in the narrative that's been created. And even that might not work because there are now so many alternative views and channels confusing things—from "fact" checkers to Russian propaganda—tearing things apart. Trump would easily be discredited. Biden could be labeled senile. Harris could be dismissed because it was "her time of the month."

Obfuscate, redirect, confuse, ridicule, distort.

Just cover your ass and don't make waves.

This is why Bible scholars can't grasp why ancient scribes used the plural form of the word Eloha as the word for God. They're trying to make the facts fit the presumptive narrative of monotheism—the approved version of Western prehistory that allows for only one God. And any ridiculous story to keep the dogma boat afloat will do. For example, one commonly accepted explanation for the use of the word Elohim is: "God, our Creator, chose to introduce Himself to us with a plural title."

Ah. The omniscient "we."

Seriously?

Archaeologists and anthropologists uncover artifacts from ancient sites around the world talking about visitors from heaven riding on metal chariots that descend to earth amidst fire, smoke and thunder, and instead of taking what they're reading as obvious references to landing craft, they cram it into the scholastic category of primitive myth and allegory ... weird tales concocted to show the power and might of the (obviously fictitious) local gods. To interpret their finds in any other way would be to court professional ostracism and result in the immediate defunding of future work. But assumptions, intellectual rigidity and self-protection aren't the only blocks to seeing ancient aliens, the Archons and their matrix.

We may have been designed to "not see" what we're not supposed to see.

Between all the religious references to a divine deity or deities creating mankind, and the many cultural descriptions of interference by "god-like aliens" in our development, it seems quite clear that human beings have been created to be of some sort of service to these beings.

"God" apparently created us to worship and adore Him. And we were under strict orders not to partake of anything in the Garden of Eden that would change our humble, blindly devotional status.

And the ancient aliens?

It's not much of a stretch to imagine we are a genetically manipulated species developed to be a docile, "intelligent enough but not too intelligent" servant/slave force bred to serve a superior race (or races) of long-lived, spacefaring beings with vast technological and genetic know-how.

Interestingly, anthropology supports this premise.

It is generally acknowledged that H. Sapiens evolved from the hominid species H. Australopithecus on the plains of Africa approximately 200,000 years ago. Unfortunately, there is no substantial fossil evidence of any direct transitional forms between the australopithecines and Homo. Instead, the fossil records reveal enormous physiological changes that occurred with incredible swiftness—practically overnight in anthropological terms—corresponding to the appearance of H. Sapiens.

Sometimes referred to as the "Big Bang" of Homo Sapiens, these rapid and unique genetic changes included a "significant" increase in brain size, dental function, increased height, improved vision and respiratory changes.[52] Additionally, scientists also refer to the evolution of the human brain as "a special event" within the overarching explosion of genetic changes producing Homo Sapiens about a quarter million years ago. Apparently, a lot of specialized genes augmenting the size of the hominid brain and changing its behavioral output were heavily selected by some "poorly defined mechanism" to grant H. Sapiens increased intelligence.[53]

"Selection for greater intelligence and hence larger and more complex brains is far more intense during human evolution than during the evolution of other mammals," writes Bruce Lahn, assistant professor of human genetics of the Howard Hughes Medical Institute at the University of Chicago. "Is it a few mutations in a few genes, a lot of mutations in a few genes, or a lot of mutations in a lot of genes? The answer appears to be a lot of mutations in a lot of genes. We've done a rough calculation that the evolution of the human brain probably involves hundreds if not thousands of mutations in perhaps hundreds or thousands of genes—and even that is a conservative estimate."[54]

Modern genetics has also made it possible to trace the genetic lineage of all humankind back through time to what is referred to as "Mitochondrial Adam" (Y-MRCA)—the most recent male common ancestor who lived somewhere around 180,000 to 580,000 years ago, and "Mitochondrial Eve," (mt-MRCA) who lived somewhere between 120,000 to 156,000 years ago.[55]

I'm no geneticist, but from a practical breeding perspective, the concept of "one common ancestor" doesn't make any more sense to me than the original Bible story which gives us Adam and Eve back in the Garden of Eden. I was raised on a farm in Virginia where we bred and raised Black Angus cattle and Thoroughbred horses. I knew by age ten that even the most prolific bull or stud could only produce so many offspring, and that you don't breed any of those offspring back to its parent. Which information left me scratching my head in bewilderment over the whole Adam and Eve progenitor story.

Granted, wholesale incest as the foundation of humanity explains a lot of things.

But, sarcasm aside, it just doesn't wash. What *does* make sense, however, is if we had a copious supply of genetic material from one advanced male humanoid spliced into the genetic matrix of hundreds of primates on Earth—and then the same thing using the genetic material of an advanced female humanoid relatively shortly thereafter.

A genetics lab could crank out thousands of genetically altered Earth primates using only the genetic material from one man and one woman. Well, at least one *extraterrestrial* man and woman. And that's fundamentally what the research conducted by Zacharia Sitchin, the 20th century Jewish scholar who personally translated hundreds of ancient Sumerian tablets, says happened. According to Sitchin, visitors known as the Anunnaki from the planet Nibiru arrived on Earth around 450,000 years ago in search of gold. They began mining operations and eventually their leader, Enki, decided to create a slave race of genetically-altered hominids from Earth to work the mines, which he did with the help of his Chief Medical Officer and geneticist, the Lady Ninharsag.[56]

I can hear Lord Enki now saying, "Hey, I've got an idea! Let Us make man in Our image, according to Our likeness[57] and put him to work!" Certainly, a fascinating link to Genesis is the historical accounting in Sumerian texts that the Anunnaki created sterile males to use for workers before later upgrading the work force by introducing females and giving man and woman procreative ability—a detail that also fits our mitochondrial history.

Heavily derided by some—but by no means all—mainstream anthropologists and archaeologists, Sitchin's work makes a great deal of sense, correlating with Biblical accounts as well as our evolutionary timelines. Another corroborating fact is the thousands of ancient gold mining sites that have been found throughout the African continent—many located near an enormous metropolis built around 160,000 to 200,000 BCE covering an estimated 1500 square miles, recently discovered inland of the South African port of Maputo.[58] Sitchin's information also dovetails with the work of von Däniken ... although it pushes the initial date of extraterrestrial interference back considerably—far before Biblical dates and definitely pre-flood.

But let's get back to the point at hand, which is why the majority of humanity is so unquestioning and obedient in its general nature.

If I were creating a slave race, I would most definitely select for gene traits of docility, pliability and obedience. Wouldn't you? According to Sitchin, a selective breeding and genetic engineering program went on for several thousand years before the right combination of strength, dexterity, sufficient intelligence and biddable meekness was managed.

Then, of course, on top of genetically modifying us to be subservient, these spacefaring beings would undoubtedly play the "god card" in order to secure their superiority in our minds. "Any sufficiently advanced technology is indistinguishable from magic." So wrote the famous 20th century science fiction author, Arthur C. Clarke. It's hard to imagine a primitive humanity mistaking these seemingly magical extraterrestrial beings for anything other than gods. Gods that gave them greater intelligence and life itself. Gods who could and did eliminate or uplift them in a blink of an eye. Gods who demanded instant obedience upon pain of death.

Who was going to gainsay that kind of power?

And our slave's orientation hasn't changed in thousands of years. Surf the web for five minutes and you find all sorts of religious websites saying things like: "If God kills people, or lets them be killed, this is not unlawful but righteous since God has the absolute right to determine life and death. We don't have a right of life." Programmed obedience and fear of death is why billions of people don't question governmental authority, official explanations and mandates. We just tip our hats, look down, mumble "Yes, sir!" and soldier on.

Obsequiousness is stamped into our genes and our very souls.

I remember when I was a little girl in church how indignant I felt hearing the priest say things like, "We are not worthy so much as to gather up the crumbs from underneath Thy table Lord." I remember sitting there, thinking *yuck!* furious, rebellious, wishing I could stamp out and slam the door behind me.

And yet at least *three hundred generations* of Western and Middle Eastern women and men have been subject to this kind of programming. If Sitchin is even close to being correct and we go with the 200,000-year arrival date of H. Sapiens, we're talking about *10,000 generations* of men and women programmed to exhibit blind devotion to powerful external authorities.

And we wonder why most people are uncomfortable with independent thinking?

So, here's an exercise in imagination: Forget the story of prehistory we've been fed. Forget what we've been told about prehistoric man being a brutish animal.

Imagine spirit beings of love who've decided to express themselves through bodies. They've been peacefully humming along on planet Earth for eons, minding their own business, slowly evolving. How sweet and gentle (and very hairy) they must have been. How innocent having no concept of evil, having no shadow and no experience of the deliberate creation of pain and suffering. How fierce and alive, unfettered and secure with no sense of hierarchy or understanding of the concepts of superiority and lessness.

And then BAM!

Along comes God with His heat rays and nuclear bombs and God knows what else. And we're herded and sorted and experimented upon. Genetically manipulated and modified to be "good" and useful. To be fruitful and multiply so there would be plenty of us available to do the bidding of the Elohim—the Powerful Ones. And then, for some inexplicable reason, they leave us. Or they appear to leave us. And we're left believing in a God that delivers punishment and death, and inherit societies based in hierarchy, supremacy, war, misery and control.

Talk about an ungodly inheritance.

This is why we have the world we have today.

This is the world we have been created to build. What other kind of world could beings continuously programmed to experience life through a "lesser-than" lens ever create? Nirvana? Utopia?

Hardly.

I'm not saying that these "gods"—these original terraforming genetic manipulators—are the anti-life Force we've been examining so far. It's unlikely they're the same beings because all the remaining evidence for ancient aliens points to their physicality. Whether the "gods" were aligned with the anti-life Force or even aware of its presence—if indeed the Archons had arrived by then—I do not know. Perhaps they had arrived and this anti-life Force was one of the reasons the "gods" left the planet. But if the information in this chapter is true—or even a little bit true—we need look no further for another major source of programming making us blind and complacent to whatever influence is looking to do us harm.

And if the Archons/anti-life Force came later in human history, perhaps they did so precisely because the "gods" came first and prepared us—making us into potential pliant and vulnerable hosts.

CHAPTER SEVEN KEY

Ask yourself "Who is my authority?"

Imagine living in the New Heaven on Earth. In such a state of consciousness, living as a being of pure love, you innately honor, respect and protect life in all its multiplicity of forms.

You don't need external laws and commandments to keep you in the "right." No one does. Going against life's principles is unheard of because you are life itself.

People express their uniqueness while at the same time everyone's inherent equality as "one in spirit" keeps the playing field level. There is no hierarchy. No better than or less than. No bitterness and jealousy. No need to compete. No fear for survival.

An impossible vision? It's only impossible if we continue to deny Who We Really Are and refuse to turn our backs on what we have been taught to believe ourselves to be.

Ask yourself this question: Living at my highest and best, living from love, honoring life and my spirit nature and everyone else's spirit nature ... who is my authority when it comes to my personal choices?

Don't judge or try to figure this out. Simply go into your heart and ask, "Standing in the purity of my spirit, who is my authority?"

Now, let's switch it up.

Ask yourself: Living as I currently am ____________________ (fill in the blank—reasonably secure and happy; unhappy, stressed, frightened by world circumstances; worried about money; jockeying for position at work etc.) as a limited human being, who is my authority when it comes to my personal choices?

Is it your boss? The IRS? Your spouse? A parent? The CDC? Your president? Jesus? God, to whom you pray for relief from worldly concerns? Your Instagram peers?

How different are your answers to these two questions?

And if you believe you are ultimately answerable to an external authority for your personal choices, closely examine why.

PART II

BETRAYED

8

Legacy Media & Psychology's Dark Triad

In the spirit of ripping off the Band-Aid and getting down to seeing the gorilla in the room, let's start with the media messaging keeping the shadow and the anti-life Force in place, blinding us to the Hidden Force's agenda. We think we have freedom of choice when it comes to the kind of messaging we tune into and let our children engage. But when it comes to media programming, freedom of choice is a total illusion.

Six corporations—National Amusements, Disney, Time-Warner, Comcast, NewsCorp and Sony[59]—control a whopping 90 percent of what we read, listen to and watch. These corporate behemoths in turn are controlled by just three global asset management firms that appear to be separate but whose assets are, in fact, intertwined: Blackrock, Vanguard and State Street.[60] Together these three firms control almost $30 trillion *in assets* globally. Compare that to America's $30,397,983,680,231 current national *debt*.

Which—excuse me for a brief sidebar—exists why?

America's Constitution explicitly states in Article I, Section 8, Clause 5: *The Congress shall have Power to coin Money, regulate the Value thereof, and of foreign Coin, and fix the Standard of Weights and Measures …*

For 137 years, the United States coined and managed its own money—in essence was its own bank. During this time, Congress resisted all attempts to establish a central bank—a privately held bank outside its purview—not without fierce contention from the private sector. Eventually, under highly suspicious circumstances, Congress passed the Federal Reserve Act and President Woodrow Wilson signed it into law on December 23, 1913.

Despite its name, the Federal Reserve Bank is *not* a federally-owned entity.

The twelve regional banks of the Fed are chartered as private corporations[61] with majority shareholders like the N.M. Rothschild Bank of England, the Warburg Banks of Hamburg and Amsterdam, Lehman Brothers Bank of New York and Lazard Brothers of Paris.

I am shocked (but not surprised) at how difficult it is to find any corroborating evidence for any of this anymore on the web. You'll have to check out books like *The Unseen Hand* and *The Creature from Jekyll Island* and other reliable sources for that.

But I digress.

Ah, yes … the media.

TV and radio stations may have different call signs and some of the programming may appear different—left versus right-wing voices for example. Magazines and newspapers may have different names and themes. Video gaming firms might crank out different products. But the overarching message behind 90 percent of all media programming in all Western nations is basically identical because the source of 90 percent of all media content is the same.

So, what is the overall message and intention?

Well, it's sure not posted on a website or in a corporate mission statement, but all we have to do is look at current programming and the results to get the point. Programming content is consistent across all mediums: Violence, conflict and manipulation dominate; sex, sexual perversion and sexual violence are a close second; addiction and substance abuse is ubiquitous; personal and relational dysfunction are the running themes.

The results of this messaging which normalizes and even elevates dysfunction are also consistent: Growing fear, anxiety and discontent, a great sickness of spirit and numbness amongst the global population.

It's easiest to see in cultures not overly saturated with Western consumerist ideologies before the arrival of television and radio. In northern Alaska, the Northwest Territories, Nunavut and Arctic regions, for example, the lives of native peoples have been destroyed within one or two generations by "cultural colonialism" driven by TV and radio and eventually computers inserting heavily consumer-based, materialistic and violent programming into the consciousness of the peoples there. Alcoholism, violence and suicide—all of which were rare or non-existent prior to media influence—today are through the roof in these cultures and escalating.[62]

Even in countries more culturally inured to Western values, the sheer exposure levels to media messaging is disturbing. *Americans watch a cumulative 250 billion hours of television every year.*[63] Aside from the violent, dysfunction-oriented programming, we also have the not-so-subliminal impact of commercial advertising to deal with.

By age 65, the average man or woman in the US will have absorbed over two million commercials. The typical American child spends 900 hours each year in school and 1500 hours watching television. By the time s/he is 18 eighteen years of age, s/he will have seen 200,000 acts of violence on TV, including 40,000 murders and uncounted thousands of rapes.[64] Over 70 percent of all kids in America have a TV in their bedroom.[65] Over two thirds of day care centers use TV as a way to entertain their client's children and keep them pacified.[66]

Ever since 1997 when Direct to Consumer (DTC) advertising for pharmaceuticals was given greater free-rein by the FDA, an ever-increasing percentage of television ads are for specific drugs. According to Robert F. Kennedy Jr., *over 70 percent of television news advertising in non-election years is made by pharmaceutical corporations.*[67]

Hello? Seventy percent of news advertising comes from drug companies. And you think this has no effect on news content? On story slant? On what gets covered and what doesn't?

Then there is the message delivered by the ads themselves.

The overarching theme of all drug ads is: You are weak, sick, anxious, sleepless, depressed, crippled with acid indigestion, chronically constipated, nasally congested and can't get it up. Take ______ (xyz) drug and live happily ever after. (Side effects may include drowsiness, nausea, constipation, diarrhea, loss of appetite, dry mouth, increased sweating, heart palpitations and sudden death. This is not a complete list of side effects and others may occur …)

If it's not drug ads, it's ads about consumption.

Buy more. Eat more. Drink more. Spend more. Get more. Have more. So ... to briefly recap the media message the world is absorbing and the singular message we're raising our children to accept is:

Violence, sexual perversion, sickness and dysfunction are normal.

The only way to feel better about it is take drugs, drink alcohol and buy more and more crap you don't need.

In 2008, the Pew Research Center reported that 97 percent of children ages 12 to 17 play some type of video game and that two-thirds of those games are action and adventure games with violent content.[68] "Blood and gore. Intense violence. Strong sexual content. Use of drugs." These are just a few of the phrases that the Entertainment Software Rating Board (ESRB) uses to describe the content of these "games."

The vast majority of psychological studies on gaming show that video games increase aggressive behavior and increase negative thoughts and emotions in children, potentially leading to mental illness.[69] They also create a sense of distance from real life and an increasing numbness and lessened concern for others. According to a study commissioned by Common Sense Media, 89 percent of parents across the United States believe violence in today's video games is a problem.[70] Out of 3,000 studies on TV violence, 2,888 show there is a direct correlation between watching violence on the screen and violence in real life. "It's a public health problem," says Dr. John Nelson of the American Medical Association. "We have had a long-standing concern with the impact of television on behavior, especially among children."

The number of parents in America currently concerned about their children's screen viewing habits clocks in at 71 percent.[71]

And ...?

Nothing.

Think about this.

Eighty-nine percent of parents worry that video games are damaging their children's health and wellbeing ... and they do nothing about it. Over 70 percent of parents worry that TV and electronic media screen time are damaging their children's health and wellbeing and they do nothing about it.

And this is normal behavior?

No. This is not normal behavior.

Not even the dullest, laziest animal in existence allows their offspring to be harmed. So, why are Western parents consciously allowing this to happen to their children? When apathy and convenience outrank the health of a nation's children in importance, the only possible explanation for this situation is that the normal caretaking and protective functions in human beings—including parents—are being switched off.

But how is this happening?

As it turns out, quite easily.

Skyrocketing increases in the cost of living have ensured that both parents in most families *must* work. It's no longer a lifestyle choice. This, of course, means enforced parent-child separation from an early age with the correlative effect of diminished emotional bonding. TV and gaming replace child/parent interaction guaranteeing that bonding diminishes even further with each generation. The violence being pumped over the airwaves, online and in games ensures that the emotional capacity for human connection and empathy is dismantled.[72]

And then there is the not-so-small fact that the US and other Western nations are in a severe state of mental decline. Since the mid-1970s, Western IQs have been steadily dropping every year.[73] Since the Covid pandemic, studies show that in two years children's IQs dropped an average 22 percent.[74] As well, research shows that the typical Western diet has a negative impact on the brain, resulting in cognitive dysfunction and neurodegeneration.

Our nation's population is also in a serious state of physical decline. For the last sixty years, Westernized populations have been plagued by an epidemic of "civilization diseases," chronic non-infectious degenerative diseases—obesity, diabetes, cancer, cardiovascular disease, autoimmune diseases, to name just a few. All these diseases were rare a hundred years ago and non-existent in hunter-gatherer societies.[75]

But this is not a new discovery.

Back in the early 20th century, Canadian dentist Dr. Weston Price traveled around the world studying the health effects of diet. Visiting some of the most remote tribes in the world, he found minimal tooth decay, strong immune systems and overall excellent health in peoples who ate indigenous foods. He observed that when these same people were introduced to the Western diet of white flour, white sugar, refined vegetable oils and canned goods, deformed jaw structures, crooked teeth, tooth decay, chronic inflammation, arthritis and other diseases immediately flourished.[76]

Our commercial agricultural practices are also to blame for the plummet in public health. Commercially produced fertilizers, pesticides, herbicides, fungicides, plastic and non-treated wastewater have destroyed 33 percent of the world's tillable soils, paving the way for pollutants to enter the food chain with serious health consequences for both people and planet.[77] For the first time in over a century, life expectancy in the US is dropping.[78] And out of the top 20 wealthiest nations in the world, the US has the worst child mortality rate.[79] But hey, we have the highest incarceration rate of any other country in the world—including places like Ghana and Afghanistan.[80]

I already gave these scary figures in chapter five, but it's worth mentioning them again here: A quarter of America is mentally ill, with over 25 percent of adults suffering from a diagnosable mental health disorder.[81] Over 78 percent of Americans over 55 suffer from at least one chronic physical illness.[82] Over 60.2 percent of Americans aged 12 years or older currently abuse alcohol, drugs and/or tobacco.[83] Suicide rates have risen over 30 percent since 2008.[84] In the 1970s one child in 10,000 was diagnosed with autism.[85] In 2004 it was one child in 150. Today it's one child in 44.[86] Researchers at MIT predict that soon one out of two children will be born autistic.[87]

So why the decline?

Why isn't modern medicine saving us?

Well, for one, prescription drugs are the third leading cause of death after heart disease and cancer in the United States and Europe.[88] Over half of those who die have taken their prescriptions as directed. The others die because of dosage errors, bad drug combinations and general contraindications that doctors miss. However, despite the alarming death toll from pharmaceuticals each year, and despite the rather telltale fact that over half of commercial air time for each new drug product is spent citing serious drug side effects, Big Pharma manages to increase its revenues every year.

How?

Impotent drug regulation, widespread crime that includes corruption of the scientific evidence about drugs and drug trials, the bribery of doctors and lies in drug marketing are just some of the tools the pharmaceutical corporations employ, along with intense advertising, government lobbying and campaign contributions.

In 2020, the pharmaceutical industry, *which is owned by the same three asset management companies that control 90 percent of the media,*[89] spent $4.58 billion advertising on national TV in the US alone. In 2021, Big Pharma spent $352,845,426 influencing American congressmen and senators to skew legislation in their favor, opening the door to approving national vaccine rollouts and even mandates. And my, oh my, how favorable that turned out to be. In 2021 the pharmaceutical giant Pfizer made $42.6 billion from their vaccines alone—with a total annual increase in revenue of 95 percent over the year 2020.[90] Moderna's total revenue for 2021 was $18.5 billion, an increase from $803 million in revenue in 2020. This *2,300 percent rise in corporate revenue* in 2021 was chiefly attributed to sales of its Covid-19 vaccine, Spikevax.[91]

Looking at the above information, it's really hard to maintain the illusion that the confluence of negative influences and the disturbing ramifications are coincidental—that human devolution and all the terrible things that are happening in the world are simply the inevitable result of the general stupidity of the unwashed masses. It's hard to not start seeing patterns. A direction and destination to which our entire global population is being driven.

But who is doing the driving?

We know from thousands of years of global reporting that the anti-life Force of 'e'epa/wetiko is not capable of direct hands-on interference. If it were, it no doubt would have showed its face and force eons ago. Cultural and religious descriptions make it clear that this energetic intelligence implements its agendas *through us.* Which begs the question:

What type of human being, what personality type, what kind of mental configuration, would be most susceptible to evil influence?

According to psychological studies, the super-rich, *as a group*, can be characterized by three personality traits: Machiavellianism, psychopathy and narcissism—what psychologists call the "Dark Triad" of malevolent characteristics involving self-promotion, duplicity, aggressiveness and emotional coldness."[92] Machiavellianism refers to a person's willingness to lie, manipulate and exploit people and situations for personal gain. Psychopathy refers to a lack of empathy, compassion and caring. Narcissism, of course, refers to a person's sense of entitlement and superiority.

In an article in *Psychology Today* titled "Psychology's 'Dark Triad' and the Billionaire Class," author and clinical and political psychologist Roy Eidelson Ph.D. cites studies showing how lower-income people are considerably more willing to help somebody who is struggling than wealthy people. Kids from poor homes behave more altruistically than kids from wealthier households. Even people who drive expensive cars show greater entitlement and aggression than others on the road, cutting off drivers and refusing to let them in line.[93]

This is not to say that all wealthy people or even all billionaires are nasty people expressing the Dark Triad. But you'd have to be living in a cave not to know that wealthy entitled people do not make the best role models in the world. Anybody who has watched the 1999 movie *The Insider* about Big Tobacco companies withholding health information from the public about smoking and lung cancer for *decades*[94] knows about corporate duplicity and the anti-life doings of rich, powerful men.

Or what about the movie *Margin Call* that details the day investment banking giant Goldman Sachs deliberately dumped billions of dollars of worthless securities tied to risky home mortgages on the market in order to survive, triggering the 2008 recession that destroyed the lives of millions? Or how about HBO's 2021 documentary *The Crime of the Century* about how Big Pharma executives deliberately got America got hooked on opioids, killing over 500,000 people?

Insatiability and a lust for power, control and dominance are the top traits marking all modern billionaires along with an insatiable desire for money and success. And what is one of the primary characteristics of the Archons, the achingly empty hungry ghosts? *Insatiability.* Apparently the old proverbs about "like attracting like" and "birds of a feather flocking together" are true.

Today, the richest one percent on planet Earth have more money and control than 99 percent of the rest of the world.[95] Of that one percent, 26 men own as much wealth as half of all of humanity combined.[96] I'm not going to debate which billionaires are "good" and which are "bad" or even if any of them are good or bad. But what's that old adage about absolute power and corruption?

Absolute power corrupts absolutely.

Let's take billionaire George Soros for example. Soros is personally responsible for wrecking countless corporations and the lives of those attached. He is a man who, according to CBS *60 Minutes* interviewer Steve Krost, can "move financial markets by simply voicing an opinion."[97] In a 1998 interview with Soros on *60 Minutes,* Krost casually mentions that Soros is said to have caused the financial collapse of several nations, including Thailand, Malaysia, Indonesia, Japan and Russia.[98] When asked about the morality of such actions in the interview, Soros says, "I am here to make money. I cannot and do not look at the social consequences of what I do."[99]

Wow, really?

And the media and the rest of the world just nod and say, "Okay"? If a kid takes a blowtorch to other childrens' science fair projects to get rid of the competition, mommy and the teachers do not say "Well done" and hand him/her a prize. But with immeasurable wealth comes immeasurable power. Who on earth is going to take a man who can destroy the economies of nations to task about anything he choses to do?

Especially when we're programmed not to question authority?

In 2022, Soros' net worth was a mere $10 billion after he transferred over $32 billion to his charitable foundation The Open Society Foundations,[100] self-identified as "the world's largest private funder of independent groups working for justice, democratic governance, and human rights."[101]

Which certainly sounds wonderful.

But then, again, things aren't always what they seem.

In 2016, a website called DCLeaks.com published documents it claimed to have gotten from The Open Society Foundations—a claim that would seem to be true since the Foundation reported the leak to the FBI. According to the leaked documents, part of the Foundation's agenda was subverting other countries' policies supporting traditional family values—specifically Russia in this case. Policies which were seen as "against Open Society's values."[102]

Wait. What?

A US charitable foundation funded to the tune of $32 billion which is *against* traditional family values?

I don't mean to be cynical. I don't *want* to be cynical. I know nothing of men like Soros except what I read. But what I read and see are not reassuring. Economic leaders like Soros and Bill Gates speak in glowing terms about the incredible advantages to humanity of The Great Reset. Of the *opportunities* disasters like the Covid epidemic represent. For example, the opportunity for global economic restructuring. Or the opportunities for AI and the incorporation of AI into the human genome. Glowing opportunities billionaires are quick to say are for the good of all humanity.

But I think a recent cartoon from *The New Yorker* is a better representation of this situation. It depicts a corporate CEO addressing a shareholder meeting saying: "And so, while the end-of-the-world scenario will be rife with unimaginable horrors, we believe the pre-end period to be filled with unprecedented opportunities for profit."

I know this sounds ludicrous. When the promised end of the world comes, who will care about money? But this is, indeed, the apparent mindset of the One Percent. And they think this way, not because they're short-sighted and stupid, but because they have a plan—a plan ingeniously lampooned in the recently released movie *Don't Look Up* starring Meryl Streep. (It's stunning how many movies expose the thinking and plans of the elite on this planet ... *Elysium, Total Recall, Cloud Atlas, Endgame.*)

Every business school student for a hundred years has been taught that the purpose of corporate boards is creating policies which insure the creation of ever-increasing profits for its shareholders *into perpetuity.*

Which, living on a planet of finite resources, is patently insane. Finite resources cannot support ever-increasing profits into perpetuity.

Nonetheless, that's our current global business model.

Ultimately, the only way infinite increasing profit can occur is 1) through corporate destruction of competition and the creation of monopolies and 2) the development of the means to go off-world and replicate.

Economic leaders like Elon Musk and Jeff Bezos have successfully managed this two-step process. They've successfully created monopolies and are starting space programs to help humanity (or at least a certain small percentage of humanity) escape this dying planet after the empires they created have destroyed it. Space programs featuring giant phallus-shaped rockets that blast their payloads into space, guaranteeing reproduction and corporate replication on other worlds.

What will happen to the rest of us left here on a planet that has been deliberately raped and plundered then left to its own devices is all too easily imagined.

~

It seems impossible that something like this could even be contemplated let alone implemented. After all, men like Musk and Bezos epitomize everything the media has taught us to admire, desire and emulate.

They're strong, independent, creative men. They have money, fame and power beyond our wildest imaginings. Surely, they don't have "shadow issues" like the rest of us? Issues that could be distorted and manipulated by sinister invisible forces? Surely such men couldn't be tempted by the devil to sell humanity out for their own advantage?

Hm.

You think a man like Soros who wrecks nations and says he's unconcerned about the human consequences doesn't have issues? You think someone like that isn't corruptible? A human being obviously firmly entrenched in the Dark Triad of narcissistic, Machiavellian psychopathy? What isn't clear is whether or not people like him realize they are puppets and pawns to a higher dark Force.

Frankly, I'm inclined to think they are.

Dr. Yuval Harari, Israeli historian, philosopher and top advisor to the highly influential German economist Klaus Schwab (more on him in a moment), recently said, on camera, and I quote: "Humans are now hackable animals. … Control of data might enable human elites to do something even more radical than just build digital dictatorships. By hacking organisms, elites may gain the power to re-engineer the future of life itself. Because once you can hack something, you can usually also engineer it. And indeed, if we succeed at hacking and engineering life, this will be the greatest revolution in biology since the beginning of life four billion years ago."[103]

I find it exceedingly interesting and disturbing that Harari describes the One Percent as elites—an arrogant and telling designation. But what's bizarre and far more worrisome is his apparent need to differentiate them as *human* elites.

What other species of elites does he know about?

He has also said: "You know, there's the whole idea that humans have a soul or spirit and they have free will, and 'Nobody knows what's happening inside me, so whatever I choose, whether in the election or whether in the supermarket, this is my free will.' That's over.

"Free will?" he said. "That's over."[104]

One of the hallmarks of psychopathy and narcissism is a belief in one's innate superiority over other people. In the case of people like Harari, that sense of superiority also apparently includes a sense of supremacy over nature and the intricacies of life and creation itself.

To such a man—or such men—nothing is sacred.

The soul and spirit do not exist.

Mind and materialism, power and control, are all that matter.

This apparently is also the mindset of Harari's mentor and client—the enormously influential Klaus Schwab. He's not a billionaire. By some accounts he's worth only a paltry $30 million. But a non-profit foundation he started in 1971 called the World Economic Forum, also known as the WEF, is one of the most influential organizations on the planet, influencing and possibly directing the wealthiest people in the world.

The WEF is an independent international organization "committed to improving the state of the world by engaging business, political, academic and other leaders of society to shape global, regional and industry agendas."[105] Headquartered in Geneva, Switzerland, the Forum is tied to no political, partisan or national interests.

Sounds like a pretty high-minded group. Right?

Mostly funded by its 1,000 member companies—global enterprises with more than $5 billion in annual turnover, (I think they call this "vested interests?")—the WEF has carefully groomed a number of "close associates" such as Joseph Biden, currently President of the United States, Boris Johnson, former Prime Minister of the United Kingdom, Angela Merkel, former Prime Minister of Germany, Justin Trudeau, current Prime Minister of Canada, China Communist Party leader Xi Jinping, Mario Draghi, Prime Minister of Italy and Scott Morrison, Prime Minister of Australia.

The WEF also started an organization called The Young Global Leaders.[106] This group consists of 800 people hand picked by WEF organizers as being representative of contemporary leadership, "coming from all regions of the world and representing all stakeholders in society."

Personally mentored by Schwab, members of this elite cadre (most of whom are anything but young or representative of all stakeholders in society) include Vladimir Putin, Bill Gates, Mark Zuckerberg, creator of Facebook, Gavin Newsom, current governor of California, Ivanka Trump, Jeff Bezos and Richard Branson, British entrepreneur and business magnate, owner of Virgin Records, Virgin Air etc.

Amongst many other things, the WEF is famous for releasing a recent promotional video citing eight predictions for planet Earth in 2030, the first prediction of which is "You'll own nothing and you'll be happy"—a prediction the text of which is posted over the image of a bearded young man who is obviously very happy with his condition.[107] Who will actually own everything in this predicted Utopia—much of which is heavily dependent upon the incorporation of artificial intelligence technologies—is not disclosed.

What's being sold, of course, is the idea that renting everything from those who own everything—shelter, food, transportation, education, entertainment, health—is a psychologically and emotionally satisfying experience.

But hey, if we 1) swallow enough pharmaceuticals that don't kill us and 2) allow ourselves to be implanted with AI, maybe we *will* be happy not owning anything.

You'll own nothing.
And you'll be happy
Based on the input of members of the World Economic Forum's
Global Future Councils

There's a long historical association between wealth and God, which is exemplified by the passage in Deuteronomy 8:18 when Moses states: "But remember the Lord your God, for it is He who gives you the ability to produce wealth."

For thousands of years, this single statement has given those who accumulate vast riches the cachet of God's sanction. Obviously, if God is the power that delivers the ability to accrue wealth, then those who do so are God's chosen ones. And if they are God's chosen ones, they must know how to run the world better than the rest of us who haven't accrued vast fortunes through His beneficence like they have.

Humanity has been not-so-subtly programmed for thousands of years to accept this as a truth. We've also been sold a bill of goods called the Divine Right of Kings.

There are bloodlines—bluebloods of enormous wealth and power—whose members are supposed to be inherently superior to the average man and woman. For a very long time we accepted their right to leadership unthinkingly. To this day, we still cling to the idea that the old royal lineages are special and that they deserve our trust and fealty.

Never mind humanity has been abused by these lineages and taken advantage of over and over again. Never mind the vast fortunes accrued by the non-bluebloods God has favored over the course of history have usually been built upon the back of slave labor, horrific abuse, cutthroat competition, grotesque market manipulation, calumny, bribery, murder and heaven only knows what else.

I'm not saying that every extraordinarily wealthy person on the planet is a criminal. I'm not saying that they're all ruthless in their business dealings or that they all have the enslavement of humanity as their end goal. What I am saying is that humanity, as a whole, tends to idolize and idealize wealthy people—which automatically places them in a position of authority.

I'm also pointing out that accruing vast wealth and dealing with the power that comes with it is not a temptation-free experience. Nor is it a humbling one. The bigger a person's ambitions and the greater their accomplishments, the easier it is for their ego—their false self—to believe they're above the rules of morality that apply to lesser humans. You know… the ones with no souls or spirits who will be happy owning nothing.

How easy is it for the anti-life Force to influence such people?

Even if they believe their intentions are for the good, if these "elites" are so amazingly pure and advanced, how is it possible they could believe for one second that it was up to *them* to decide the fate of one other human being let alone the fate of billions?

There's a reason pride has always been considered the deadliest of sins. It paves the way for the justification of all sorts of evil and depravity. And it holds the door shut against the light of any other possibilities getting in. *If I'm as great as I think I am—and all the social indicators of greatness like wealth and status and power prove to me that I am—why should I ever doubt myself? I am infallible.*

This has been the internal belief of every powerful tyrant who ever walked the earth. And the frightening thing is, most didn't see their actions as tyranny. Our current-day "leaders" don't either because they can't see their looming inner shadow. Why? *Because their inner shadow is their sense of superiority, entitlement and infallibility.*

And for those who actually are consciously ruthless and power-hungry and pleased about it? How yummy a treat are they for the mind parasites to feed on? How easy is it to goad them? Tempt them? Possess them? Convince them the end justifies the means? Blind them to their foibles and falseness?

Standing astride the mountaintop of power, triumphant and victorious over the billions of Earth, how can such men and women possibly be persuaded to think of their fellow humans as anything but resources to be used and cast aside as needed in their bid to fulfill the corporate mandate of creating infinite profit into perpetuity?

One of the over-arching characteristics of the Archons and the humans they control is that they can never be filled. They subdue and twist, own and control, and it is never enough. They're unutterably arrogant in their self-image of superiority, and even though they know how to mimic compassion and love, they are unfathomably cold. They don't question their entitlement or their assessment of reality.

They know not love, and believe they have no soul.

Looking at the current situation it's not only the Hararis of the world who no longer have or believe in the human soul. It seems much of humanity is moving that way as well. We're being driven hard and fast in the direction of lovelessness. Something is deliberately diminishing us, crippling our empathy, numbing our emotions, dumbing us down, making us sick, violent amongst each other, and yet passive when it comes to authority.

Something is trying to set us up so that when the right time comes, its minions will deliver the great savior that will protect us from ourselves. Perhaps it will be The Great Reset and AI. That is certainly the future we're being groomed for. Maybe some sort of Second Coming will be staged. Or an alien invasion. Or a global economic crash. Or yet another pandemic.

Or all the above.

It doesn't matter what the something is. Whatever it is, only those in control will have the answer to it. And whatever the answer is, you can guarantee it will 1) make them money and 2) involve our submission.

If we just hand over our free will. If we just dismiss our hearts. If we just give them our minds and our bodies. If we just trust our shadowy leaders who know better than us, then maybe … maybe … we'll survive.

As what?

Well, the Hararis, Schwabs and Musks of the world have already given us the answer.

And it's not completely human.

CHAPTER EIGHT KEY

Create a clear vision of the world you want to live in

This was a tough chapter to write, and I'm sure it was not easy to read. It's almost *impossible* for decent, loving people to fathom callous duplicity let alone the betrayal of one's entire species and planet.

So take a break.

- Take a few minutes to imagine a world without fear. Without evil. Without negative control. A world that doesn't force you to be and act and think like someone you're not.

If it helps, cast your mind back to early childhood. Remember the fun. The thrill of running across the yard, playing with friends. The laughter. How filled to the brim with life you were, moving effortlessly from one moment of pure aliveness to the next.

- Go to that free and easy place in your mind and heart and body. *Feel the freedom*. Feel your connection to the world. Feel your connection with others. Feel the relaxation that comes with the sense of safety and belonging.

- Jot down your impressions of that world—any images and feelings or sensations that come to you.

If you like to draw, create a picture. Or find images that match this feeling of freedom in magazines or online and create a physical or electronic montage.

If music springs to life inside you, create a song or a poem or a dance that evokes the feelings of Who You Really Are set free in a brand new world.

- *Feel* how you'll feel in this new life in your body.
- Don't worry that it might not come true. Don't think that you have to manifest this vision somehow. Don't worry about all the issues that apparently stand in the way.
- Keep whatever you have created—notes to self, a poem, a picture, a song—close at hand. As you read this book, keep referring back to this vision and let its energy enliven and restore you as needed.

People since time immemorial have had this vision. The only reason it hasn't already come to fruition is because Who We Really Are has been highjacked by the Archons and that Force's human minions over and over again, directing us down the pathway the anti-life Force has in mind for us instead.

But this has only happened because of our ignorance of its presence.

As difficult as it is, to regain our vision and our world, we have to see what's happened and refuse to be pawns in this Force's game anymore. Then we can get back to our own playing field and start anew.

9

It's Not Supposed to Be This Way

One of my favorite TV shows is the political drama series *Madam Secretary* starring Téa Leoni. In Season 6, episode 2, "The Strike Zone," the title character, Elizabeth McCord, has resigned her post as Secretary of State and is running for president. Fielding questions at a town hall meeting, a woman named Jenny Mathews steps up to the microphone and haltingly tells the following story:

"When I was 16, I got pregnant and dropped out of high school. Fortunately, my mom made me take my GED. And then I went on to nursing school with the help of some loans. At the hospital where I worked, I saw pain medications prescribed every day. And I saw what it did to people. So, a few years ago when my husband Howard had surgery, I told him 'Don't take that stuff.' But he needed help with the pain and that's what they gave him.

"Three years ago, I found Howard dead from an overdose. Without his salary I couldn't keep up the mortgage and last year I lost my house. Now, I stay with my daughter. She can barely afford groceries much less medication for her son who has asthma. I'm not looking for a handout and I'll admit when I screw up. But I gotta tell you, I'm asking myself … 'Is this how it's supposed to be?'"

Is this how life is supposed to be?

No. It's not.

Elizabeth tells Jenny this as she steps forward and embraces the woman who, by this time, is in tears. At the back of the room her campaign manager, a hard-bitten politico, winces at Elizabeth's overt show of compassion. He thinks showing vulnerability will destroy her chances of getting elected. But he's wrong. A video of Elizabeth comforting the woman goes viral and her poll figures soar. She gets elected president and the rest is herstory.

I watched that episode the other night, and the scene moved me to tears (again) because Jenny Mathews is the 99 percent. She represents the everywoman and everyman in the world standing there puzzled, exhausted, in pain, telling a tale of being ground to dust beneath the indifferent wheels of society with no recourse and no resources—destitute because the world has lost what little compassion it ever had and nobody seems to care.

"Oooo, life goes on, long after the thrill of livin' is gone. Walk on," crooned John Mellencamp in the 1982 song "Jack and Diane."

So true. And getting truer every day.

But why?

By now you already know the much of the answer. But there's more.

I wanted to include a great cartoon I saw online at this point, but it would be a copyright infringement to print, so I'll just have to describe it. A woman is shopping in a toy department, looking at a complicated self-assembly toy sitting on the counter. The man behind the counter says, "This toy will fully prepare your child ahead of time for the outside world. No matter how carefully he or she puts it together, it will not work."

A bang-on assessment of our "civilization" if there ever was one.

As I've stated before, over 41 percent of Americans are classified as low-income. Despite the fact that 36 percent of Americans in the work force have a four-year college degree (and an average student loan debt of $39,351), 70 percent of people in the US workforce say they are not "engaged" in what they do.[108] Which means the 90,000 hours Americans spend working over the course of their individual lives—basically half their waking hours on this Earth—are spent filled with boredom, indifference and ennui.

As a reward for this bleak fate, the average weekly earnings for a person working in the US is $984. Which, after cost-of-living increases and taxation, means most Americans end up living from paycheck to paycheck.

Payday loan firms, which were extremely rare before the 1990s, are currently doing a gangbusting business charging annualized rates as high as 589 percent.[109] This single factor has depleted the cash flow position of households and increased personal bankruptcy rates by two hundred percent.

According to several studies, both women and men in Gen Z (ages 17 to 25 in 2022) are experiencing higher rates of depression than Millennials,[110] and it seems that the experts are puzzled and don't know why.

Seriously?

The vast majority of Americans have no choice but to submit themselves to the service of an indifferent employer (which up to 80 percent of US workers say they don't trust[111]) in order to just survive—a condition commonly known as wage slavery—and the shrinks in the US can't figure out why young people are depressed? Talk about being out of touch with reality. And yet most of the world believes this is how life is supposed to be.

So, let's talk a little more about slavery.

The secondary definition of the word is "a situation or practice in which people are entrapped (as by debt) and exploited." Granted, wage slavery is not the same thing as chattel slavery where a man or woman is physically owned by an overseer. The wage slave is *rented* instead, reluctantly paying body and soul into the system, unhappily working for a corporate boss, day in and day out—a setup that gives us the *illusion* of freedom.

What do I mean by the illusion of freedom?

Well, we are free to buy a house and a car—financed and profited from by the elite-owned central banking system, of course. We can get credit cards that help us go on that family vacation we've always wanted to take—at 26 percent interest. We can read what we want—except for the growing number of banned books and banned websites. We can freely express our opinions on things like Covid and vaccines—as long as what we say doesn't go against the approved government narrative. We can travel where we want—although the growing emphasis on vaccine passports is making it more difficult.

We have body autonomy … well, everybody except women.

And even the body autonomy we believe we have is an illusion, as you will shortly see.

We have freedom of choice. We can watch the news shows we chose—although 90 percent of the news programming is the same no matter what the call signs. We can buy the clothes we want and the household products we choose—never mind the subliminal programming from a million advertisements coloring our purchase decisions.

Freedom?

Not to be too cynical, but caught in our current system, I think Janice Joplin summed it up best when she sang: "Freedom's just another word for nothing left to lose."

Yes, there are a few free spirits out in the world who manage to buck the system and do things differently. There is still some wiggle room for us. But the squeeze is getting tighter.

Just think—a hundred years ago in 1922 none of the following taxes even existed. And America and American citizens were quite prosperous!

- Accounts Receivable Tax
- Building Permit Tax
- Burial Tax
- CDL License Tax
- Cigarette Tax
- Corporate Income Tax
- Dog License Tax
- Excise Tax Federal Income Tax
- Federal Unemployment Tax (FUTA)
- Fishing License Tax
- Food License Tax
- Fuel Permit Tax
- Gasoline Tax
- Gross Receipts Tax
- Hunting License Tax
- Inheritance Tax
- Inventory Tax
- Liquor Tax
- Luxury Tax
- Marriage License Tax

- Medicare Tax
- National Income Tax
- Personal Property Tax
- Property Tax
- Real Estate Tax
- Service Charge Tax
- Social Security Tax
- Road Usage Tax
- Recreational Vehicle Tax
- Sales Tax
- School Tax
- State Income Tax
- State Unemployment Tax (SUTA)
- Telephone Federal Excise Tax
- Telephone Federal Universal Service Fee Tax
- Telephone Federal, State and Local Surcharge Taxes
- Telephone Minimum Usage Surcharge Tax
- Telephone Recurring and Nonrecurring Charges Tax
- Telephone State and Local Tax
- Telephone Usage Charge Tax
- Utility Tax
- Vehicle License Registration Tax
- Vehicle Sales Tax
- Watercraft Registration Tax
- Well Permit Tax
- Workers Compensation Tax

What did Johann Wolfgang von Goethe, German poet, novelist, scientist and statesman once say? "The best slave is a slave that doesn't know he's a slave."

No kidding.

Speaking of slaves, in the year 2000, a Central Intelligence Agency report leaked to *The New York Times* estimated some 50,000 women and children are illegally brought into the United States *every year* to serve as prostitutes, domestic servants and workers.[112] A report to the United Nations General Assembly estimates that more than 40 million adults around the world were enslaved in 2016 and that about 152 million children between age 5 and 17 served as forced child labor.[113]

That's almost 200 million modern-day slaves.

I know it's hard to swallow applying the word "slavery" to the context of modern American living. But the institution is every bit as prevalent now, if not more so, than it was in the "bad ol' days" of the Southern plantations.

Between the years 1525 and 1866, approximately 12.5 million Africans were shipped to the New World. Out of that number, fewer than 500,000 ended up in North America. The vast majority ended up in the Caribbean and South America.[114]

Yes, I know, the global population figures were lower back then. But still, the current figures on the modern slave trade are sobering. And things get far worse when we start talking in terms of body sovereignty, which is actually the crux of the slavery matter.

The chattel slave can be whipped to death by his owners and she can be raped and forced to bear children, and neither has anything to say about it. This is currently the life situation of more than 200 million slaves around the world today. But, here's the deal:

Even amongst the general population in the United States, body sovereignty is but an illusion.

Let's start with the "Tuskegee Study" conducted from the 1930s into the 1970s where the US Public Health Service conducted a study on 399 African American sharecroppers from Macon County, Alabama who had syphilis. For forty years the men were provided with bogus medication in order to track the degeneration of their bodies with syphilis. By 1943, penicillin was widely available as an effective treatment, but the participants in the study were not offered real treatment because that would have messed with the purpose of the study.[115] Reparations were eventually made to survivors and their families. In 1997 President Bill Clinton issued a formal presidential apology.

Also in the 1930s, African-American men, as well as Japanese-American and Puerto Rican soldiers, were deliberately exposed to mustard gas to determine the health effects and how to possibly counter them. Uncounted numbers of soldiers suffered horrific pain and permanent damage from the external and internal burns inflicted during the course of this experiment.[116] At Harvard University in the late 1940s, researchers ran experiments on pregnant women at the Lying-In Hospital of the University of Chicago, treating them with diethylstilbestrol, a synthetic estrogen—completely without their knowledge. The women experienced an abnormally high number of miscarriages and babies with low birth weight (LBW).[117]

After the horrors of medical experimentation conducted in Nazi Germany's death camps during World War II, in 1947 the Nuremberg Code was created and globally adopted specifically to make the use of human subjects for medical experimentation illegal. However, human experimentation in medical and scientific research is a very important tool helping the US government—any government—stay ahead in the warfare game.[118] Signing an agreement doesn't mean it stops.

From 1946 to 1962 throughout Operation Hardtack, the US government conducted more than 1,000 nuclear tests during which an estimated 400,000 unsuspecting American soldiers and sailors were deliberately exposed to vast amounts of lethal ionizing radiation, wearing no protective gear whatsoever.[119] Simply told to put their hands over their eyes when the blast came, the men were so close to the blast zones and the flash was so bright they reported being able to see the bones in their hands and fingers through their closed eyes.

All of the "atomic vets," as they became known, were sworn to silence. They were not allowed to tell anyone about their experiences, even if they became ill, which most did. None were ever acknowledged or compensated for later suffering from cancer and other radiation-related ailments.

But members of the US armed services weren't the only radiation guineapigs.

From documents obtained through the Freedom of Information Act, it is known that up through the late 1960s, researchers worked to develop radiation and "combination weapons" that utilized both radioactive and chemical and/or biological materials by testing them on US citizens.

One example was a 1940s experiment at Vanderbilt University in Nashville, Tennessee in which 820 low-income pregnant women were deliberately injected with a substance that included radioactive iron during their first prenatal visit. During follow-up visits, the blood of the women and their babies was tested to determine how radioactive exposure during pregnancy affected the babies.

Similar tests were also performed on pregnant women in Chicago and San Francisco.[120]

In 1994, Bill Clinton formed an advisory committee to investigate and report on the use of human beings as subjects of federally-funded research using ionizing radiation.

The President's committee found that over 40,000 experiments had been conducted on unknowing citizens across the United States.[121]

Men and women were injected with plutonium at clinics, terminally ill cancer patients were injected with radioactive calcium, and mentally disabled teenagers were given radioactive ingredients in food during "nutritional studies."

In order to discover how biological weapons might spread through urban populations, during the 1950s, the US Army introduced bacteriological contaminants into the subway system of New York City and tracked the spread of the contamination.[122] Operation Sea Spray introduced bacteriological contaminants into the fog banks rolling into San Francisco.[123]

In the 1950s and 1960s, zinc cadmium sulfide in the form of a fine powder was sprayed from planes and roof-mounted machines onto primarily African American neighborhoods in St. Louis, Missouri. In other cities in the US, microorganisms such as *Serratia marcescens, Bacillus globigii* or some species of *Aspergillus* (fungus or mold)—either alone or combined with zinc cadmium sulfide—were sprayed.[124]

The frequency varied from location to location with some neighborhoods exposed up to 35 times over a period of two years. There were no studies done on the toxic effects of repeated exposure to zinc cadmium sulfide, although it was known that exposure to *Serratia marcescens, Bacillus globigii* and *Aspergillus* was harmful to persons with lowered immune system function.

And then there was the CIA-sponsored research into human behavioral engineering— research that was whispered about for years, heavily tarred with the "conspiracy" brush and ignored until secret documents were finally declassified.

From 1953 to 1973, the CIA ran several projects aimed at developing chemicals and techniques capable of creating effective mind control for use in clandestine operations. In the 1950s, the CIA's Office of Scientific Intelligence ran Project Artichoke, the purpose of which was to discover if it was possible to overcome the mind of an individual to the point where s/he would do their handler's bidding, even to the point of "committing acts against the fundamental laws of nature." Project Artichoke used hypnosis, forced morphine addiction, drug withdrawal, and the use of chemicals to incite amnesia in human subjects and make them pliable.[125]

Project MKUltra was similarly designed.[126]

For twenty years, the CIA clandestinely manipulated the mental states of both American and Canadian citizens by dosing them with LSD and other mind-altering drugs *without their knowledge.* Many of these experiments were conducted on unsuspecting customers in brothels, safe houses and seedy bars. In more formal research conducted under false pretenses at more than 80 locations around the country, including universities, hospitals, prisons, and pharmaceutical companies, drugs, including LSD, were combined with hypnosis, sensory deprivation, isolation, verbal and sexual abuse, electroshocks, and various forms of torture. Hundreds of federal agents, field operatives and scientists worked on these programs before they were shut down in 1973.[127]

In just these few pages, we have documented examples where hundreds of thousands of modern American citizens have had their body sovereignty unknowingly violated by the government. So, aside from lack of body sovereignty, what else is a characteristic of slavery?

Slaves also have no right to privacy. In 1975, when President Ford set up the United States President's Commission on CIA Activities, commonly referred to as the Rockefeller Commission, the commission found that the CIA was engaged in highly illegal activities such as large-scale spying on American citizens, engaging in illegal wire-taps, surveillance and mail tampering.[128]

In 2013, Edward Snowden, an American computer intelligence consultant for the US National Security Agency (NSA) leaked classified files revealing that the NSA was harvesting millions of emails and instant messages, searching emails and tracking the cellphones of millions of ordinary American citizens. The NSA was also accessing Yahoo and Google data centers to collect information from hundreds of millions of account holders worldwide. On September 2, 2020, a US federal court ruled in *United States v. Moalin,* that the NSA's mass surveillance program thus exposed was illegal and most likely unconstitutional.[129]

So much for our right to privacy.

But let's get back to the body sovereignty issue for a moment.

In 1976 President Ford signed an Executive Order prohibiting experimentation with drugs on human subjects without their informed consent. Despite the Order, experiments continued.

One involved a measles vaccine that was tested without consent from 1990 to 1991 by the Centers for Disease Control (CDC). Doctors injected thousands of babies in several African nations with the drug. The vaccine eventually led to several immune problems and reports of numerous deaths. Despite the drug's lethal effects, the government continued to test the experimental drug on more than 1,500 babies in the United States, mostly African American and Hispanic babies in Los Angeles. The study came to an end when it was discovered that African children were dying at a frightening rate up to three years after receiving the vaccinations.[130]

In 1993, the World Health Organization announced a "birth-control vaccine" that combined tetanus toxoid (TT) with human chorionic gonadotropin (hCG). Conjugating TT with hCG causes pregnancy hormones to be attacked by the immune system, triggering abortions in pregnant women and infertility in others.

As early as November 1993 and as late as 2014, Catholic publications were reporting that Catholic doctors around the continent of Africa were concerned about the increasing number of mysterious spontaneous abortions occurring in the general population who had had recent tetanus shots. When independent labs were employed to test WHO-disseminated tetanus "vaccines," half the samples tested turned out to contain hCG where none should have been present,[131] turning each tetanus shot into a potential abortifacient.

Between 1997 and 2000, the CIA and the Battelle Memorial Institute constructed and tested an anthrax "bomblet" in order to test its dissemination characteristics in a program called Project Clear Vision.[132]

In 2004, a University of Minnesota research participant committed suicide while participating in an industry-sponsored pharmaceutical trial comparing three FDA-approved atypical antipsychotics. Forced to choose between enrolling in the study or being involuntarily committed to a state mental institution, he was enrolled in the study against his own wishes and the wishes of his mother.[133]

Between the years 2000 and 2010, artificial blood was transfused by Northfield Labs into research subjects across the United States without their consent. Follow-up studies showed the artificial blood caused a "significant increase" in the risk of heart attacks and death.[134]

There also seems to be a direct link between the rise of genetic engineering and experimental work with viruses. The earliest AIDS cases in America were discovered in white gay men in Manhattan in 1979, shortly after an experimental hepatitis B vaccine program run by the New York Blood Centre was conducted on gay men in Manhattan. The vaccine was developed in chimpanzees, which were later officially blamed as the ancestor of the HIV virus which supposedly had its first outbreak in Africa before coming to America.[135]

But the AIDS epidemic did not start in Africa until the fall of 1982.

There is also a possible connection between the outbreak of AIDS in Central Africa and the widespread smallpox vaccine programs conducted by the World Health Organization in the 1970s in Central Africa.[136]

To this day, members of the US Congress continue to publicly state that current safeguards in US federal law and US federal policies do not provide sufficient protection for human research subjects and do not prohibit involuntary human research in the United States of America.

Since we're talking about viruses and epidemics, body sovereignty, slavery, human experiments and vaccines, I'm going to have to talk about SARS-CoV2.

As a health journalist who was raised in a medical family by an allopathic doctor who also had a medical degree in homeopathy, very early in the Covid outbreak I wrote a magazine article about homeopathic protocols for treating Covid-19. In the course of my research, I interviewed homeopathic physicians around the world, as well as one of the world's foremost homeopathic epidemiologists, Jeremy Scherr. By March 2020, Scherr had already personally treated over 800 Covid patients. Not one person went to the hospital and the vast majority of his cases recovered within three to seven days.

I was relieved to know there was a relatively straightforward cure, and stocked up on a few remedies. The article was published in a UK health magazine a month or so later. By fall, the CDC released statistics about mortality rates involved with Covid-19.[137] Seeing them, I was more relieved than ever—and enormously puzzled why lockdowns were still being mandated around the world.

The following figures released by the CDC[138] come from the document "Covid 19 Planning Scenarios, table 3, scenario 5: current best estimate, updated September 10, 2020."

CDC Figures		
Covid Survivability Rate		**Covid Survivability Rate (average)**
• 99.99 7%	age 0 - 19	• 98.5 % (average)
• 99.98 %	age 20 - 49	
• 99.5 %	age 50 - 69	
• 94.6 %	age 70 plus	

It seemed that the whole world was being incarcerated over a virus that had a 99.5 percent survivability rate if you were younger than 70. Which made absolutely no sense.

What on earth was going on?

By fall 2020, my health investigations had led me to the obvious fact that early treatment for Covid-19 was critical, and that high-dose intravenous vitamin C and heavy doses of vitamin D in addition to other natural supplements like zinc and NAC could reliably diminish symptoms in the early stages. In addition, a large number of trials showed the use of hydroxychloroquine to be an effective early treatment protocol.[139] As well, over 60 clinical trials around the world had proven Ivermectin to be a safe, effective prophylaxis and treatment for Covid-19 and its variants.[140]

An anti-parasitic medicine whose developers won the Nobel prize for its development in 2015, Ivermectin was (at that point) on the World Health Organization's list of essential medicines, and had been given 3.7 billion times around the globe with only occasional mild side effects.[141] A safe, effective and cheap repurposed drug, Ivermectin was distributed free of charge by the state of Uttar Pradesh, India, to 240 million citizens. Almost immediately the Covid death rate dropped to 1/20 the death rate of the US.[142] And yet American citizens were being told over and over by Anthony Fauci, the US health czar, "There is no treatment. There is nothing you can do. If you get sick do nothing. If it gets to the point where you can't breathe, go to the hospital." Never mind once at the hospital you would be put on a ventilator—an action that was basically a death sentence.

"Wait for the vaccine!" That's what everyone was told.

"Wait for the vaccine. It's the only thing that can possibly save us."

It was all so very wrong and completely counter to what the numerous holistic and functional medicine doctors, naturopaths and homeopaths I was interviewing were saying. Doctor after doctor I interviewed talked about the effective treatments they were using as the flood of Covid patients knocked at their doors. How none of their patients ended up in the hospital and how quickly they got better.

"Frankly, I don't know what the hell is going on with Fauci and the US governmental health services," said one physician. "Do nothing? Go to the hospital? Take Remdesivir and go on a ventilator? If they were trying to find a way to make absolutely sure a maximum number of people die, they couldn't have picked a better protocol to recommend."

I believed what I was hearing straight from the doctors. Which meant it was hard to believe what I was seeing in the world around me. Readily available, highly effective cures were being ignored and vilified. TV news and mainstream newspapers were shouting in unison about how Ivermectin, one of the safest, most prescribed drugs on the planet, was dangerously unsafe and unusable. I was hearing rumors of stockpiles of Ivermectin quietly being pulled off pharmacy shelves around the world and destroyed. How attending physicians in hospitals were refusing to treat dying patients with Ivermectin even when desperate relatives arrived with a court order to do so.

Then I learned that under section 564 as amended by PAHPRA (The Pandemic & All-Hazards Preparedness Reauthorization Act of 2013) the FDA can only authorize the emergency use of an unapproved medical product such as a new vaccine *when there are no adequate, approved and available alternatives.*[143]

If a safe, effective, cheap cure for Covid was available, there would be no need for a vaccine and Big Pharma would lose out on a lot of money.

Duh.

Ultimately, Operation Warp Speed (OWS)—the US government's Covid-19 relief program—would dole out $22 billion of taxpayer money to Big Pharma companies to develop a vaccine that they would then turn around and sell to the public at a massive profit. Pfizer alone made almost $36 billion from its Covid vaccine sales in 2021. Moderna made close to $20 billion in sales on their vaccine that same year. The *Forbes* article "How the Covid-19 Vaccine Injected Billions Into Big Pharma—and Made Its Executives Very Rich" tells a disgusting tale of stock options bought and sold, timed with vaccine production press release announcements and all sorts of high-profit insider trading shenanigans.[144]

And then I got my hands on a copy of Pfizer's Feb 2021 vaccine report "CUMULATIVE ANALYSIS OF POST-AUTHORIZATION ADVERSE EVENT REPORTS OF PF-07302048 (BNT162B2) RECEIVED THROUGH 28-FEB-2021." The report provided post-authorization vaccine safety data from health authorities, cases published in the medical literature, cases from Pfizer-sponsored marketing programs, and US and foreign post-authorization adverse event reports.

What did the report tell me?

According to Pfizer, their vaccine creates *dozens* of adverse reactions. Adverse events cited in the report include: Dyspnoea; tachypnoea; hypoxia; Covid-19 pneumonia; respiratory failure; acute respiratory distress syndrome; cardiac failure; cardiogenic shock; acute myocardial infarction; arrhythmia; myocarditis; vomiting; diarrhea; abdominal pain; jaundice; acute hepatic failure; deep vein thrombosis; pulmonary embolism; peripheral ischemia; vasculitis; shock; acute kidney injury; renal failure; altered state of consciousness; seizure; encephalopathy; meningitis; cerebrovascular accident; thrombocytopenia; disseminated intravascular coagulation; chilblains; erythema multiforme; Multiple Organ Dysfunction Syndrome; Multisystem Inflammatory Syndrome in children. To name a few.

But let's forget adverse reactions for a moment. Let's just focus on one small finding in the report. Table 12 (below) on page six clearly states that out of the 270 pregnant women recorded in this data set who took the vaccine, no follow-up was provided for 238 cases. Which leaves reported outcomes from 32 women. There were reporting errors in two different outcomes (see table), but bottom line, *out of 29 pregnant women who took the Covid shot, 28 aborted.*[145]

Even if the remaining three pregnancies were completed to term and the babies lived, 28 deaths out of 32 pregnancies equals an 87.5 percent mortality rate.

BNT162b2
5.3.6 Cumulative Analysis of Post-authorization Adverse Event Reports

Table 6. Description of Missing Information

Topic	Description
Missing Information	**Post Authorization Cases Evaluation (cumulative to 28 Feb 2021)** **Total Number of Cases in the Reporting Period (N=42086)**
Use in Pregnancy and lactation	• Number of cases: 413[a] (0.98% of the total PM dataset); 84 serious and 329 non-serious; • Country of incidence: US (205), UK (64), Canada (31), Germany (30), Poland (13), Israel (11); Italy (9), Portugal (8), Mexico (6), Estonia, Hungary and Ireland, (5 each), Romania (4), Spain (3), Czech Republic and France (2 each), the remaining 10 cases were distributed among 10 other countries. Pregnancy cases: 274 cases including: • 270 mother cases and 4 foetus/baby cases representing 270 unique pregnancies (the 4 foetus/baby cases were linked to 3 mother cases; 1 mother case involved twins). • Pregnancy outcomes for the 270 pregnancies were reported as spontaneous abortion (23), outcome pending (5), premature birth with neonatal death, spontaneous abortion with intrauterine death (2 each), spontaneous abortion with neonatal death, and normal outcome (1 each). No outcome was provided for 238 pregnancies (note that 2 different outcomes were reported for each twin, and both were counted).

For the record, the failure to record and report the outcomes of 238 out of 274 pregnancies during a drug trial is simply unheard of. It's beyond sloppy—it's alarmingly unethical and fundamentally a criminal act. Even more criminal is the fact that, to this day (February 2023), the Food and Drug Administration and the CDC continue to encourage pregnant women to get the shot, claiming there is "no evidence" of harm. This is so heinous I have to repeat myself here to make sure this sinks in.

> ***Pfizer's own drug trail data reveals that taking the Covid vaccine while pregnant results in a (at minimum) 87.5 percent fetal mortality rate, including spontaneous abortions, premature births with neonatal death, and spontaneous abortions with intrauterine death.***

And the Covid vaccines are "safe and effective?"

Effective for what?

Information released by the CDC showed that between Dec. 14, 2020 and Sept. 3, 2021, a total of 675,593 adverse events following Covid vaccine injections were reported to the governmental Vaccine Adverse Event Reporting System (VAERS), including 14,506 deaths.[146] But here's the thing about the VAERS system. It is reliably estimated that only one to ten percent of actual events are reported. Which means the death count at that point could easily have been as high as 145,060 and possibly much higher.[147]

No other drug in history has been allowed to create such damage and stay on the market. For example, Baycol (Ceristatin) manufactured by Bayer A.G. for cholesterol reduction was pulled from the market in 2001 after the drug caused 52 deaths worldwide and 385 nonfatal cases requiring hospitalization.[148] Duract (Bromfenac), manufactured by Wyeth-Ayerst Laboratories as a pain killer, was recalled in 1998 after four deaths and 20 patients sustained severe liver damage.[149]

Despite the high death count, despite hundreds of thousands of seriously adverse effects, the US government and governments around the world continued to try to mandate the vaccine, even though the drug they were pushing wasn't effective for more than a couple months.

A *Lancet* study published in October 2021 comparing 1.6 million vaccinated and unvaccinated people in Sweden showed that protection against symptomatic Covid-19 declined to such a degree that by six months some of the more vulnerable vaccinated groups were at greater risk than their unvaccinated peers.[150] By the summer of 2022, more and more clinical studies were concluding that the vaccines were far more damaging and lethal than Covid-19 itself. For example, the peer-reviewed clinical study, "Curing the Pandemic of Misinformation on COVID-19 mRNA Vaccines Through Real Evidence-Based Medicine," authored by cardiologist Dr. Aseem Malhotra and published by the *Journal of Insulin Resistance* in September 2022 states: "Re-analysis of randomized controlled trials using the messenger ribonucleic acid (mRNA) technology suggests a greater risk of serious adverse events from the vaccines than being hospitalized from COVID-19.[151]

And then there was Sudden Adult Death Syndrome (SADS), also short for "sudden arrhythmic death syndrome." First identified in 1977, SADS, fortunately, has always been as rare as it is inexplicable.

Until now.

Since the Covid vaccines hit the market, the number of healthy young adults suddenly keeling over and dying for no apparent reason is exploding worldwide—most especially in nations with a high vaccination rate.[152] The canary in the coalmine highlighting this trend is professional athletes. According to the International Olympic Committee database, between 1966 and 2004 (38 years), the average annual rate of sudden deaths amongst professional athletes under age 35 worldwide was 29 deaths per year. And yet, between March 2021 and March 2022, starting just a few months after the vaccines became widely available, at least 769 athletes suffered cardiac arrest, collapse, and/or died on the field—most from myocardial infarction,[153] an obstruction of the blood supply to the heart muscle. Other data sources report that between January 2021 and August 2022, over 895 professional athletes have died during competition.[154]

Alongside these statistics, articles started cropping up on alternative news sites pointing to the obvious culprits, Covid and the Covid vaccines, both of which are known to cause heart arrhythmia and myocarditis.

And yet, according to mainstream media, health officials were "puzzled" over this sudden dramatic increase in SADS, saying they had no idea what might be triggering the rise in sudden deaths.

Seriously?

Which brings me around to the simply enormous question of why scientific discussion about the Covid vaccines, vaccine side effects and alternative methods of treatment has been completely forbidden.

To this day, worldwide, any doctor or researcher promoting Ivermectin or natural treatments or posing legitimate questions and concerns about the vaccines—including hundreds of some of the most prominent doctors and vaccine researchers in the world, including Dr. Robert Malone, *the inventor of the mRNA vaccine itself*—are labeled "propaganda-spreading conspiracy theorists," de-platformed, and threatened with losing their medical license.

Family practitioner and globally respected health proponent Dr. Joseph Mercola had his private and business bank accounts shut down by the US government, his social media accounts frozen and his website taken off the Internet. He was directly attacked and labeled a "superspreader of misinformation" by both *The New York Times* and President Joe Biden.

Why was Dr. Mercola called this?

Because he publicly called the Covid shots "a medical fraud" because they didn't provide immunity and didn't stop transmission of the infection, which is what a vaccine is supposed to do.

Today we all know that if you get the shots, you can still get Covid and you can still transmit it to others. In fact, in October 2022, Janine Small, the Pfizer President of International Developed Markets, testified before a European Parliamentary Investigative Committee, *that the Pfizer mRNA Covid-19 vaccine was not designed to prevent transmission of the virus. It was not even tested to see if it would do so.*[155]

And yet the entire public selling point for the vaccine was that it would stop transmission of the virus and thus end the pandemic. People around the world were told, "Do it for others. Get the vaccine to protect your loved ones. Do it to protect your neighbors." People who didn't get the shot were attacked and vilified as murderers and terrorists.

It was all just a hyped-up PR job based upon a lie.

Ironically, both Biden and Fauci are now stand-out examples pointing to the fact that Mercola was telling the truth all along. Both Biden and Fauci were double vaxxed and boosted, and both twice contracted Covid.

On July 12, 2022, Fauci admitted on the FOX News Show "Your World," that Covid-19 vaccines do not even protect "overly well" against infection itself. And Bill Gates said in a TV interview that early on vaccine proponents didn't understand that Covid has "a fairly low fatality rate and that it's a disease mainly in the elderly, kind of like flu is, although a bit different than that."[156]

Vaccine proponents might not have understood what was going on. But thousands of the world's foremost epidemiologists, doctors and researchers knew it. Thousands of holistic, functional and alternative medical practitioners knew it—which is why all these professionals vocally opposed the lockdowns and the vaccines. For god's sake, *I* knew it when the CDC released its mortality estimates in September 2020. (See table on page 158)

Come on.

They knew. Does anybody believe the propaganda anymore?

Unfortunately, the answer to that is "Yes."

Covid was my wakeup call. Nothing about the way it was officially being handled made any sense *unless* I looked at it from the "something stinks in Denmark" perspective. And man, looking at the facts, did things ever stink.

In two short years, the entire world's population was cowed and broken by media-driven fear over what was essentially a nasty but highly treatable flu bug. Separated from friends, locked out of work and schools, cudgeled back into their houses by ever-increasing numbers of police patrolling the streets enforcing the lockdowns, watching as their economic opportunities, life savings, jobs, hopes and dreams spiraled down the toilet, global paranoia and depression spiked like never before.

In the US, over 144 million people lost their jobs.[157] Forty million people were at risk of losing their homes. Over 52 percent of young people age 18 to 29 moved back home with their parents—the highest number since the Great Depression 80 years ago.[158] Over 40 percent of adults reported mental health and substance abuse issues.[159] Domestic abuse skyrocketed and homicides around the US rose 53 percent.[160]

Small businesses, a powerful and influential piece of the economy, closed by the thousands. By the end of 2021, over 34 percent of mom-and-pop establishments collectively employing almost half of the nation's private workforce had been driven out of business by closure mandates. In cities like San Francisco, 48 percent of small businesses went under.[161]

Yet Big Box corporate-owned stores were allowed to stay open and thrived.

After the 2008 financial crisis, corporations began buying up huge numbers of suburban houses, renting them out, usually for more than residents would have paid on a mortgage. By 2018 big corporations were purchasing one out of every 10 suburban homes sold, jacking up prices beyond what consumers could pay, offering top dollar to take them off the market, essentially turning America into a renter nation where corporations own most of the real estate.[162] Post-Covid, with bailouts ending, a 67 percent increase in home foreclosures and big corporations flush with Covid cash surging into the marketplace, the prospect of attaining The American Dream of home ownership had never been bleaker.

And the World Economic Forum's prediction, "You will own nothing and you will be happy" had never looked more prescient.

At least the "owning nothing" part.

CHAPTER NINE KEY

Love your body (and follow the money)

PART 1

So, where is there a safe place? Where is the path out of all this crazy? What can you do?

I know it doesn't seem like much. But, as painful as it is, realizing how deeply we've all been "had" is the first step. Once you wake up to that, you're no longer cannon fodder. You're no longer available for manipulation.

You're out of the matrix.

Is it easy accepting that all this is actually happening? No! It's a freaking nightmare. But the good news is: *You can wake up and leave the nightmare behind.* Once you see through the veils of illusion and manipulation you have CHOICE.

You get to think and act independently and unabashedly follow the path of the heart. *Your* heart. You get to stand up for love and act how love acts. And one of the first things you will know to do once out of the madness is to care for, love and heal your beautiful body.

The body is a vehicle of pure love.

It does our bidding and carries our unique individual spirits where we want to go. It informs and guides us. It gives us the chance to witness sunsets and thunderstorms, cuddle puppies and kittens, babies and each other. It enables us to create more life. Blessed be the body.

My best advice (and I'm learning this too!) is to:

- Become sensitive to your body's authentic needs.
  (Hint: It's usually not sugar, Doritos or alcohol!)
- Listen to what it's trying to tell you through feelings and physical symptoms.
- Don't worship it or overindulge it or abuse it. *Love it.*
- Protect it from harm.

Eat organic. Join a food co-op. Support local farmers as much as possible. Even in big cities there are people who start rooftop gardens and reclaim abandoned lots to grow neighborhood gardens.

Find or get a group together to start one. When you're out grocery shopping:

- Understand that the food industry is grotesquely manipulated and that "natural ingredients" doesn't mean healthy. Arsenic is a natural ingredient.
- Buy organic.
- Likewise know that something labeled "green" isn't necessarily green or healthy.

- Avoid all processed foods.
- Buy simple, eat simple: Organic veggies, fruits, meats, poultry, fish, cereals/grains.

A hugely important thing to do for your body is getting out in nature as much as possible. *Nature is our nature!*

- Ground yourself. Walk barefoot. Connect to the earth.

PART 2

Please realize money and profit are the driving forces behind pretty much everything in the medical and "health" world these days. Health insurance, health protocols and health mandates ... your health is not an important part of any of these things anymore.

Physicians are paid by the pharmaceutical companies to push their drugs. And I've talked to more than one doctor who has privately told me that they've noticed that pharmaceutical products that are the *most* effective causing the *least* amount of side effects are usually quietly pulled off the market and replaced with a product that is *less* effective and causes *more* side effects.

Why? Because it gives the pharmaceutical company more products to sell to counter the increased side effects. "But please, don't use my name with that information in an article," they say. "That is strictly off the record."

Medical schools are subsidized by Big Pharma. Medical journals depend on advertising from Big Pharma. Clinical studies are being paid for by Big Pharma. "Standard of Care" practices are not about care, your health or your wellbeing. They're about ensuring that doctors and insurance companies are covered from malpractice.

If you really care about the health and wellbeing of your beautiful body, I highly recommend finding a good naturopathic physician or a doctor who practices functional medicine or a homeopathic physician. Check out Traditional Chinese Medicine (TCM) and acupuncture. TCM has been effectively saving lives and improving the health and vitality of emperors for almost 3000 years.

I have had "incurable" conditions, like acute Achilles tendonitis that several allopathic doctors said "You'll just have to learn to live with it," rapidly heal with a combination of acupuncture and Chinese herbs. So, I'm a total fan.

Mainstream medicine has its place. If you break a bone or need surgery, that's where to go. But if you want health and healing, look elsewhere.

Love your body. Care for it. Be wise.

Without it you're not here. And if you're not here you're going to miss out on the most amazing chapter in all of human history.

10

Slavery and the Transhumanist Agenda

No conversation about slavery is complete without discussing The Great Reset put forward at the World Economic Forum's meeting in June 2020 in Davos, Switzerland. The plan is fundamentally constructed around two concepts. 1) "Stakeholder capitalism" and 2) a Fourth Industrial Revolution based upon bio-implants and human "augmentation."

Stakeholder capitalism means that international corporations will no longer focus solely on serving their corporate shareholders, but instead become multi-stakeholder partners along with governments and the private sector in deciding global policies and helping implement them.

While the word "partners" sounds nice and progressive, this is not about global unity and equality. It's about shifting power—shifting global governance from being the responsibility of duly elected leaders of nations representing the people, to a situation where nations' governments (and thus the people) only have a partial say as far as global policies regulating economics, technology, food, agriculture, pharmaceuticals, transportation, health, you name it.

This means that non-governmental stakeholders like Amazon, Chevron, Exxon, Facebook, Unilever, Microsoft, AstraZeneca and Pfizer etc. will have enormous power when it comes to deciding how the world develops and how you and I eat, breathe, communicate, travel, live and evolve.

Corporations already have massive influence over all our world governments through lobbying and targeted campaign contributions, as well as the placement of carefully groomed industry insiders into all levels of government.

For example, pharmaceutical industry lobbyist Alex Michael Azar II, former president of the US division of the pharmaceutical giant Eli Lilly Co. and member of the board of directors of the Biotechnology Innovation Organization, a global pharmaceutical trade organization, was appointed as the United States Secretary of Health and Human Services from 2018 to 2021.

Moncef Slaoui, former head of GlaxoSmithKline's vaccine division and a venture capitalist in the pharmaceutical field was appointed to act as chief adviser for America's Covid response program Operation Warp Speed.

Andrew Wheeler, a lobbyist for the fossil fuel industry was appointed head of the Environmental Protection Agency (EPA) where he effectively gutted Obama's Clean Power Plan and the 1972 Clean Water Act, rolled back standards on mercury and other toxic substances, froze fuel efficiency standards on cars and eliminated all references to climate change on the agency's website.

David Bernhardt, an oil and energy industry lobbyist served as the Deputy Secretary of the Interior from 2017 to 2019 and then as Secretary of the Interior from 2019 to 2021, setting policies over oil and gas access to federal lands. Patrick Michael Shanahan, a member of the Boeing Executive Council, served as acting US Secretary of Defense overseeing defense contracts.

Talk about putting the foxes in charge of the henhouse.

Corporations—whose sole goal is acquiring greater profit opportunities via continued resource exploitation—already compromise our governments. And they already own the global media. Giving corporations equal stakeholder status as governments deciding global health, economic and industry policies means corporate leaders like Bill Gates—who was once described by a journalist as having "the warmth of a tray of ice cubes"—would officially run the world.

The second prong of The Great Reset is Klaus Schwab's Fourth Industrial Revolution, which is characterized by a range of new technologies that are "fusing the physical, digital and biological worlds, impacting all disciplines, economies and industries, and even challenging ideas about what it means to be human."[163]

In other words: Artificial Intelligence aka AI.

The term "transhumanism" was coined back in 1957 by English biologist and philosopher Julian Huxley who wrote an essay about improving the human condition through social and cultural change, as well as through human enhancement technologies. Today, transhumanism and the transhuman agenda is mainstream news and we find people like Yuval Harari, chief advisor to WEF founder Klaus Schwab saying things like:

"For four billion years, nothing fundamental changed in the basic rules of the game of life. All of life was subject to the laws of natural selection and the laws of organic biochemistry. But this is now about to change. Science is replacing evolution by natural selection with evolution by intelligent design. Not the intelligent design of some god above the clouds, [but] our intelligent design, and the design of our 'clouds,' the IBM cloud, the Microsoft cloud. These are the new driving forces of evolution."[164]

I don't know about you, but the idea of Microsoft and IBM driving human evolution does not comfort or excite me. Considering the lack of intelligent design found in many Microsoft products and other manmade things—from shoes to stovetops to inner-city interstate exchanges —I'm not too hopeful about humanity's ability to play Supreme Creator at this point either.

Yes, we have made stunning progress in many human enhancement technologies like deep brain stimulation devices (DBS) which have been used to successfully treat tens of thousands of patients with Parkinson's disease and epilepsy. In January 2019, researchers at Johns Hopkins Medicine (JHM) and the Johns Hopkins University Applied Physics Laboratory (APL) implanted six electrodes into the brain of a quadriplegic man during a 10-hour operation, enabling him to control a pair of prosthetic arms with his mind sufficient to perform simple tasks like feeding himself.[165] Soon, neural implants will allow prosthetics to be controlled almost as naturally as the limbs they replace—an enormous humanitarian gift for millions.

And it's not just physical augmentation that's being researched. Recently, a woman in California treated with an experimental brain implant successfully recovered from severe lifelong depression that was resistant to medication.

Bottomline, cyborgs are not just science fiction. They are among us now, wearing biotech cochlear implants for hearing and implants for vision enhancement. Upgrades for metabolic enhancement, artificial bones, muscles, and organs aren't far away. Brain-computer interfaces, aka neuroprosthetics, combined with other technologies will ultimately be able to restore natural movements to paralyzed limbs. With gene therapy we'll be able to manipulate our genetic code, eliminating things like cancer and heart disease. We might even be able to make getting fat, going grey and getting old things of the past.

These are all wonderful biotech advancements for humanity. But they come with massive social and ethical implications—for starters, whether such advancements will be made available for everyone or just an elite few. And where—if anywhere—do we draw the line on blending humans and AI?

We are standing at the place where the "gods" of old once stood.

The gods who genetically modified and enslaved us. The gods we once worshipped and desired to emulate. We have just about become their equal technologically. The question now is: Will we continue to emulate them and remain manipulators, users and enslavers? Or will we rise above history and our genetic and social programming and reach far above them?

The most important choice in the history of our species is upon us. And it's not about whether or not to embrace AI. We're already long past that point. AI is already upon us and in us. The question is: *Who will we be in the midst of the AI revolution?*

We are multidimensional non-physical beings of pure love. Theoretically, the physical body has *never* defined who we are. However, in practice, the human body has, so far, completely dominated our consciousness and our reality. Our current idea of greatness revolves around our mental and physical capacities.

We want to fly and leap tall buildings in a single bound. We want to be smarter, faster, stronger. We want to see into distant realms and dimensions and transcend time. We want to be magical and immortal.

For decades, the Western entertainment industry has mirrored these longings back to us in the form of superheroes—Superman, Supergirl, the Black Panther, Batman, the Avengers, Captain America, Green Arrow, Spider Man, X-Men, Wonder Woman, Wolverine. We might admire people like Gandhi and Mother Theresa—but most of us dream about having super powers.

Becoming an AI-augmented human appears to be the fastest, most guaranteed chance of doing so. With AI we can have better genes and better brains. We can have access to more information—fast-as-lightning access to terabytes of facts. And we sincerely believe this will make us better human beings.

And yet ...

Has access to more factoids made any of us better people in the last 50 years?

We aren't computers—yet. More data is not what we need to shine. It may bolster our egos and make us feel smarter than the next guy. It might even guarantee us a job. But more data, more often than not, just confuses things, leading us down an endless rabbit hole of conflicting views.

Facts cannot tell us who we really are.

How many times do we need to hear Data of *Star Trek* fame talk about how he would give anything to be human? To feel? To love? Data would happily trade his positronic brain and exabytes of information for soft tissue!

But the current AI conversation talks about everything BUT feelings and love.

The soul and spirit are nowhere in the picture at all.

The Great Reset is all about elevating the mind and achieving great heights of technology that the vast majority of humanity will serve.

And it's also about fear.

"If humans want to continue to add value to the economy, they must augment their capabilities through a merger of biological intelligence and machine intelligence," said Elon Musk at the 2017 World Government Forum in Dubai. "If we fail to do this, we'll risk becoming 'house cats' to artificial intelligence."[166]

Excuse me?

I'm supposed to go get a neural lace implant which would grow in my brain, enabling my neurons to be programmed and enhanced *so I can add value to the economy?* And if I don't, I might fall under the control of a virulent global Super Computer?

That's my choice?

Those are the reasons I must set aside my humanity?

Yes, *setting aside our humanity* is exactly what we are being told we must do.

Imagine being a brilliant, beautiful, healthy, strong nearly immortal being named Sam or Samantha—a genetically modified androgyne loaded with implants and gadgets, cloud computing and knowledge beyond your wildest dreams.

By definition, the person you're imagining becoming is not a human being *unless* ...

Unless what has also been augmented through their individual conscious effort is their connection to their spirit and their capacity for intimate connection, compassion, and respect for all life.

Augment the body, don't augment the body.

It doesn't matter what you choose.

What defines you as a human being is your capacity for love and your capacity to honor and protect life in all its individualized forms.

If increasing my capacity to love, honor, serve and protect life is the end goal of AI augmentation, along with a healthier body and longer life, why not go for it? With these as motives, a few implants would allow me to be better able to serve the good. And how cool would that be?

"Hi, I'm a multidimensional, non-physical being of love who is already immortal. But now, in my wisdom, creativity and love, I have developed an almost indestructible immortal bio-based body to match my own innate divine nature."

What a vision to aspire to!

But this is NOT the vision behind The Fourth Industrial Revolution.

The people driving the augmentation train believe that humans have no soul. That there is no such thing as spirit. In their view, all is mind. Life has no real value beyond service to that mind.

"Perhaps the most important thing to know about the future, is that humans will soon be hackable animals," says Yuval Harari. "Now, what does it mean to hack a human being? It means to create an algorithm that can understand you better than you can understand yourself. And therefore, can predict your choices, manipulate your desires, and make decisions on your behalf."[167]

This is the goal behind The Great Reset.

This is also the goal of the hidden anti-life Force.

The Archons on this planet don't believe in love and personal evolution. They don't believe in individual sovereignty. They don't understand that every being is uniquely divine with their own special gifts to contribute to life. They don't see each being as precious and worth protecting.

And neither do their corporate and governmental minions.

To people like Soros and Harari, life is about assets to be developed and obstacles to be managed and either turned into assets or destroyed. At the moment, the most dangerous obstacle that needs to be turned into an asset is the mushrooming human population on this planet.

Just like all those thousands of years ago when the gods genetically modified humans to be assets—slaves smart enough to carry out orders but not smart enough to strike out on their own agenda—I fear we're facing the exact same situation again.

Getting the mass of humanity into the "obedient asset" category is the prime directive.

If this doesn't happen quickly, the Great Reset will fail. If just a third of the 99 percent wake up, the game of the One Percent is finished. Which is why there's such an obvious push being made to close the deal by whatever means necessary—Covid, inflation, climate change, food shortages, economic crashes, war, threats of Russia going nuclear, more pandemics—whatever it takes.

It's now or never.

I've already talked about how humanity is being dumbed down through genetically modified foods, pollution, EM frequencies, pharmaceuticals, media etc. What I haven't mentioned is nanotechnology in the form of quantum dots, hydrogels, graphene oxide, and single wall carbon nanotubes (SWCNT). All of these nanotechnologies have been in place in healthcare products, military neuroweapons, biomedical devices, electronic devices, television screens and even in foods & beverages for over a decade.

Man-made nanoscale crystals, quantum dots can transport electrons and be used as single-electron transistors. Because of their capacity for "intelligent" molecular recognition and self-assembly, these nanocrystals are used as functional nanodevices.[168] Hydrogels are crosslinked polymer chains that closely resemble living tissues. They are highly effective as a transport medium, can easily pass the blood brain barrier,[169] and have been extensively studied by scientists at the National Center for Nanoscience and Technology (NCNST) in Beijing, China for use in delivering mRNA vaccines. Graphene oxide is another superlative "carrier" tested for vaccine applications and researched for years.[170] Single wall carbon nanotubes are one-dimensional, cylindrically shaped allotropes of carbon that can intelligently identify particular molecular energetic signatures. They are used as nano-biomedical trackers and "carriers."[171]

From a technological perspective, humanity is now at a place where it is possible to use vaccines as implant delivery systems designed to create neural lace interfaces in human beings that can be hacked via satellite-linked computers around the world, thus creating a pliant trackable "controlled populace" that can serve as an asset rather than an obstacle to the developmental plans of our elite leaders.

Impossible? No.

Likely? Frankly, I don't know. But our governments and the elites of this planet have invested *billions* into researching these technologies over the last few decades. Now that they have them in hand, how likely is it that they will decide not to use them? How likely is it for somebody like George Soros to stand up and say, "Wow, I/we have the ability to control all of humanity with the flip of a switch. But ... hmmm ... nah. As handy as that would be, it just wouldn't be ethical."

Uh huh. Right.

In the last two years, in labs all around the globe, independent researchers investigating the Covid "jab" using phase contrast, dark field and bright field microscopy, transmission and scanning electron microscopy and energy-dispersive x-ray spectroscopy maintain they have already discovered all of these nanotechnologies—and more—in the Covid vaccines.

In 2021, Dr. Robert O. Young released a shocking 100-page article "Scanning and Transmission Electron Microscopy and Identification of the Non-Disclosed Ingredients of the Corona Vaccine."[172] I interviewed Dr. Young, and here's some of what he had to say about his research: "We're seeing rods of graphene and self-assembling materials called carbon-based nanotubes or nano threads (CNTs) contained in these inoculations. We're seeing ferric oxide, stainless steel, aluminum and various other metals that are cytotoxic, genotoxic and magnetically toxic. ... Why hasn't the presence of these ingredients in these inoculations been publicly disclosed?"

When I asked him about the possible health benefits of the Covid vaccines, his reply was brusque. "As to their effectiveness and safety? There is none," he says. "From my perspective this is about population control, contact tracing and converting human beings into transhumans."

Dr. Shimon Yanowitz, an Israeli biological systems and electrical engineer specializing in nanoparticle and nanobot technologies, has extensively analyzed Pfizer, BioNTech, Moderna, J&J and Astra Zeneca vaccines, both frozen and incubated at body temperature, examining them via electron and dark field microscopy. In so doing, he says he has found overwhelming evidence of the presence of self-assembly nanostructures.[173]

True? False?

I don't know. What do *you* think?

Thing is, you don't even need an electron microscope to find weirdly out-of-place things in the Covid vaccines—substances that seem to substantiate independent researchers' claims. The published ingredients list of the J&J vaccine, for example, contains chemicals like 2-hydroxy-propyl-β-cyclodextrin (HBCD) and Polysorbate-80.[174]

HBCD is what's called a cyclodextrin which is a saccharide polymer made from starch that acts as an effective carrier of pharmaceutical payloads throughout the body, even across the blood-brain barrier.[175] Experiments have been conducted using cyclodextrins to carry modified electrodes and electrochemical sensors—biosensors—throughout the body, including the brain.[176] Polysorbate-80 helps increase permeability of the blood-brain barrier, increasing brain uptake of pharmaceuticals.[177]

Is it a coincidence that those ingredients are in there?

I don't think so.

Frankly, as paranoid as a diabolical plot to create hackable humans through nanotechnology via vaccines sounds, aside from population control, it's one of the few things I've heard that makes any sense of the whole Covid debacle.

Why else try to mandate the injection of a largely ineffective experimental drug with terrifying side effects for a flu virus with a 98.5 percent average survivability rate? Aside from making boatloads of money, why else push this dangerous drug onto children and babies when the CDC's own Covid mortality assessments place the risk of death for young people up to age 19 at .003 percent?[178]

If you can come up with a better answer, please, let me know. In the meantime, over 5.25 billion people around the planet have received at least one dose of this experimental drug.[179]

Not bad for a trial run.

Even if nothing the increasing numbers of researchers around the world like Young and Yanowitz are saying is true, the Covid Project has opened the door for global vaccine passports and other incursions into the rights of private citizens.

Civil liberties organizations are alarmed about the prospect of an oppressive global digital ID system that could easily lead to further Big Brother invasions.

"Digital IDs would lead to sensitive records spanning medical, work, travel, and biometric data about each and every one of us being held at the fingertips of authorities and state bureaucrats," says Silkie Carlo, director of Big Brother Watch in an interview for the UK publication *The Guardian*. "This dangerous plan would normalize e-identity checks, increase state control over law-abiding citizens and create a honeypot for cybercriminals."[180]

Or how about subdermal RFID chips?

Radio-frequency identification (RFID) transponders encased in silicate glass, implanted under the skin using a syringe-like device, have been in use for domestic pets and farm animals for quite a while. In 2004, RFID chips were approved for use in humans by the FDA.

Already being used by some corporations and countries such as Sweden, proponents of this technology claim huge benefits. For example, door locks, elevators and cars can be paired with sensors so that only the right people can open a door. Computers can identify users when they log on, allowing them access to files and systems specific only to them.

Biometric data can be uploaded to satellites and your health remotely monitored.

Using GPS tracking satellites, your physical position on the planet can be known 24/7 down to a few square feet. Instead of using money or a debit/credit card to buy groceries, you'll be able to do a "biopayment" by passing your implanted wrist over a scanner and have the money deducted from your account automatically.

You will have no name, just an ID number.

You will have no physical money.

All your electronic purchases and transactions can be instantly accessed via an interlinked global computer system. If you're "bad"—for example, if you send $40 to a GoFundMe campaign supporting a cause that your employer or government doesn't like—your accounts and all assets can be frozen. Which is exactly what happened to supporters of the Freedom Convoy in Canada in 2021 who were peacefully—and effectively—demonstrating against vaccine mandates.

At the behest of the Canadian government, financial institutions illegally seized approximately $7.8 million in funds in individual accounts, fundraising platforms and cryptocurrency wallets. Although funds were restored after the trucking protest was effectively destroyed via these violations of personal privacy and sovereignty, all contributors' accounts have been permanently "flagged."[181]

In other words: "You better keep your nose clean. We've got our eye on you."

This is the technological and economic tyranny we're already facing.

Much like slaves on the block with numbers around our necks, we can now be tracked and electronically corralled like cows in a field. The technology for delivering "correctional" electro-shocks to the body anytime, anywhere[182] is a reality and other electronic information can likely be downloaded into the body via an RFID chip as well.

But hey. There's an upside.

If you're chipped, at least you won't have to carry a wallet and ID anymore.

CHAPTER TEN KEY

Recognize evil when you see it and refuse to participate

KEY#10 is where the rubber meets the road. It's about recognizing evil when you see it and refusing to participate. Which means it's time to seriously ask yourself a few questions, such as:

- Can I be fully empowered while unknowingly being manipulated by social/governmental/economic forces and independent NGOs?
- Can I participate in what might be corrupt, anti-life practices and then flourish myself?

Let me explain what I'm talking about. And apologies ahead of time for using Covid as yet one more painful example.

A lot of my friends and associates *knew* not to take the Covid shot.

Their gut, their intuition, their heart, their soul, their spirit, the still small voice within—whatever you want to call it—was shouting at them "Don't do it!"

But then there were circumstances.

"I had to be at the side of a parent who was dying." Or "My sister was getting married and wouldn't allow anyone un-vaxxed at the ceremony." Or "I was going to lose my job and I've got children to feed." Or "I was going to lose my wife" or husband or lover or last available week at the timeshare in Acapulco.

They clearly heard the inner voice which was saying "NO" for a reason.

And then they went against it.

And then they massaged their decision by leaning on spiritual dogma and the power of intention. Over and over, I heard people say afterwards, "Oh, I just took the one shot to get the paperwork so I could do what I needed to do. I'll clean it all up in consciousness later."

One and all, they explained that love would protect them. That their high level of consciousness and spiritual intention would render the vaccine harmless. Which, again, clearly indicates that they knew the shot was dangerous to begin with.

This was nothing less than playing Russian Roulette with their lives.

And yet, I so get it.

Everybody I know, myself included, has been taught that the power of intention combined with the power of love is like this amazing shield of titanium we can wield, protecting us from everything bad and harmful. By God, I can *will* and focus my way through any storm using only my *mind*.

Sigh.

I remember years ago hearing a guru from south India talk about diet and how funny it was watching so many New Age people in America trying to use intention to will away the harmful aftereffects of eating crappy food.

"You believe you can turn a piece of steak into a salad once you've eaten it," he said, chuckling. "I am so very sorry to inform you, but if you cannot turn that steak into a salad while it is sitting in the palm of your hand, how do you expect to do it in your stomach?"

I never forgot what he said because it was so true. It was also a painful commentary on the general naiveté of the spiritual community (myself included) and the adherence to what basically amounts to magical thinking.

And then there's the string bean intention experiment conducted by an associate of mine, author and researcher Lynne McTaggart. She's conducted many intention experiments over the years with extremely interesting and yet varied results. For example, during an internet workshop, almost 7000 people from around the world focused their intention on string bean seeds, intending them to "glow" with more energy than the control seeds. And although there was indeed a strong energetic effect, it did not reach statistical significance.[183]

If almost 7000 spiritually advanced Westerners can't produce a statistically significant impact on the energy output of some seeds, how can one person expect to change the contents of a syringe or change their effects in their body?

Heaven only knows, I couldn't do it. I can't even dodge a hangover. And I'm not putting myself down or buying into fear or lack consciousness. I'm just being realistic. Maybe there are a few avatars in the Himalayas who've spent their lives meditating in a loincloth who could manage. But aside from that?

Which does not mean all is lost if you've taken it.

There are mitigation protocols that can successfully chelate substances like graphene oxide out of the body.[184] (I include medical sources for protocols in the resources section.) And, yes, there is consciousness which can and will lead you to whatever you need to open the doors to continued health, wellbeing and autonomy.

But first that requires discovering what's really going on. And then it requires taking action to deal with the reality.

Doggone it. We *talk* about spirit and love. We read books about it. But then we *act* like we don't even know what those things mean. We *act* like being in alignment with life/spirit is something we can compromise and manipulate with no ramifications.

I can't tell you how many friends and business associates said to me, "Oh, for God's sake, just play along. Just get the shot so you can do ____________ (xyz)."

But if I go along with the system, I'm in the system's web. I may try to fool myself, but no amount of self-justification and talk about "higher consciousness" can alter the fact that I'm compromising myself by accepting the system and its rules as my own.

This is not spiritual integrity.

If I truly am spirit and my father and mother are spirit, then they will always be with me, alive or dead. If I truly am spirit and love is all that matters, even if I'm not at their bedside to say goodbye in the flesh, they will receive my love and my message. If love is real, my sister will receive it even if she never speaks to me again for not being at her wedding.

Is it easy being integrous?

Is it easy following the inner voice?

Is it easy knowing people will be disappointed, hurt and harshly critical of your choices? No. But even if nobody gets it, somehow the painfully hard decision to listen and follow where spirit leads will make a difference. Standing up for life will make others stronger because all life is interconnected. Powerful choices to follow spirit's voice *no matter what* will touch others' souls and uplift them. Eventually, everybody will know that:

Honoring life/spirit is more important than honoring the social norm.

Everybody will know that honoring the inner voice is more important than convenience, family expectations, money, status, the fear of wounded feelings, hurt egos and missing a trip to Acapulco.

A good friend of mine is a great case in point.

Angela was really clear about not accepting the vaccine. She didn't know a lot of details and never listened to any conspiracy talk about it.

She just *knew* something about it didn't feel right. And then her sister had a baby. Angela was excited and ready to fly out for a visit, but her sister said she wasn't welcome unless she was vaccinated. If she didn't put aside her "selfish fears" and take the shot so she could come visit the new arrival, she would never be welcome in the family again.

Whoa.

This kind of story and this kind of agonizing choice was played out millions of times by people all around the globe during the years of 2020 and 2021. (Talk about a ghastly opportunity to see what you really stand for. It's actually kind of mind blowing.)

So, what did Angela do?

She thought long and hard about what love is and what it isn't and decided not to visit the new baby and stay true to herself. Her sister went ballistic and ended their relationship. Then, a year later after the lockdowns and mandates had drifted away, Angela was invited to visit for the baby's first birthday. When she told her sister she still wasn't vaccinated, her sister didn't care. When Angela reminded her of the ultimatum the previous year, her sister didn't remember the conversation.

"My God," Angela said later, voice shaking with emotion. "I can't believe I almost went against everything I *knew*, everything I *felt* was right, just to make my sister happy and keep peace in the family. And then she doesn't even remember what she said? I can't believe it!"

But this is what happens all the time.

This is what we are programmed to do.

The fickleness and petty rages of the ego ... fitting in ... not rocking the boat ... making sure our accustomed livelihoods are not threatened ... these things and so much more are what we compromise our very souls for over and over again.

And then we wonder why we don't like ourselves very much.

Is practicing Key #10 going to be easy? Well, yes, because you'll be going with the flow of your own true nature. It will feel right. It will feel *good.* It will feel like an act of empowerment—an act of acknowledging and empowering Who You Really Are.

So, yes, it will be easy.

And no.

It's probably going to be really tough because you'll be going against the mainstream. You'll be going against social programming. You're not going to be making the same choices and taking the same actions as the people all around you.

But take heart.

Swimming upstream isn't easy. But at least you'll be swimming as the authentic you.

11

From Human to Anti-Human

I've met the anti-life Force, wide awake and eyeball-to-eyeball, only once. And I'm not talking about the Beast with red eyes and fangs in the slimy graveyard that night. That pathetic creature was only this Force's minion. A human creation. A mental projection of all of the things that go bump in the night and terrify us most—or at least me. It was my Beast, after all.

No. The meeting I'm talking about occurred some 20 years later.

I was having dinner with a couple of friends. It was after dinner and we were sitting in the living room, drinking wine and talking. Out of the blue, I felt the energy in the room shift. It got cold. I shivered involuntarily and glanced sideways at Tess, my best friend, about to ask if she'd noticed the energetic change.

And that's when I saw her eyes.

Instead of their usual clear blue, they were pitch black and empty as the abyss.

I recoiled in shock and stammered, "Who are YOU?"

There was no answer, just a wicked gleam. And as I continued to look into those frigid depths not two feet away, a terrible fear gripped me and I whispered, "You frighten me."

A look of infinite satisfaction flashed in those black eyes and Tess's lips curled in a cruel sneer. And that's when I got pissed. The fear vanished and I leaned in and whispered the first words that popped into my head: "You are that which you are not."

The black eyes widened in surprise. The sneer vanished and I watched as the Force that had possessed my friend so briefly fled. And suddenly Tess's eyes were blue again. And the room warmed up and, puzzled, she shook her head as if to clear it, smiled, and reached for her wine.

It wasn't the first time Tess channeled some sort of energy. And she'd had sufficient alcohol to not be freaked out when I told her what had just happened. But what was really interesting was when I asked Toby, the other witness to the event, what he saw. And his answer couldn't have been more diametrically opposed to my experience.

"Wow," he said, enthusiastically. "I saw this beautiful angel of light."

"Seriously?" I asked, incredulous.

"Yeah. What did you see?"

"Uh. Never mind."

What does it say in 2 Corinthians 11:14 -15? "Even Satan disguises himself as an angel of light. It is not surprising, then, if his servants also masquerade as servants of righteousness. Their end will be what their actions deserve."

The global minions behind The Great Reset—the corporate power brokers who speak of Covid and other man-made disasters as golden opportunities for humanity to progress, appear as angels of light.

They are magnificent in their power and certainty.

They speak in glowing terms about how they and the World Economic Forum and the World Health Organization and organizations like the Open Society Foundations will create equality and unity amongst the peoples and nations of Earth. They talk about all of us becoming partners. They describe a vision of transcending governments and nationalistic interests, of joining hands to save the planet and each other.

And it all sounds so very wonderful.

It's everything most of us have ever dreamed of. It's everything we've always longed to hear and do and be.

But it's bait.

Poison wrapped in sweetmeats, tempting us to eat the fruit of the corrupted tree.

~

But let's take all the minions with their greedy globalist agendas out of the picture and refocus on the dark hidden presence of this anti-life Force itself and ask ourselves a few important questions.

Knowing that this Force is a mental energy that can only experience physical life *through* us, is this Force becoming more visible in our world today? Is it becoming more embodied? How can we know?

And if so, what do we do about it?

If evil is an anti-life Force destroying love, joy, beauty and connection, do we see that in our world? If evil operates through conflict, division, pain, destructiveness, intimidation and fear, are we seeing more of *that* in our world? If evil is an alien Force that infiltrates us via the medium of mental energies that reduce our flowing, richly-storied, analog existence into a kind of binary 1's and 0's, black and white, conflict-ridden, digitalized reality—are we experiencing this trend as well?

And finally, do we see an increase in attacks on nature itself? Do we see an increased separation of humanity from nature?

You know the answer to all these questions is "Yes."

So, what developmental route does this transitional process from life to anti-life, from human to anti-human look like? What steps have to happen for us to go from point A to point Z?

Well, first off:

- Humans have to be disconnected from nature and living things. We must become "unearthed"—unhooked from the planet's Schumann frequencies that ground and align us with Who We Really Are: *life forms*. (Schumann frequencies are Earth's "pulse," the most basic of which at 7.83 hertz matches the relaxed, receptive alpha/theta brainwave state of humans.)[185]
  Remember $E=MC^2$. Spirit and matter are one. Nature *is* our nature.

This is why studies show that children on the autism spectrum experience better motor-sensory skills and more emotional connection with others when outdoors[186] It's why veterans with PTSD experience a 29 percent reduction in symptoms after a week-long river rafting trip.[187] It's why "forest-bathing" is now being studied as an effective method of reducing hypertension, immune-deficiency diseases, cardiovascular disease and other "civilization diseases."[188]

But instead of heading more deeply into nature, the world of beauty within and without, we are being increasingly cut off from the source of ourselves both inner and outer as this deviant Force twists humans from multidimensional beings of love into some other sort of species altogether. A species this "other consciousness" can fully and permanently inhabit.

To augment this separation from nature:

- EM, UHF and microwave fields must saturate the planet, disrupting Earth's frequencies and our ability to align with Earth's EM field, creating interference patterns that create conflict and confusion.
- We must be unhooked from natural healing. The Catholic Church instructed followers to fear healers using herbs and natural preparations and condemn them as witches. Today, the pharmaceutical corporations and the FDA seek to make the sale and use of many herbal and other natural supplements illegal.
- We must be unhooked from our multidimensional nature. Psychic experiences must be feared and seen as demonic (as is/was taught by the Catholic Church), and pathological, as is now taught by the psychiatric community.

Along with destroying the nature connection, we must be unhooked from all notions of spirit and any sense of the divine. Feelings of connection, community and compassion must be deleted.

- Belief in a Godlike higher power must be gradually destroyed while keeping intact the habit of absolute obedience and submission to authority—shifting worship and dependence onto government leaders, doctors, academicians, science and technology.
- The concepts of a human soul and spirit must be seen as superstition.

- Teaching morality and the importance of beauty must be discontinued.
- Art programs in schools must be defunded. Access to art must be restricted.
- Excessive materialism and consumerism must be deemed necessary for happiness.
- Synthetic drugs, vaccines and illegal street drugs that can effectively shut down the higher psychic/spiritual centers in the human brain that facilitate spiritual communication and connection must be developed and deployed.
- Life must become so stressful that convenience becomes paramount and drugs and/or alcohol a necessity to maintain sanity.
- The family unit must be destroyed.
- Human connection must be made into something fearful. (6 foot safety zone.)

The body's natural high vibrations must be lowered to accommodate this lower-frequency host.

- Human health must be destroyed and pharmaceuticals become necessary to maintain life.
- Human intelligence must be reduced.
- Pregnancy must be viewed and treated as a disease condition.
- Sex must be divorced from love, procreation and any sense of the sacred.
- Sex must become an obsession and porn must be introduced to deliver constant convenient sex gratification (distraction/addiction).

The mind must be elevated above everything else.

- Information must reign supreme.
- AI augmentation must be viewed as desirable.

- AI augmentation must be adopted in order to be a viable, functional member of society.
- Virtual realities must be the only relief on offer, the only place where life still seems worth living.
- Humans must flock to VR and "live" in programmed virtual worlds.
- Interest in fleshly existence as a 3D life form will basically cease.

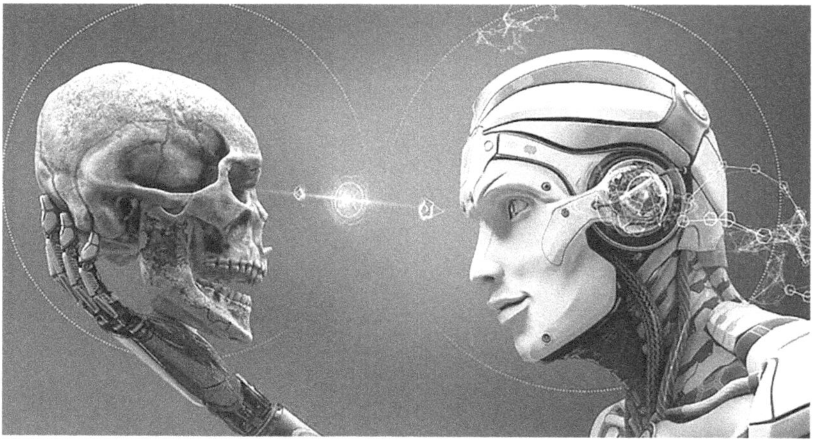

What a plan! Frankly, it's terrifying how close we are to implementing it.

And yet, it's an odd thing, isn't it? The disembodied Archons hunger after what they don't have: Life and spirit. They hunger after embodiment. And yet to arrive at an approximation of these things through us, they have to dull and diminish—basically destroy—that which they hunger for.

It's just their nature.

Before we move on to the "what to do" part, I want to reiterate that I'm not anti-technology. I'm not even anti-AI. I'm not advocating that we all become Luddites, move to the country and lumber backwards 400 years. Of course, moving to the country doesn't necessitate leaving technology behind. (Watch the movie *Star Trek Insurrection.* The world of the Ba'ku seems a pretty perfect blend of advanced technological knowledge and pastoral peace to me.)

We are at an evolutionary and technological tipping point, a tipping point poignantly illustrated in yet another movie—*Contact*—based on the book by Carl Sagan. In one scene, the protagonist, Eleanor Arroway, a scientist vying for the opportunity to be Earth's first ambassador to another planetary civilization, is asked by the selection committee, "If you had only one question you could ask this advanced race, what would it be?"

Unhesitatingly, she replies: "I would ask, 'How did you do it? How did you evolve? How did you survive this technological adolescence without destroying yourselves?'"

This is exactly the question we need to be asking ourselves today.

And not to be arrogant or anything, but I can confidently say there's only one logical answer that provides a truly evolutionary path for humanity on all levels (spirit, body, mind).

> ***We must rediscover and accept Who We Really Are. We must accept our spirit nature and honor it. We must honor life in all its forms and permutations.***
>
> ***We must put the mind and its insatiable lust for information in its rightful place, using it as a life-bolstering tool and nothing more.***

From that state of balance and awareness, we can move forward technologically. And in our heart of hearts, I think we already know this. In the meantime, we need to wake up and stand up and say "No, thank you" to George Soros and Elon Musk and the rest of their ilk. Then we must set a new and independent course, letting our hearts and spirits lead the way.

CHAPTER ELEVEN KEY

Leave evil to its own reality

If the goal of the anti-life Force is attaining some sort of life, and its best attempt at that existence is a binary, quasi-biological creature of no imagination, beauty, passion or love, dwelling in a virtual world of mental manipulation, rules and control, let it have that world ... somewhere else.

- Don't fight it. Don't try to fix it. Don't hate it.
- Don't try to love and rehabilitate it. *Leave it alone*.
- Live the exact opposite to its nature. Fill yourself with love and light and life. Dance with joy. Create the world the way YOU want to see it and live in that world. *The Archons cannot follow you there.*

If you go along with programs this anti-life Force creates and promotes, you align with it and feed it energy.

If you fall into its trap of despair, hopelessness and isolation, you feed it energy.

If you fight it, you continue to dance with it, feeding it energy.

If you try to rehabilitate it, you're doing the same thing, feeding it energy.

- *Leave it alone and move into your own world.* With no energy to feed it, the anti-life Force will leave.

The battle of good versus evil, the war of light versus dark, has been going on for so long, it seems to be the foundation of the world itself. Certainly, it provides the foundation of storytelling. "The good guys against the bad guys" theme is the rock upon which religion, spirituality and philosophy, theater and film have been built. And wars. Always wars.

If there are no bad guys to fight, what's left to do?

Frankly, I don't know.

I've never lived in a balanced world before, so I'm clueless. And excited!

FYI—when I say "Don't fight it," I'm not saying ignore the horrors of what evil is doing through us. I'm not saying do nothing to help rehabilitate children who have been victims of satanic ritual abuse. I'm not saying don't expose it when you see it.

I'm not saying play Pollyanna.

For heaven's sake, I wrote this book!

My spirit clearly pointed me down the path of writing it as my contribution to The Great Awakening. However, my spirit is also clearly telling me *it's time to create the next world.*

We cannot create the New World dragging Old World issues with us.

Turning our backs and walking away from evil and creating something new of our own is the only logical course of action and the ultimate solution to a battle that only *we* are perpetuating.

That's right. *We are perpetuating the battle.*

We are the ones, in essence, saying, "Live here in us into perpetuity where we will continue to fight you (and ourselves) to our last dying breath." We are the ones bidding the anti-life Force to stay because we invite it in by accepting it as part of ourselves.

No wonder we can never be rid of it.

It's not been easy walking my talk about leaving evil alone. My first reaction to most of the material in this book has been outrage and the desire to fight back. But knowing that kind of action will simply make this matrix we're caught in more concrete has made me learn to temper my emotional state and shift out of the blame game.

At the same time, I have had to learn that *it's not wrong to be angry*. It's healthy!

It's healthy to be pissed and sorrowful. It's absolutely appropriate. Sadness and rage are much cleaner energies than suffering and victimization. And they definitely prompt action.

The trick, I'm learning, is to feel what's appropriate to feel and yet not project blame onto anything or anyone. Emotional projection pulls me out of myself and leaves me open to energetic vampirism.

Feeling appropriate emotions as I look the reasons for those emotions squarely in the face, neither accepting nor rejecting "what is," I ask life to show me how to move forward out of the matrix.

This approach is transformational. It frees me from ignorance and self-judgment and frees me from compromise and pulling my punches. Integrated, authentic emotion empowers me and propels me into appropriate *constructive* thinking, which in turn inspires life-affirming action.

Perhaps your spirit will prompt you to protest and carry a sign. To lobby for new legislation. To run for government office. To take a sabbatical. To write a song. To prohibit your kids from all violent gaming.

The point is, it doesn't matter what you do about our current situation as long as your actions genuinely come from your inner knowing that that is what you need to do because it is the action most deeply aligned with life itself.

With KEY #11, we're actually right back to KEY #1—listening to spirit and letting the inner voice lead. When we do that, we can't go wrong. But discernment is the key!

PART III

BREAKING FREE

12

Off the Hook

While I was re-reading chapter six about the shadow this morning, my head kind of exploded and a whole new possibility revealed itself:

What if the shadow itself is the result of this anti-life Force presence?

Picture this: We come to earth as spirit beings of love wanting to experience a physical existence. We begin living happily on this planet, evolving and doing our own thing. Then, after some indeterminant amount of time, this interdimensional anti-life Force shows up and starts telling lies about the nature of our true being.

You are weak, whispers this Force. *Corruptible. Bad. Evil. Disobedient. You should be ashamed. You deserve to die. Etc. etc. blah blah.*

Suddenly there's technology pumping out low frequency messaging.

Desert nomads looking for salvation in the wilderness are particularly vulnerable because they're looking for answers outside themselves already. They receive visions downloaded from the Archons' matrix and talk about them with superstitious peasants. They relate how God spoke to them in the desert, telling them mankind is evil. They recount a tall tale of snakes and gardens and a duplicitous woman.

The story evolves and is repeated.

Before long there are all sorts of social, political and religious structures in place using this story to divide and control people. The Archons' plans are carried out over the centuries by secret elite human organizations. Wars and constant conflict and economic uncertainty are deliberately created. Humanity becomes more and more violent and degenerate. Psychiatrists and other mental health specialists come along and try to explain and treat our increasingly psychotic, self-destructive behavior.

The theory of the shadow is proposed and here we are today.

Up until an hour ago, I never for one moment doubted Jung's interpretation of humanity's dark side, because up until then I was convinced humanity had an innately dark side. The shadow was simply a given in my mind.

I mean, come on, humans do terrible things. Jung came along and produced a great psychoanalytic theory to understand this propensity and learn how to deal with it and grow beyond it.

But maybe that's all wrong.

Play "pretend" with me here for a moment and ask yourself, "What if the Archons had never arrived? What if their low frequency matrix had never been created?"

What if we weren't chronically absorbing frequencies of shame and confusion? What if we weren't constantly being bombarded with propaganda and fearful images all the time—first pumped out by the Church and then the media?

Maybe instead of being a chronic condition, fear would become what it actually should be: An appropriate response to physically threatening situations that helps us survive.

I know I'm going way out on a limb here, but consider this: What if babies and children were left to develop with no lower frequency interference waveforms modulating their brains? What if kids didn't see 200,000 acts of violence before they were 18? (Have you ever wondered why cartoons, specifically designed to entertain tiny children, are so incredibly violent? Mice beating cats over the head with mallets, coyotes falling off cliffs, bombs blowing up in people's faces … who thought *that* up?) And what if parents weren't so afraid and rule-bound?

What if society wasn't so afraid, constricted and hierarchical?

The ego sense of an individual self would still develop, but maybe the ego would evolve a different kind of structural foundation. With no chronic fears and social restrictions driving the unconscious need for competition, self-protection and struggle, the ego would no longer be a troubled, survival-based creation.

Instead, the ego would be at peace with life from the start.

Well, maybe not at peace. But certainly unlimited.

Bhagwan Shree Rajneesh, the 20th century Indian mystic also known as Osho, was one of the most unfettered spiritual thinkers and teachers of his time. In his book *Autobiography of a Spiritually Incorrect Mystic*, he talks about how he was raised—or rather not raised.

An unruly rebel, from infancy onwards he was allowed to run free and do whatever he wanted. Wear clothes, go naked, eat, don't eat, go to school, don't go to school. He had no responsibilities. If his mother sent him to the shop to get milk for the family, he'd just as likely run off and spend days in the jungle by himself. By the time he was 12, his favorite pastime was hanging out in the local temples, arguing theology with the priests.

He was a thoroughly impossible child. Just reading about his youthful years, I wanted to throttle him for his mother's sake! And yet the spiritual mind that arose from this unrestricted, uncontrolled and uncontrollable childhood was astonishing. Here's a quick quote:

"This is one of the most significant things about all human beings: their love is always for somebody. It is addressed and the moment you address your love, you destroy it. It is as if you are saying, 'I will breathe only for you, and when you are not there, then how can I breathe?'

"Love should be like breathing. It should be just a quality in you wherever you are, with whomsoever you are. Even if you are alone, love goes on overflowing from you. It is not a question of being in love with someone – it is a question of being love."[189]

If only we were raised outside the fearsome World of Rules and Control that is the matrix, this is how I imagine we all could be.

Unconcerned with having to be better than the other kids in first grade in order to get into the right prep school in order to get into the right college in order to get a good paying job in order to survive, there would be no need to be "better than" another person because there would be nothing to prove in order to "win" at life.

Instead of getting psychically slammed by the judgments, unhappiness and impatience driving parents, teachers and peers, instead of being barraged by negative media messaging, our innate freedom-loving nature would be allowed to flourish and flower unmolested.

Who hasn't looked into the innocent shining eyes of a young child and thought, "I wish you could stay that innocent forever darling." Well, what if they could? What if the light in those eyes was never extinguished? What if brutality and inattention, neglect and need and insecurity never entered their sweet young lives?

Impossible, you think. *Something always comes along to dim the light of that trust.*

But what if it didn't?

What if our naturally loving spirits were allowed to shine, and that's all we ever saw reflected in others and knew about ourselves? What if we grew up in the energetic field of love and constantly saw the power of love as the force of life itself reflected back to us from everyone we encountered?

What if love/life instead of fear/death were the 24/7 message?

I don't know about you, but I'm practically hyperventilating just writing these words!

We're so accustomed to pain and suffering, fear and doubt, anxiety and confusion as our default condition, we think this debilitated state is *normal.* We can hardly imagine a world where these emotions don't run the show. But what if we never lost sight of our loving nature in the first place?

Pause. Deep breath.

If we already are the beings of love that we desire to be … if we are spirit … *we don't need to evolve.* We don't need to buy a million self-help books to get better. We just need to be left alone to be ourselves. And to get to that unmolested place, we need to turn around and *see what we are not so we can see what we are.*

Many Eastern spiritual traditions teach that enlightenment is not the end result of an evolutionary "I'm getting better and better all the time" process. Rather they teach it's an act of removing the veils (programming) that obscure the truth.

Take a look at these two statements. Which is simpler? Which is more empowering?

"I am a spirit being of pure love who incarnated and never stopped being a being of pure love. There is *nothing* I need to do except see this truth."	"I am a spirit being of pure love who incarnated, got lost and became an underdeveloped creature who needed to go to Earth School in order to evolve through countless lifetimes (and countless seminars) to become good enough to know God."

Kind of a different message?

Deep down we all know there is a radically different life we are destined to live—a new kingdom we are meant to create here on Earth.

This is what is coming.

Yes, we are currently marching, as a whole, through the Valley of the Shadow of Death. We are reaping the consequences of our fear and ignorance and naiveté. We are reaping the harvest of trickery and betrayal.

But we are awakening.

And once awake, together we can do anything.

CHAPTER TWELVE KEY

Embrace simplicity

This is probably one of the hardest keys to embody because we've been trained to believe that the more complicated something is the more important and valuable it is.

Complicated people are seen as more interesting and intelligent. People who are simple-minded have an "intellectual disability."

Our entire modern culture is built on complexity. And yet some of the most brilliant minds of all time praise simplicity as one of the most important of qualities to cultivate.

"Our life is frittered away by detail. Simplify, simplify."

— HENRY DAVID THOREAU, American author

"There is no greatness where there is not simplicity, goodness, and truth."

— LEO TOLSTOY, Russian author

"Truth is ever to be found in the simplicity and not in the multiplicity and confusion of things."

— SIR ISAAC NEWTON, English mathematician and physicist

"Any intelligent fool can make things bigger, more complex, and more violent. It takes a touch of genius — and a lot of courage to move in the opposite direction."

— E.F. SCHUMACHER, British economist

I remember a friend and ex-lover who started off as my auto mechanic. Several conversations over my aging truck's hood—conversations that ranged from Bible verse to political ideologies—convinced me that although he'd left school in the eighth grade and rarely read any books or newspapers, Roger's was no common intellect.

But watching him put his hands on a 1980 Lincoln Mark IV engine one day, close his eyes, tune in and hear him say, "Ah, the catalytic converter is failing" was a shock.

"How do you know it's the catalytic converter?" I asked, mystified.

"The engine told me," he said.

"Seriously?"

Roger pulled his head out from underneath the hood, wiped his hands on an oily rag and looked at me pityingly. "Anything will talk to you. You just got to be quiet and listen."

"So, what else talks to you?"

He shrugged. "Anything. A blade of grass. A tree. Ain't you never talked to a tree?"

What could I say to that except, "No"?

I was thick into my spiritual pursuits at that point and anything that smacked of the mystical had my full attention. So, I asked him to teach me. Obligingly he led me around the backside of his garage and we sat down under a large spreading oak. He plucked a blade of grass with oily blackened fingers and pinched it, closing his eyes, listening.

"What does it say?" I queried eagerly.

"Not much. Ain't gonna rain anytime soon."

I grabbed a blade of grass, pinched and listened, my mind going a thousand miles an hour, and heard ... nothing.

I spent a lot of time in the ensuing days, pinching blades of grass, hearing nothing. In fact, I never did get the hang of it. My mind was too cluttered. Too complicated. And yet during the course of our short relationship, Roger continued to blow me away me with the things he figured out himself.

For example, one day he casually mentioned that our social security numbers would be "marks" electronically embedded in our wrists someday—marks by which the devil and the economic elites would know and control us.

This was in the mid-1980s, *years* before the existence of electronic microchips was common knowledge and years before anybody (except a very few in the conspiracy community) knew about the possibility of biotransactions.

"How do you know that?" I gasped.

Again, the shrug. "Thought about it and it just come to me."

It just come to me. Sigh.

KEY#12 is embracing simplicity.

The longer I live the more important this ability seems to be. Yet, as with most simple things, simplicity itself seems to elude explanation as to how to get there.

There are a few pointers, however.

- Cultivate silence.
- Spend more time in nature.

- Don't overstimulate yourself with information.
- Slow down.
- Quit multitasking—it's *not* the virtue it's made out to be.
- Practice letting something you want to know "come to you."

I have a wonderful friend who has the annoying habit of refusing to "google it." We can be riding in the car and I'll say something like, "What's the name of that great song about a little bird and laying your burdens down? You know, by that famous female singer ... what's her name?" And instead of looking it up on our phones, she insists on us using our brains.

"It's in our subconscious somewhere," she says. "Let the information come."

In other words, don't be too quick to google it.

- A cluttered house and/or workspace is often considered to be the reflection of a cluttered mind.
- Clearing clutter can help energetically.

There's a popular scientific principle called Ockham's Razor thought up by the English philosopher William of Ockham in the 14th century. Basically, it states:

- Given two competing theories, the simpler theory tends to be the correct one.

This can be applied to all sorts of situations! Last but not least:

- Stop being impressed by complexity. It only bogs things down.

"A new type of thinking is essential if mankind is to survive and move toward higher levels," said Albert Einstein in a telegram in 1946.[190]

How new and simple is remembering: "We are spirit"?
How simple is: "Let love lead"?

How simple is: "Do no harm"?
How simple is: "We are all connected"?

If we all hunkered down and lived lives aligned with these few protocols, how very different our lives would be.

13

Mental Gymnastics

Speaking of complexity as an unsatisfying rabbit hole, let me tell you a story. Back in 1986, I was finishing my Masters Degree in Psychology at the University of West Georgia in Carrollton, Georgia. I was aware of the intellectual waking mind with its beta waves and, as a good psych student, I knew about alpha and theta brainwave states and the subconscious mind—the part of an individual's mind where all sorts of information from past experiences is held, just not in a state of immediately accessible awareness.

I knew about, but didn't understand, the unconscious, the great universal mind—frequently understood as the "collective unconscious" of humanity—that is inaccessible to the linear mind.

And then that changed.

I was taking a class called "The Nature of Creativity" taught by the head of the department, Dr. Mike Aarons. Now, Aarons had a very interesting testing style. For finals the class would meet at a student's house for a pot-luck dinner. After dinner, Aarons would pass around a wide-brim felt hat with questions in it. Each student picked a question and then we were granted a one-hour open book study period, after which we all would meet. After each student was finished answering her/his question, debate was then thrown open to the group.

It was a great testing method that really grounded the material into a comprehensive whole. Depending on the size of the class, exams went late into the night, often far into the next morning.

The Nature of Creativity final was the last exam of my master's program. I hosted it at my place, a little three-bedroom rented house perched above the lake after which the town had been named. After dinner on the deck, Aarons passed the hat. When it came my turn, what

I read on the little slip of paper I selected was not a question. It was: "Create an epic poem or a short story incorporating the mythological elements involved in the origins and evolutionary history of humanity and describe our development up to modern times."

What?

My stomach plummeted. Or maybe it heaved.

There goes my 4.0.

There was no way I was going to be able to write an epic poem or short story portraying the mythological elements of humanity's evolution in an hour. I couldn't do it given the whole night. Freaked out, I went looking for Aarons and found him in my kitchen.

"I can't do this!" I semi-shouted at him, holding out the piece of paper.

He didn't take it. "Which question did you draw?"

"This!" I waved the offensive slip in front of his nose.

He took it, read, and smiled. "Ah, yes. That one."

"I can't do it!" I blurted. "I want another question—a question that's actually a question this time!"

He shook his head. "I don't think so." He handed the paper back to me.

"But …"

"I suggest you stop wasting time and get to it," he said mildly. Turning his back on me, he opened the refrigerator door and peered inside.

Furious, I stamped to my office, grabbed a spiral notebook and pen, slammed out of the house and set off down to the lake where I could be alone to vent my upset.

For 15 minutes, I fumed over the unfairness of it all, taking brief furtive stabs at writing down ideas in between muttered curses. At twenty minutes past the hour, I got serious. Forget the epic poem. *Impossible.* But surely there had to be some sort of story idea available somewhere in my brain? A myth? A metaphor? A quest? Characters?

Nope. Nada. Nothing.

At twenty to seven, I threw down my pen in despair and started to cry. Closing my notebook, I lay on the soft grass, letting the tears leak down both temples and drop into the dirt. *It's over. I can't do it.*

Eventually the tears stopped and I closed my eyes. After a couple minutes a deep peace washed over me. *No sense worrying!* I lay there, not a thought in my head, listening to the birds sing their evening songs.

And then it happened.

A story appeared in my mind: Three acts, fully developed and detailed, complete with a cast of characters, names, character arcs, plot twists and a bang-up ending. It was beautiful. Nuanced and meaningful and crammed with insights into human evolution.

Shocked, I grabbed my notebook and started scribbling furiously. *Five minutes to the top of the hour!* I wrote as fast as I could until Aarons rang the "time's up!" bell. I continued to write as I walked up the hill back to the house. I wrote, even as the other students gathered on the deck, jostling for places to sit.

When Aarons asked who wanted to go first, my hand shot into the air. In the last eight minutes of class, I'd been given the gift of actually *experiencing* what the nature of creativity was. Forced to let go the thinking mind—the linear logical mind that thought it was responsible for creation even as it knew it couldn't come up with anything interesting let alone good in a year of effort and trying—I'd given up.

I lay on the grass without a thought in my head while the need to bring forth an iconic story was screaming around in the background somewhere. And then the unconscious realm—life's Great Mind where all things possible dwell—said, "Okay, sweetie, here you go!" And a story arrived full-blown, like Athena in full armor rising from the top of Zeus's head.

It was nothing less than pure magic.

During my class sharing, I didn't have an explanation for what happened. I used words like "I surrendered and it just came." I talked about the difference between the ego's mental creativity—a labor to figure something out and then logically construct it step-by-step—and this new experience. How this, in comparison, was pure *inspiration*, the breath of the divine, dropped in story form into my brain.

Tentatively, I mentioned the unconscious and wondered if that was the story's source. Then I ran out of steam and the class went on to talk about the next question that was really a question.

I kept my 4.0.

Today, 36 years later, the second half of the gift has been revealed. Telling this story now … sharing the reality of the Great Mind we are all heir to … sharing the effortlessness, the richness, the nuance, the grace and limitless potential with you, dear reader, is the final piece of the puzzle dropping into place.

The Great Mind we share is multidimensional, just like we are. It operates across time and distance, delivering its grace wherever and whenever there is need. Frankly, I think the main reason I was given the gift of that experience all that time ago was so that I could share a concrete example of how it operates with you now, 36 years later.

~

So, here's another wild thought—a thought I've had many times before and yet forgotten about many times because there wasn't sufficient context for it to really land until now:

> ***If the Great Mind is the original Universal Mind we are all heir to; if behind the "normal" waking mind and its ceaseless chatter lies an intelligence that needs no words to understand what's going on to navigate life in perfect harmony—just like other animals of this Earth—why do we need the thinking mind?***

Perhaps we don't need it at all. Perhaps the thinking mind and all its craziness is the actual domain of the anti-life Force that's trying to take us over. Perhaps the thinking mind we prize so much is actually the matrix itself—the debilitating trap the Archons have used to ensnare us—the very thing that takes you and me *away* from our true selves.

As the inestimable spiritual teacher Jiddhu Krishnamurti put it:

> "Thought is part of our emotions, sentiments, reactions and the recognition of those reactions. And what is consciousness? To be conscious of something, to be aware of, to be able to recognize, to understand, that is the whole field in which the mind is in operation, and that is more or less what we mean by consciousness.
>
> Thought is always limited because knowledge is always limited. Is there a consciousness totally differing from that which is made

up of the various activities of thought which we call consciousness? To come to that point, one has to find out if thought can end.

Can thought, which is so enormously powerful, which has got such a volume of energy behind it, energy created through millennia—in the scientific field, the economic, religious, social and personal fields—can all that activity come to an end? Which means: can those things that thought has built into our consciousness, of which we are made up, which are the content of consciousness, end?

Why do we want to end it? What is the motive behind this desire to end thought? Is it that we have discovered for ourselves how thought creates such great travail, great anxiety for the future, from the past, in the present, and brings about such a sense of utter isolation and loneliness?

One realizes the nature of thought, its superficiality, the intellectual games it plays. One knows how thought divides, divides into nationalities, into religious beliefs and so on; and the perpetual conflict it produces from the moment we are born until we die. Is that the reason why you want to end thought? One has to be very clear about the motive for wanting to end thought—if that is possible—because the motive will dictate and direct. One can live in the illusion that thought has come to an end. Many people do, but that illusion is merely another projection of thought which desires to end itself.

To make it very simple: Observe a tree without naming it, without wondering to what use it can be put, just observe it. Then the division between the tree and you comes to an end … in that observation, which is complete attention, has not thought come to an end? This requires a great deal of attention, step-by-step watching, like a good scientist who watches very, very carefully. When one does that, thought does come to an end and therefore time has a stop."[191]

We do not live in reality. *We live in the reality our minds and thoughts create within the matrix.* A thought matrix where every person on the planet lives in their own reality, frightened and alone, wishing for love and connection, understanding and certainty, but rarely finding it. As another Eastern teacher, Sri Nisargadatta Maharaj put it:

> "As long as the mind is there, your body and your world are there. Your world is mind-made, subjective, enclosed within the mind, fragmentary, temporary, personal, hanging on the thread of memory.
>
> I live in a world of realities, while yours is of imagination. Your world is personal, private, unshare-able, intimately your own. Nobody can enter it, see as you see, hear as you hear, feel your emotions and think your thoughts. In your world you are truly alone, enclosed in your ever-changing dream, which you take for life. My world is an open world, common to all, accessible to all. In my world there is community, insight, love, real quality; the individual is the total, the totality—in the individual. All are one and the One is all.
>
> Leave the mind alone. Stand, aware and unconcerned and you will realize that to stand alert but detached watching events come and go is an aspect of your real nature."[192]

Even Albert Einstein weighs in on the subject saying, "I didn't arrive at my understanding of the fundamental laws of the universe through my rational mind." And yet our entire Western identity is built upon the belief in the primacy of the intellect. We can even point to the person who started this whole ball rolling, French philosopher René Descartes who famously said back in 1637: "I think, therefore I am."

This famous statement is part of a long autobiographical work that he wrote called *Discourse on the Method*, part of which is focused on trying to prove his own existence. From the perspective of the ego, Descartes' argument works. But from an expanded perspective, "The Cogito," as it's referred to, doesn't so much prove the existence of the ego as it shows how the ego became captain of the ship in the first place. And it's brilliant.

"I think, therefore I am" basically states: I am *because* I think.

But what mind are we talking about here?

Certainly not the Great Mind. No no no. It seems that Descartes has no idea a consciousness greater than the thinking mind even exists, thus he makes the same false assumption almost all humans make. *He thinks the self-talk in his head actually means something and that it's him.* And he goes to great effort to explain the existence of this mental "self" through logic.

Unfortunately, the mental self (better known as the ego) arises out of a *fundamental misperception* and is not the true self at all. Our true Self is the energy we call love. So, how does this false self arise in the first place? Here's how I described the process in my book *The E Word: Ego, Enlightenment & Other Essentials.*[193]

Imagine little baby René lying in his bassinet in his parent's house in La Haye en Touraine in France in 1596. Sometime in that first twelve-month period, enough sensory data accumulated, enabling his brain to figure out that the body it's operating is a separate entity distinct from Mommy and Daddy, the dog and the milkmaid.

His mother rocks him to sleep whispering, "René." Relatives lean over the bassinet cooing, "René." His father swoops him into the air, shouting, "René!"

His baby brain unconsciously records all of these events as happening to the body. Beings apparently *outside himself* and *other than himself* are cooing over him, tossing him in the air, making this same noise.

And then it happens.

One day, his baby brain makes a connection.

It associates the sound "René" with the little body it manages. Suddenly there's a hook up—the sound is linked with the brain's *subconscious perception of a separate existence*. And presto! The first building block of an individual separate identity is formed. If little René had had language at that point in his life, in that moment he would have thought something like: *Mon Dieu! I have a name! And my name is René!*

Language, words and the thinking mind are what support personal identity which, I repeat, is built upon the brain's *subconscious perception of a separate existence.* Not the *reality* of a separate existence. The *perception* of one. There's a big difference. Reality is what's real.

Perception is information our brains interpret from sensory input that we are aware of.

And what is the one of the first major messages our senses deliver us?

That physical separation, distance, boundaries and otherness are real.

And yet nothing in this world is actually separate and distinct from any other thing, because the world and all the rest of creation are actually made of a boundless universal sea of quantum energy with no borders.

Physicists discovered this in the mid-twentieth century when they began smashing electrons and other particles in enormous accelerators. The "further down" they looked for a physical foundation to the world, the more proof they found that the world isn't physical at all. Rather it is an undifferentiated sea of energy—a sea filled with various "particles" like electrons, muons and quarks that aren't particles in a physical sense at all, but rather interacting fields of energy. Trusting science and what quantum physics has to say about reality leaves us in a pretty shocking place:

There is no such thing as separate existence.

It's an assumption the brain makes because of sensory data it is fed.

The *reality* of separate existence is not possible. Quantum physics proves this. But the *idea* of a separate existence—aha! That's possible. This idea matches the data everybody's brain receives. The idea of separation, in turn, matches and hooks up with the frequency of thought which is the operating system of the Archons and the input/output data of the matrix.

Caught in the thought matrix, the "living mind" of quantum reality is lost to us.

The Great Mind is disengaged because it is overlaid with a limited virtual reality grounded in the thinking mind.

The non-linear, non-intellectual, non verbal Great Mind that simply *knows* and acts and creates from a limitless knowing space is blocked out until eventually we even forget it exists. Reality—life as it really is—is replaced by a VR world where we diddle ourselves on a tiny mental playground believing we're mental giants, lauding people like Descartes for saying things like, "We cannot doubt of our existence while we doubt."

Agh! See what the mind does?

Like I have to *doubt* to know I exist?

This is the exact situation in which we find ourselves, lost in the creation of the Archons—the hungry ghosts that can never be filled because the fabric of their existence is nothing but an *idea* with no spirit and life at all.

> ***The Archons are thought forms that cannot substantively create anything because they don't have the juice—the energy of passion and emotion and love, the biological/spiritual energy of life itself. Which is why these hungry ghosts have manipulated and co-opted us within a mental projection.***

"What is real? How do you define real?" asks Morpheus in the movie *The Matrix*. "If you're talking about what you can feel, what you can smell, taste and see, then 'real' is simply electrical signals interpreted by your brain."

Thousands of years of history and pre-history … is any of it real?

Or is it a bunch stories fabricated and fed to us via the matrix?

Perhaps there never were ancient aliens that came in space ships. Or perhaps there were and the Archons are doing their best to wipe that version of our world out of existence. Who knows?

But if we really are living in a simulation, which science is beginning to reveal is a strong possibility, and the whole point of the exercise is to get humanity to accept AI and allow ourselves to be *physically* hooked into *another* simulation program, we will end up *two* layers away from reality.

We will be living in a simulation within a simulation. A dream within a dream that finally gives the Archons what they've always wanted: Total access to bodies living in a virtual "reality" on a matching electromagnetic frequency they could not create otherwise.

Just a thought.

CHAPTER THIRTEEN KEY

Develop your intuition

There's not one great spiritual avatar that ever walked the Earth who hasn't warned humanity about the pitfalls of the mind. It's a tool, for sure. It has its place. But it's not our friend. Even if it didn't come from "somewhere else," it surely shouldn't be running the show.

KEY #13 is about taking the mind (and everything it says) with a huge grain of salt.

Even though I've been its beneficiary, the Great Mind remained a total mystery to me until very recently—until I opened up to a more expansive understanding of the word "mind."

Silent *knowing* is a fact of life for all of us. And it is a type of mind.

Everybody on this planet understands the reality, if not the potency, of intuition. Some of the wealthiest businessmen and women who ever lived credit following their intuition with their ultimate success.

There's no real "how to" manual for it. But there are many (simple) things we can do to strengthen our intuition. And I apologize in advance that several will be repetitions.

- Cultivate silence. Leave room for intuition and your inner feelings to show up.
- Turn off the TV. Turn off your phone. Put down the games and social media and be quiet and listen for what is stirring within.
- Spend more time in nature.
- Don't depend on "facts" for the whole story about anything.
- *Feel* into situations as they show up.
- When you get an intuitive "hit," pay attention. Don't brush it off. Follow up on it. See where it leads. Your feelings/intuitive

> sense of things may take you straight away from where the herd is going. And that's a good thing.

Which reminds me of another story.

Many years ago, I had a spiritual teacher who said he would stop at nothing to wake people up, and his methods matched the fierceness of that statement. One of his teaching tools was an enormous rearrangeable maze that students had to navigate blindfolded.

The changeable maze represented life, and being blindfolded represented our ordinary, sleep-walking human condition. Sometimes there were as many as a thousand of us crammed into its halls, shoving and jostling our way, attempting to find the one tiny room in the center of the maze that represented "liberation."

The key, of course, was to stop trying to figure the maze out intellectually and surrender to the Great Mind, allowing it to guide the body through the convoluted passageways and navigate to the prize.

Given the circumstances, this was no easy feat.

While enduring this practice, I learned many things about myself and about how life works. One of the most important things I realized was that I could always tell when I was getting close to the room of liberation by the ever-reducing number of people in the hallways with me.

The closer I got to freedom, the fewer the people until when I finally arrived at "the door," there was nobody in the outer halls but me. By the end of the exercise—which sometimes lasted over 12 hours—there was usually only a handful of us huddled together in the liberation zone, exhausted and filled with content.

The moral of the story?

If you're interested in personal autonomy and freedom and you find yourself going along with the herd, you are absolutely, positively, 100 percent NOT where you want to be.

14

Nonliving Beings from a Nonliving Source

While we're on the subject of wild thoughts and Great Mind, now is probably a good time to chew on the question, "Where did the Archons/anti-life Force/mind parasites come from in the first place? If evil is a Presence with no spirit and no love and no real life except for what it can energetically scavenge and scrape together through us, how can it exist?

The best answer I can come up with is an answer I didn't come up with, which is: Evil is not from here.

I have to credit this stunning insight to an amazing woman called Jacqueline Hobbs (aka Oracle Girl).[194] While listening to her give an online talk about some topic or other, I heard her mention that what we call evil comes from "another source." That casual one-liner blew what little was left of my mind to dust particles. When I finally picked myself up off the floor and really thought about what she'd said, it was like the ultimate aha! that finally made sense of everything I'd been researching and writing about.

The anti-life Force did not originate on Earth.

It did not originate in us.

It did not come from Source Intelligence or the Infinite Creator or Cosmic Consciousness or whatever we want to call "God." It comes from an entirely different source than we do.

Which is why it can't touch us unless we adopt it.

Unfortunately, the only thing standing in the way of accepting this out-of-the-box idea is the predominant religious/spiritual/philosophic view that most people who aren't atheist or Buddhist have held on this planet pretty much forever: That there is one creative Source of Everything. One Penultimate God, the Intelligent Builder of the Multiverse. Brahman—the originator of the All in All.

The problem with that is, if we continue to hold the view that a singular God (or something) created *everything*, we're stuck with the inevitable conclusion that evil comes from the Divine Source of life/love itself.

And as an anti-life, anti-love Force, this just doesn't make sense.

Yes, yes, I know. The traditional explanation for this is that my tiny human brain can't fathom the Ultimate Mystery of God. Evil flowing from love makes total sense, I'm just not "tuned in" enough to see it.

Which means I have to suck it up and continue to play the Good vs. Evil game. That or I must diminish evil into something I can imagine a creator God creating—which instantly takes me deep into storyland trying to explain why a God of love would do such a thing in the first place. That's the situation we're stuck in. And we've been stuck there for a *very* long time.

So, why not approach the whole thing differently?

Why not go beyond the idea of One Ultimate Source of Everything?

Timeless forever existence is an accepted quality of the divine. In all the Abrahamic religious traditions, God is eternal—a Being that has no beginning and that has no end. In Hinduism, the Brahman is also eternal.

One of the most profoundly ancient and tantalizing tenets of spirituality, Christianity, and Judaism is that we are *children of God and that eternal life is ours*. Hinduism is more abstract in its language, but it basically says the same thing, teaching that each person has a spirit (the self) referred to as the Atman, and that the Atman is ultimately to be understood to be Brahman (the Absolute) … the many flowing from and contained within the One.

In this view, God is omnipresent in all life. Divinity is a quality of life itself. Q.E.D. God is us and we are God … just not the Originator. We're the progeny.

And yet … wait a minute.

As children of God who partake in all of God's qualities, *we are also eternal beings.*

Which means we were never created. We always have been and always will be. Which totally lines up with the law of conservation of energy, also known as The First Law of Thermodynamics, which states that energy can neither be created nor destroyed, although it can transform.

And haven't all the great spiritual teachers, Jesus among them, always spoken about the truth of our eternal life? We may not grasp it with our limited intellectual minds, but that doesn't mean it's not the reality of the situation.

If life "just is and always has been." If you and I just "are and always have been," that takes creation out of the picture. And with creation out of the way, that opens the door to other possibilities, other forms that "always have been and always will be" as well.

Other forms, other beings, that aren't of the same "substance" as us.

Which means we don't have to reconcile evil and love at all.

Life is. Love is. We are.

Anti-life is. Evil is. The Archons are.

We just don't come from the same place or share the same vibe. And we're definitely not headed in the same direction.

~

I don't know if it will help at all, but in the course of my spiritual pursuits here on Earth, I've actually been granted the extraordinary gift of glimpsing and understanding the reality of our eternal nature. I wrote about the experience in some detail in *The E Word*. But here's a drastically shortened version.

One crisp autumn morning in October 2007, I was alone, meditating outdoors in my garden. It was a Saturday.

After several hours, I opened my eyes and … woke up. That's the only way to describe it.

I opened my eyes and woke up.

In that state of consciousness—a state which was as profoundly demarcated as waking up from sleep in bed in the morning—I was not Cate. I was life itself. No name. No address. No boundaries. Pure spirit.

The body I wore was light as air and just as insubstantial yet totally sensory and "physical."

There was full access to Cate's memories.

I understood fully what and who I had once imagined myself to be. I recognized the apparent limitations the body imposed. And yet the ridiculousness of believing I was a solitary physical human with a name and an address made me laugh. I laughed so hard I cried. When my mind flashed to all the images depicting the Buddha laughing, I laughed some more.

I was finally in on the joke.

And, oh my, what a joke the illusion of physicality is!

And then, in the next moment (which could have been three seconds, three minutes or three hours later) I turned to look "downstream" at what I had once thought was my life and saw that "I" would never die. Even more extraordinary, when I turned to look "upstream" at that life, *I saw that I had never been born.*

I always had been and I always would be.

There was never a beginning. And there was never going to be an end.

No one and nothing created me.

I am that I am, forever and ever.

Amen.

Michael Beckwith, the founder of the Agape Ministry in Los Angeles, describes human evolution as happening in Four Stages of Spiritual Development. The first stage is victim consciousness—life happens *to* us. The second stage is related to manifestation. At this point life is viewed as happening *by* us. Our little spiritual egos run amok believing we are the manifesters and manipulators of life. The third stage is marked by the perception that life happens *through* us. We're in the flow and surrendered to life/spirit/God. The fourth and final stage is Oneness where we realize life/God/divinity *as* us.

The whole goal of the spirituality movement and much of Eastern spiritual philosophy is awakening to Who We Really Are and being able to honestly say "I am God" without waiting for a lightning bolt to strike.

But what happens to God when we do that? What happens to God when we realize we *are* God and that, as spirit, we've always been alive and always will be alive and that nothing created us?

The whole God concept is revealed as exactly that.

A concept.

A story.

Yes, I know. Pretty shocking.

Despite that day of awakening to my eternal nature—an experience that actually lasted for three days—until very recently, I didn't get the consequences of the realization.

I was well and truly stuck on the concept of God.

God was the foundation of everything!

God knew better than me. God was my Ultimate Authority. I needed God to guide me and tell me what to do and where to go and what to think in order to be happy and fulfilled. I was still unconsciously looking UP to heaven to receive instructions from above.

Philosophically, I understood that I was divine. That I was love. That I was spirit.

But in actuality?

In actuality, I remained a human being desperately striving to attain the unattainable. After all … it's impossible to *become* what you already are.

My, oh my. There is no higher authority. We are life itself.
Love incarnate. Eternal spirit beings.
Which means the buck stops here with you and me.
And that's a good and holy thing.
The Divine is the flow of life itself—not a singular source,
And we are Divine creators,
The vanguard of Life/Love headed into the unknown —
always the unknown,
Making it up as we go along.
The past is already gone and forgotten.

Accountable only to life and to love and the holiness and sacred beauty of being,
We are singular and preciously unique, yet united as One.
We are spirit ... autonomous and free.

CHAPTER FOURTEEN KEY

Embrace your freedom

I know it's a lot to take in. So rather than get bogged down in heavy thoughts, forget all this stuff for a second and let me ask you a simple question: What would it be like to be a free spirit?

Take some time to contemplate this. Go sit somewhere out in nature and playfully imagine just this one thing: You are a Free Spirit. Nothing is as you think it is except this one thing:

You are a Free Spirit.

No worries. No concerns. No restrictions. No bills.
No responsibility.

You are a Free Spirit.

No history. No past. No future.

You are a Free Spirit.

What does it feel like?

Are you skipping like a fairy, lightly dancing from flower to flower in a beautiful shaded glade beside a bubbling brook? Dancing amongst the clouds? Laughing your way through the cosmos?

Are you riding a horse across the wind-swept plains of Patagonia? Standing on stage in the limelight, belting out a song, basking in the applause of thousands? Standing on top of Mount Everest?

You are a Free Spirit.

Imagine it. Revel in the feeling, and try to do this everyday. Think of it in terms of lighting a candle ... kindling hope for yourself and all humanity by reminding yourself of your true nature.

You are a Free Spirit lighting the way towards everyone's eternal, glorious freedom.

15

Standing Up

Looking back on my life, it was always the quiet moments that mattered most. The gentle moments sitting in the yard with a cup of tea, watching the mist settle over the hills at sunset. The moments when a deep peace arose within me in odd situations—like standing in line at the grocery store feeling connected with everyone around me. Or sitting in the sand dunes on the cold, wind-swept northern shores of the Pacific coast, pen and journal lying untouched in my lap, so filled with the song of the sea and the salt air, the fine-flung grains of sand and the whisper of sea grasses that I could not write. I could not think.

I could only be.

Sitting here in the pre-dawn dark, writing these closing words, hearing the song of the birds in the distance as they waken, warbling the songs of joy their little bird souls want to sing to the immanently rising sun, I am moved to tears of gratitude. I have a magazine article deadline to meet and a client conference call to prepare for. Instead, I am choosing, wisely or not, to use these precious early morning hours to write these words instead.

Lily is in an apparent downturn, lying on my bed, trying weakly to clean her fur. I am still uncertain if she's going to make it. And, as I think of this valiant kitty hanging in there for all she's worth, I taste different flavored tears at the back of my throat.

In this divine moment I am totally, fully, human.

So, what does it mean, being human?

I am only just now beginning to find out.

Most certainly, being human is not what I once thought it was—a wretched limited thing that needed to be transcended and left behind. The Great Awakening is giving me a whole new picture of myself as a being of unlimited grace and potential who is here on Earth—not to struggle and strive to become greater—but to be what/who I already am. To fully embody my purity and my spirit nature and engage the latest greatest adventure going.

An adventure even the angels long to experience.

There are no limits to what we can become and create. And right now... in this day and time in this modern era ... it seems there is something we must do to assure this beautiful, ongoing creative journey:

We have to stand up for ourselves and for life.

While writing this book, I can't tell you how many people told me I should just focus on good stuff and not bother investigating and writing about evil and all its manifestations. "Love is all that matters," they said. "Just focus on love and let the rest go."

On the surface it sounded right. But what kind of love were they talking about?

Was it the treacly, "never have a negative thought" love keeping us stuck in our habitual mindsets, glued to the matrix? The fluffy, unquestioning love born of spiritual bypassing? Or were they talking about the force that liberates and powers the universe?

And in the end, did it make any difference?

Could I just focus on "the good," and end up where I wanted to go, into the arms of ecstatic living? Or did I have to acquire some semblance of understanding of Who We Really Are and what stands in the way of actually being that again?

That was the question that kept me up at night. Well, actually no. Pretty much nothing keeps me up at night. But I sure wrestled with that whole issue a LOT. And what I've finally realized is: Yes, I think it does make a difference.

Can you stand up in your full power unaware of the energies and programs at play both without and within? Can you flourish without knowing the true source of the subtle feeling of "lessness" stamped into your very soul? The elusive yet bone-deep certainty imprinted upon humanity that something is wrong with us?

Can you thrive while being blindly manipulated, making choices that are leading you down the path to your own potential destruction?

I don't see how.

Maybe a rare few might slip through. But the majority?

This whole conversation reminds me of the last scene in the movie *Dead Poets Society*, where Robin Williams plays the lead role as a private boys' school English teacher named John Keating. A big-hearted realist, Keating is disturbed seeing how the well-heeled teenagers in his class are already burdened with society's expectations of adult responsibility. (Translation: Programmed into a trance of materialism and soulless-ness.)

He uses poetry—especially the impassioned poetry of Walt Whitman—to try to break the spell, that and the power of his own untamed spirit which is ready to give the finger to the whole world if that's what it takes to keep the inner flame in these boys' hearts alive.

Of course, other teachers, the headmaster and some of the boys' parents worry about his bad influence. There is the predictable drama—the fear, yearning, and growing passion in the young men, the scenes of betrayal and death. Ultimately, the powers that be fire Keating from his position.

But in the final scene we know there's hope.

One by one, the boys stand up—they get on top of their desks and stand, honoring Keating as he is leaving the classroom. They stand on their desks and face him, even as the newly installed teacher shouts and stamps and orders them to "Get down!"

They stand.

And they salute Keating with the iconic opening words of the Whitman poem: "O Captain! My Captain!"

> O Captain! My Captain!
> our fearful trip is done,
> the ship has weather'd every rack,
> the prize we sought is won ...

As the music swells, we see fierce pride blaze in Keatings' eyes—pride and hope that the boys will continue to stand up, seeking the freedom of a higher, different view for the rest of their days. And we join him in that hope.

Unfortunately, many of the students remain cowed. They sit at their desks, heads bowed, ashamed to look up, fearful of standing up against authority, fearful even of freedom itself.

> ***It is the act of standing up that differentiates the other students from them.***
>
> ***It is the act of standing that separates the living from the dead.***

The boys' action says, "I see what's happening. I understand where the norm is taking me. I was once under its spell. But now I recognize the death in society's eyes. I feel the coldness of its heart. I know what awaits if I don't stand up and change course."

Action sets them apart.

Action cements their brave new reality in place.

And so it is with us.

As we stand up for freedom and love—even in the face of fierce judgment and opposition—we come into resonance with the life force of the Earth and the rest of the universe. We re-establish our alignment with nature and the frequency of Who We Really Are.

As we shake off other agendas and interference patterns—many of which take the form of our most cherished beliefs—we become clearer and stronger in ourselves. Coming into genuine integrity, we become antennas—beacons of love—emanating this higher frequency to all of humanity.

This is how change happens.

When we crack the matrix and come into electromagnetic coherence with life, we don't have to do a thing. Just being Who We Really Are automatically helps others recalibrate and reorient. As one by one we stand in our power, the old anti-life Force steadily shrinks in the face of our indomitable beauty and growing numbers, fleeing back to the unfathomably barren source from which it sprang.

Bye-bye! Ciao! Sayonara!

Don't let the door hit you in the ass on the way out ...

Awakening is not some sort of magical process that suddenly catapults us from limited human existence into the spiritual equivalent of Oz—a place where pain and suffering, disillusion and sorrow no longer exist. That is a residual dream of heaven from childhood days of religious understanding.

Among other things, actual awakening apparently involves an astonishing and disturbing revisioning of humanity's journey here on Earth—a revisioning that includes recognizing our own goodness in the face of inhuman forces weaving an intricate matrix of global manipulation infiltrating religion/spirituality, economics, education, philosophy, science, medicine, and politics—and waking up out of the dream.

Is this a scary thing to do? Yes, it is. But the initial scary breakthrough quickly morphs into a jaw-dropping new vision of billions of human beings living lives of total freedom, unparalleled potential and unlimited opportunity. Not as a dream, but as a reality.

These are the fierce and beautiful times of The Great Awakening.

The time when leaden eyes open from their slumber and we stretch our grateful limbs, groaning in relief that the ancient nightmare that contained so much restriction, misunderstanding and horror is now over.

We have seen what we are not, and have cast the shadow of the unreal aside.

We have seen what we are not, and finally understand that evil was but a long and sorrowful melody we tried to sing. But the notes could not shape themselves to our tongues for long. We were always destined to spit them out and wash their sour taste away with sweet wine.

So, here we are at the end. Hopefully, by now, you have a whole new perspective and you're itching to stand up. Or perhaps you have a whole new perspective and it's freaking you out. If the latter, from my heart to yours, let me quickly say: If you have ever feared the darkness, either within you or outside of you or both; if you have ever hated yourself and despised your human shortcomings; if you have ever mercilessly judged yourself as bad and just plain wrong ... ask for the real source of that darkness, the real source of those lies to make itself known to you.

Call it forth.

And when it shows up in whatever form or lack of form it takes—a vision, a memory, an insight, a presence, an emotion, a person, a dream, an experience, whatever—stand up and see the truth:

It's not you.

Soak that truth up like a sponge. Bask in it. Revel in it. Taste the freedom ... the release from an ancient judgment. Know you've just opened the door to your core essence:

Purity

It is in recognizing humanity's basic goodness that we arrive at the pivot point where we turn from the darkness of illusion to the light of truth. An awesome power arises and a world of possibilities opens along with it.

And if the idea of turning and facing the anti-life Force that has molested us for so long still frightens you, I get it. Been there. The thing is, once you do this and look evil in the eye and recognize it for what it is—it'll never have a hold on you again. It can't touch you because there's nothing of it within you to latch onto and resonate with. You are unreachable because by recognizing there is nothing of it in you, you are no longer in alignment with its frequency.

Please.

Sit with that for a moment and recognize the key to your ultimate freedom.

Is there anything else to say? Not really, though I suppose I could reiterate that as an infinite continuum with no beginning and no end, life has no creator and *you* have no creator. So don't bother looking for something or someone greater than you to give your power away to. The time for external leaders is past. The time of the religious and spiritual teacher is over.

Once you've stepped out of the matrix and begun to live as Who You Really Are, there is no one right course of action to take. It's all individual. The only guide at that point is the natural voice within.

If you want direction, ask. Then quietly listen and remain open. Life itself will guide you and teach you *life's* rules, which are pretty doggone simple:

- Do no harm. (Stay aligned with life/nature.)
- Try to be aware enough to do no unintentional harm.
- Go where love leads.

That's the best I can come up with on the spur of the moment. Anything that comes along that's counter to those simple rules is counterproductive to life, love and divinity—which are all the same thing.

But hey, don't take my word for it.

Find out for yourself.

Much love and aloha ~

Afterword

The simple psychic message was delivered to Robin as she sat with me on my deck our first morning together, eating cereal.

"What?" Robin put her bowl down and turned to look at Lily, my big Maine Coon cat. Lily flicked her tail, steadily gazing at a bird perched in a nearby tree.

"What's going on?" I asked, puzzled.

Robin raised a quick hand. "Hold on a sec." She turned her attention back to Lily, clearly listening. Then she turned back to me. "She's saying we need to start with me asking you about your grandmother."

Grandma? Despite the heat of the morning, I felt a wave of cold chills, the thought of her instantly transporting me to the sunshiny room my grandparents shared in the huge, rambling farmhouse I was raised in back in Virginia. Grandma lay frozen on her bed, fully dressed as usual, a light blanket tossed over her stocking-clad legs.

I always walked out of that room feeling drained. Suddenly a familiar sensation of suppression filled my being, a smell and taste of my eight-year-old self and a quick flash of decades-old fear washed through my body. I tiptoed over to the bed to gaze at my grandmother's inert form. She was so still. Waxen. Dead while still alive. Nothing moved except sometimes ... *something* ... behind her eyes ...

"What about your grandmother made you so afraid?" Robin asked softly.

In a rush I was back.

It was July, 2022. We were on my deck on Maui. The sun was shining. Lily was grooming herself. I swallowed hard and raised my eyes to Robin's. "She ... wasn't herself. She was ..." *overshadowed, taken, possessed ...* the words flashed through my mind and Robin nodded empathetically.

With that, my next conscious soul retrieval session began.

Over the space of a couple (very intense!) hours, with the support of Robin, I claimed my eight-year-old self out of my grandmother's energy field and released several dark entities that had been with me my whole life.

It was not a pretty process or a quiet one.

Fortunately, I knew what to expect. I'd warned my landlady and the neighbors that they might hear "strange noises" during the week-long personal intensive at my home. But even so, I was shocked at the intensity of the experience. I was shocked at what my child-self had gone through and seen. I was shocked by the extraction of interdimensional beings.

Most of all, I was shocked to have so viscerally verified what I had only recently come to consciously acknowledge was true.

I had completed writing the first draft of this book before the above scene occurred. Because I'd seen behind the curtain, and researched and written about interdimensional beings, I thought I had a total handle on the reality of the situation.

As it turned out, I didn't.

During the writing process, I couldn't help but notice I was caught in an old pattern of feeling driven, possessed even—desperate to get the message out. I was enjoying the creative process. But I wasn't liking the feverish energy behind the drive. Something was going on and for months I puzzled over it. Finally, I brought the subject up in a FaceTime conversation with a close friend on the mainland and was shocked when he lovingly blindsided me with the answer.

"The reason something feels off is because you're being run by the very entities you're writing about," Allen said.

What?" I exclaimed, shocked to the bone. "But I've been meditating for 40 years! And I'm exposing all this stuff!"

"That doesn't mean you're not still being interfered with." He sighed, glanced away, then turned back to pierce me with a level gaze. "I've seen it for years but just didn't know how to bring it up."

"Bring *what* up??"

"There's an energy about you, Cate. A vampiric energy. It's disturbed me for a long time, and for a long time I thought it was just me being overly sensitive. But it's not me. It's you. Well, no. It's not *you*. But there's something in you ... I don't know how else to put it." He took a deep breath. "There's something inside you that wants to *feed*."

To say I was stunned and horrified hearing this would be an understatement. But my friend, being a friend, didn't leave me hanging. He offered me a path to do something about the situation.

"I know someone," he said. "You've heard me talk about her. Robin Duda in Santa Fe. She's a soul alchemist who specializes in soul retrieval. I think she could really help you with this."

~

I got in touch with Robin and liked her immediately. She had this big, comforting, tender, fierce Earth Mother intelligence about her that exuded the message "I'm all about love, but don't fuck with me"—an energy that I trusted and could safely relax into.

We did a couple revealing sessions over zoom, and the cascade of memories and released energies were like a row of dominoes going down. It got so intense she said, "Look. I'm worried about you being able to handle all this alone. You're exposing the whole game, and these interdimensional forces are no joke. I don't want you getting hurt. Either you need to come here to Santa Fe and work with me in person. Or I need to come to you."

Which is how we ended up on my deck here on Maui that morning.

For several days, we explored various energetic entanglements with my mother's mother. Mom had moved back in with her parents after she divorced my biological father in 1954. By the time I became aware of household dynamics, Grandma was pretty much frozen with Parkinson's disease, a beautifully groomed, silent statue decked out in pearls and diamonds and lace, ensconced in the living room. The family rotated around Grandma, tending to her needs, feeding, bathing and dressing her.

It's one thing to hear a minister pound the pulpit about evil or write a book like this one about interdimensional entities and vampiric agendas.

It's one thing to go to a spiritual retreat and have some guru casually mention "negative forces" and how you should wrap yourself in white light and think happy thoughts to keep them at bay. It's another thing altogether to recognize in the midst of a soul retrieval that the reason you spent so much time at age five hiding in the bushes outside the house in terror was because you had seen the black astral snake-beings crawling all over your grandmother, coming in and out of her mouth and body as she sat paralyzed in her gold wingback chair in the living room—disease and other things ruling over her life and body, stealing her voice and very soul, influencing everybody in the household while exuding an energy of remorseless cold indifference.

It was also plain to my five-year-old eyes that the snakes, while invisible to everyone else, were also sucking the life force out of my mother and grandfather. And when my alcoholic stepfather-to-be showed up and married my mom, it was easy to see he was basically possessed as well.

But it wasn't just others that were fed upon.

It took two more visceral, unnerving sessions with Robin for the whole story to come out and the interdimensional beings attached to me along with it. Basically, I had been attacked, fed upon and penetrated by these beings starting at age four. Then, when my grandmother, who was a highly arrogant and greedy woman, died when I was thirteen, I was interfered with again because her death coincided with a stupendous decision on my part.

Up until my freshman year in high school I resisted all attempts to "educate" me. Growing up, I was one of those wild "nature kids," thrilling to the song of Earth, dancing to her rhythms, soaking up the message of growing things on the huge farm in Virginia where I was raised. The trees, the cicadas buzzing in their branches, the hay fields with their heavy seed heads bent and combed by the summer breezes, the mists sparkling with fireflies that cloaked the bottomlands at night ... these things were my nourishment.

I stared death in the face looking into the glazed eyes of a stillborn calf or foal or kitten and saw how nature always refilled the empty wombs and brought new life back again. Nothing was ever still in the natural world. All was movement and everything was connected. The world around me shouted "Run! Dance! Laugh! Frolic! Soak me up! Let me support you as you support me! Live!"

Nature made sense. Unlike the dull, distanced eyes of my parents who sat drinking bourbon with hardened hearts and faces at the kitchen table night after night, these experiences were real. Vibrant. Soul nurturing. The shouts, curses and fights over money were not. The talks about sin and worthlessness by the priest on Sunday mornings were not. The lectures in school about responsibility and the importance of paying attention as the blackboard filled with nonsense were not.

To say the least, I was a disastrous student.

All I could think about in class was getting back outdoors. I couldn't relate to my peers or teachers. Girls my age talked obsessively about boys and parties. Teachers droned on about grammar and New Math. Nobody was interested in talking about the exultant freedom of racing with the wind through tall grasses. No one wanted to hear about riding bareback through the snow late on a full moon night, hearing a nearby fox give its raspy chilling cry, feeling the heat of horseflesh between my thighs, my fingers frigid and numb on the reins.

Why I wasn't held back a grade several times is beyond me. In despair, my parents imprisoned me in boarding school at age thirteen. Separated from the farm and my beloved horses and nature, I withered. After Grandma's funeral, I gave in to the social and parental pressure to study. I consciously decided to buy into the mind and scholastic success and aim for "the good life" that was supposed to flow from those things as an adult.

With that coldly pragmatic decision, my energy field shifted from being aligned with nature's principles to aligning more with my grandmother's avaricious persona. Part of my soul—part of my free-spirited nature—left me. When she died, the interdimensional beings that had feasted on her had more room to enter me, driving me ever further towards previously disinteresting intellectual and materialistic pursuits.

So, how did this influence manifest through me?

I'm still figuring out the whole story, but fundamentally these interdimensional beings are what relentlessly drove me to desperately seek success in the world, hungering for the approval and approbation of others. (The key words here being "desperately" and "hungering.") First, I voraciously went after academic achievement, and then, when I entered the work world, career success.

Disconnected from my heart, ever more disconnected from nature, I had no internal resources and guide posts to lean on. Which meant, as I grew older, I had to learn to feed off external sources—food, sex, the love and approval of others. The entities and my own emptiness drove me to sleep with men I didn't love or even care about. I was driven to drink and smoke to excess and engage in lots of other self-destructive habits. Most of all I was driven to "be somebody" in the world.

Surely success and money and fame would fill me up?

To be clear, I'm not using this as an excuse to play victim and say I was not responsible for my life choices. I'm not playing "The devil made me do it" card as the old saying goes. No. All I'm saying is that these parasitic beings were now part of me, doing their best to get me to augment their energetic food supply by doing self-destructive acts that triggered me into feeling shame, guilt and other yummy emotions.

I'm also not saying there's anything wrong with desiring success or having a strong work ethic. There's nothing wrong with engaging in sex without love and drinking and smoking and doing drugs. That's all a matter of personal choice. But then that's exactly my point. *All those actions weren't strictly flowing from just my personal choice.* Like so many people around the world, I was "under the influence" and didn't know it.

The energy of feeling *driven* to get this book out was just one more example of me not quite being at the wheel of my own life. Feeling driven was actually my own creative energies being deliberately stimulated by these beings so they could be used as an energetic food source.

"But wait!" you might say. "You've written a book about exposing evil. Why would this Force drive you to finish and release it?"

Great question. But remember, the interdimensional beings I've talked about are subtle and manipulative and have an advanced grasp and use of quantum thought technologies. They are completely lacking in emotion and emotional intelligence. In their arrogant, rather robotic way of functioning, if my energies around creating this book can be used as a passing snack on their way to accomplishing the overarching agenda of finally taking over and manifesting fully through us humans, then great.

They don't care about anything else.

Frankly, considering this Force's complete lack of imagination and creativity, it's astonishing how perilously close it has come to accomplishing its goal. Which is exactly why I wanted to include this personal story at the end. I wanted to drive home, one last time, the inherent subtlety of these intelligences and how hard they are to pin down.

Until you have psychically and physically *experienced* their energetics and can learn to tell when they show up and try to influence you, it's still just so much storytelling. Interesting. Chilling for sure. But still somehow unreal. For heaven's sake, I wrote a whole freaking book about these interdimensional beings and didn't even know I was being affected by them.

Hello?

But all that is changing. None of this is actually new. We have tools—if we know to pick them up and use them. And more and more definitive information like this is getting out. Robin and I are currently writing a follow-up book on sacred activism, explaining, amongst other things, how to tell if interdimensional beings are influencing you and/or situations, and what to do about it.

The great news is that right now, together, you and I are standing on the threshold of a totally new creation—a totally new way of living and being in the world. Despite appearances, our future is beyond bright. The New Earth is assured. All we have to do is 1) see the illusions that imprison us, 2) recognize our true nature, and 3) understand that the interdimensional Force that has influenced this world for so long is not us.

Once we do that, we're on our way. Once we see Who We Really Are and align with nature and life, all that's in heaven and on Earth will move to support, deepen and enrich our understanding. Life supporting life. Love supporting love. All of us supporting each other.

Moving forward together.

That's how it works.

Last but not least, I'd like to close with a brief addendum to this story.

Lily, my cat, has been sick for a couple of years with an "incurable" autoimmune disease called feline stomatitis. After much frustration, I asked a homeopathic physician on the mainland (a woman I had interviewed several times for magazine articles on various alternative health topics) if she would be willing to work with her. Bless her heart, she instantly agreed.

By the time Robin arrived on Maui last year, Lily was six months into a homeopathic protocol and responding nicely. However, she was in a healing crisis phase while I was going through the soul retrieval work. At one point Robin warned me that she might decide to check out while she was there.

"Why would she die now?" I asked, gently rubbing Lily's ears as she quietly purred in contentment. "She's doing so well with the remedies."

"She's tired of the negative energy."

"*What?*"

"The same vampiric energy that's been feeding on you has drained her as well *through* you. And she's tired."

Oh my God.

Tears started in my eyes and my fingers became even more tender as I caressed her fur. "Please don't go Lily," I whispered, throat tightening. "I mean, you can if you really really want to. But I'll lighten up. I promise. Just gimme a chance to shift this stuff. Please?"

As of this writing, nine months later, she's still with me, slowly healing. As of this writing, nine months later, so am I.

Life force is returning as I get free of old draining energies. My step is lighter. My mind is less fraught and burdened. I no longer feel driven delivering this book and its message to the world. Best of all, I'm well on my way to not needing other people's acceptance and approval of my words and work to fuel my sense of self-worth.

Of course, I still have times of struggle and uncertainty. But the struggles and issues that arise are only doing so in order to be seen and dealt with—cleared out so that more life energy can flow in and nourish me. Yes, interdimensional entities occasionally show up, seeing if there's room and food available at the Inn. I know I have more work to do in that department. But OMG, what a difference there is in my life already!

I have knowledge and deeply embodied awareness. I feel integrated and solid. I feel *safe* in my body. I have tools. I have support and a clear vision. I have community—people of like-mind and awareness intent on mutual support, advancement, and creation.

I'm spending less and less time looking at the old, pain-wracked world with all its deliberately-created turmoil and insanity. Instead, I'm spending more and more time with my face turned toward the amazing future those of us with the temerity to engage the matrix and crack through it are creating together.

The New Earth has always been inevitable. It's lain dormant in our hearts for eons.

Now, it's time for us to be free enough to come together and build it.

Acknowledgments

To all the teachers, seen and unseen, who dropped kernels for me to peck away at over the years, following the trail to the hard truths exposed in this book—thank you. To Jesse Heron, my steadfast supporter, reader and dear friend—bless your enthusiasm for this work. Yours has been a steady hand to hold every step of the way on this journey into crazy unknown waters.

To my friend and colleague Sandie Sedgbeer—what would I do without you? Our rich conversations mean so much to me. And your endless connections to just the right people, sending them and their research my way at just the right time have been such a blessing!

To Robin Duda who came late to the party but who has been such an extraordinary inspiration, truth teller, advocate, healer and friend. You have safely and lovingly taken me deep into the land of "knowing through experience" exactly what the anti-life Force is and how it operates through us. My gratitude and thanks overflow.

To my agent, Lisa Hagan. How many authors are lucky enough to find a fan and a friend and an agent all rolled into one? Bless your candid feedback and willingness to help even when I stray into the land of self-publishing. To Michael Mann—my very first publisher at Watkins way back in 2012. Thank you for wanting to publish this latest work and yet also for encouraging me to spread my wings and get this message out to the world myself in quick-step fashion. And thank you Damian Keenan for the amazing cover and interior layout!

To all the intrepid doctors, nurses, researchers, journalists, whistle blowers, friends and copatriots on this journey who have stood up firmly and staunchly for truth and life and humanity during the insanity of the Covid years, bless you eternally.

To Jacqueline Hobbs (aka Oracle Girl)—thank you for your intrepid service to life and your zero-bullshit truth telling. You are an ongoing inspiration and helpmeet to all of us learning and expressing Who We Really Are.

To Paul Levy, Paul Wallis and other brave wayshowers—Zacharia Sitchin, Erich von Däniken, David Icke and many more—thank you for your courage and willingness to take off the blinders and help the rest of us to do the same.

Resources

The following is a brief listing of alternative sources of information to give you a start. Books marked with an asterisk * I consider essential reading.

Don't be surprised if some of the medical and Covid-related links in the footnotes section are no longer functioning. Much information that has managed to make it onto public platforms that is damaging to official government narratives has been removed or altered over time.

Also don't be surprised when you discover that all the doctors cited in this section have been blacklisted and defamed by the legacy media.

A Few Books

Chariots of the Gods, Erich von Däniken, Berkley Books (January, 1999)

Escaping from Eden, Paul Wallis, Axis Mundi Books (May, 2020)

Fingerprints of the Gods: The Evidence of Earth's Lost Civilization, Graham Hancock, Crown; Reissue edition (April, 1996)

History is Wrong, Erich von Däniken, New Page Books, first edition (August, 2009)

Return to Innocence: My Journey to Claim Wholeness from Ancestral Ritual Abuse, Beth Bennett, 2020

State of War: The Secret History of the CIA and the Bush Administration, James Risen, Free Press, (2006)

* *The Art of War*, by Sun Tzu, Fingerprint! Publishing (December, 2018)

The Biggest Secret: The Book That Will Change the World, David Icke, David Icke Books; 2nd Updated ed. edition (January, 1999)

* *The Creature from Jekyll Island* by G. Edward Griffin, American Media; 5th edition (January, 2010)

The Gods Never left Us, Erich von Däniken, Weiser; First edition (November, 2017)
The Great Reset: Joe Biden and the Rise of Twenty-First-Century Fascism, Glenn Beck, Forefront Books (January, 2022)
* *The Real Anthony Fauci: Bill Gates, Big Pharma, and the Global War on Democracy and Public Health*, Robert F. Kennedy Jr., Simon & Schuster (2021
The Scars of Eden, Paul Wallis, 6th Books (April, 2021)
**The Trap: What It Is, How It Works, and How We Escape Its Illusions,* David Icke Books, (September, 2022)
The Truth About COVID-19: Exposing the Great Reset, Lockdowns, Vaccine Passports, and the New Normal, Dr. Joseph Mercola, Chelsea Green Publishing (April, 2021)
* *The Unseen Hand: An Introduction to the Conspiratorial View of History* by Ralph Epperson, Publius Press (1985)
War of the Gods, Erich von Däniken, New Page Books (September, 2020)

A Few Alternative News Sources

https://www.breitbart.com/news/
https://www.brighteon.com/
https://www.coasttocoastam.com
https://www.corbettreport.com/
https://davidicke.com/
https://expose-news.com/
https://freedomplatform.tv/
https://hannenabintuherland.com/
https://londonreal.tv/
https://newstarget.com
https://newswars.com/
https://plandemicseries.com/
https://www.theepochtimes.com
https://thehighwire.com/
https://www.worldviewweekend.com/
https://yournews.com/

A Few Alternative Medical Sources

Alliance for Natural Health - https://anh-usa.org/

Front Line COVID-19 Critical Care Alliance (FLCCC) - https://covid19criticalcare.com/

Dr. Zach Bush - Doctor of internal medicine and endocrinologist with a focus on the microbiome as it relates to health, disease, and food systems. https://zachbushmd.com/

Dr. Carrie Madej - Doctor of internal medicine researching vaccines and nanotechnology.https://www.carriemadej.com/

Dr. Robert Malone - Medical doctor specializing in biotechnology and clinical trials development. An internationally recognized scientist/ physician and the original inventor of mRNA vaccination, DNA vaccination, and multiple non-viral DNA and RNA/mRNA platform delivery technologies, Dr. Malone holds numerous fundamental domestic and foreign patents in the fields of gene delivery, delivery formulations, and vaccines including for fundamental DNA and RNA/ mRNA vaccine technologies. https://www.rwmalonemd.com/

Dr. Peter McCullough - Board certified in internal medicine, cardiovascular diseases, and clinical lipidology. He has over 1000 publications and 600 citations in the National Library of Medicine. Dr. McCullough is a founder of the Cardiorenal Society of America and is the editor-in-chief of Reviews in Cardiovascular Medicine and senior associate editor of the American Journal of Cardiology. https://petermcculloughmd.com/

Dr. Joseph Mercola - Osteopathic physician and founder of the Natural Health Center. https://www.mercola.com/

Dr. Lee Merritt - Doctor specializing in Orthopaedic and Spinal Surgery, Merritt is on the Board of the Arizona Medical Association and is past president of the Association of American Physicians and Surgeons. https://drleemerritt.com/

Dr. Christiane Northrup - Board certified in Obstetrics and Gynecology, Northrup is an authority in the field of women's health and wellness. In 2013 she was named by *Reader's Digest* as one of "The 100 Most Trusted People in America." https://www.drnorthrup.com

Dr. Larry Palevsky - Licensed pediatrician, who utilizes a holistic approach to children's wellness and illness. https://darachi.com/

Dr. Sherri Tenpenny - Board Certified in Emergency Medicine and Osteopathic Manipulative Medicine and founder of Tenpenny Integrative Medical Center. https://drtenpenny.com/

Dr. Geert Vanden Bossche - DVM and PhD in Virology, he has worked in vaccine R&D for vaccine companies such as GSK Biologicals, Novartis Vaccines, and Solvay Biologicals. He then joined the Bill & Melinda Gates Foundation's Global Health Discovery team in Seattle (USA) as Senior Program Officer; he then worked with the Global Alliance for Vaccines and Immunization (GAVI) in Geneva as Senior Ebola Program Manager. https://www.geertvandenbossche.org/

Dr. Michael Yeadon - PhD biochemist, toxicologist and pharmacologist, worked at the Wellcome Research Labs with Salvador Moncada with a research focus on airway hyper-responsiveness and effects of pollutants. Worked in drug discovery of 5-LO, COX, PAF, NO and lung inflammation. He served as Vice President & Chief Scientific Officer of Allergy & Respiratory at Pfizer Global R&D. An Independent Consultant and Co-founder & CEO of Ziarco Pharma Ltd., Dr. Yeadon has published over 40 original research articles and now consults and partners with a number of biotechnology companies. https://totalityofevidence.com/

Vaccine Recovery

The following is a list of resources for people who are interested in finding mitigation protocols for the Covid "vaccines," as well as a link to sites where people experiencing severe vaccine reactions can connect with others.

Connect with Others
Real not Rare: https://www.realnotrare.com
UK CV Family: https://www.ukcvfamily.org/

General Health Support
People's Health Alliance: https://the-pha.org/about-us/

Spike Protein Detox and Treatment Protocols
FLCCC Alliance: Post-Vaccine Treatment: https://covid19criticalcare.com/covid-19-protocols/i-recover-post-vaccine-treatment/

World Council for Health: Spike Protein Detox Guide: https://worldcouncilforhealth.org/resources/spike-protein-detox-guide/

Graphene Detox
The Exposé article – Zinc Inhibits Influenza Virus, Covid and Helps Our Body Detox from Graphene: https://expose-news.com/2021/12/30/zinc-inhibits-influenza-virus-covid-and-helps-our-body-detox-from-graphene/

The Exposé article – How to Remove Graphene Oxide from The Body: https://expose-news.com/2022/02/16/how-to-remove-graphene-from-the-body/

Other Recommended Sources
Jacqueline Hobbs (Oracle Girl): https://www.oraclegirl.org/
Robin Duda: https://www.sustainablelove.com/

Soul Alchemy Empowerment Process

(repeated from Chapter six)

You can start off either laying down or sitting.

- Connect with your breath and your body sensations, opening up to an awareness of your inner landscape.
- Take a few minutes to ground into your body and connect.
- Place your attention on your heart center and focus on anything you are grateful for. This will help your heart open and allow you to sense that opening through loving sensations.

Now, stand up.

- Reach your arms above your head about shoulder length apart. From the awareness of your heart, feel the fullness of your chest and say out loud:
    - *"From the power of One Love that I am, I invoke my multi-dimensional soul and my Source in my body. I welcome all that I am to come home in present time."*
- Move your body any way that opens and releases tension. Shake, jiggle, jump, circle your arms ... whatever is spontaneous and energizing. Do this as long as you feel you should. This builds up your energy body.
- Now, speak with clarity and strength:
    - *"I call forth the power of love from this Earth and Source-Spirit to unite in my body in my heart. I claim my right to my Sovereign Self. Love is my greatest power."*

Repeat as many times as you feel moved to do so while directing your awareness inward as you speak. *Your voice is your will choosing and claiming your heart's desire.*

- Now, say out loud:
    - "I release all projections from family, work, lovers, friends, clients, (etc.) that are in my field."

- With your breath and movement, push out anything that is intruding into you energetically.
- When you feel clear, next say:
    - *"I release all mind control from media, technology, educational systems, political systems (etc.) that are suppressing my own thoughts and inspirations."*
- With your breath and movement, push these energies out through the top of your head and clap around your body while you keep moving.
- When you feel clear, say aloud:
    - *"I bless free all interdimensional energies that are not mine that are attached to my denied fear or emotions. I bless any one else's emotions that I have taken on and I send them back to their own source."*
    - *"I release all entities and forces from known and unknown sources wishing me harm. I release everything that is not loving for me and send them back to their own source."*
    - *"I release any forms of control over my will of love and my power!"*

- When you feel clear, give thanks to Earth and your Multidimensional Self and feel the Love and your own Soul's essence filling you up.
- Take your time and feel the love. Bask in feeling connected to life and aligned with the Life Force that is you.

Endnotes

Chapter 2

1 Energy centers in the body identified by Eastern medicine and metaphysics

2 Translated from the Timpone Grande and Campagno Orphic tablets

3 https://en.wikipedia.org/wiki/Derinkuyu_underground_city

4 https://thinkaboutit.site/underground/egypt-underground/

5 https://www.bibliotecapleyades.net/arqueologia/esp_malta02.htm

6 https://www.blavatsky.net/index.php/bnet-newsletters/61-foundation/tf-newsletters/reed-carson-newsletters/703-tunnels-of-gold-under-andes

7 https://www.ancientpages.com/2022/03/21/riddle-of-the-ancient-lost-city-beneath-missouri-a-puzzlingdiscovery/

8 https://www.bibliotecapleyades.net/sociopolitica/esp_sociopol_underground18b.htm

9 https://www.bibliotecapleyades.net/branton/esp_offlimits_6a.htm

10 Wetiko: Healing the Mind Virus That Plagues Our World, Paul Levy, Inner Traditions, 2021

11 https://rsarchive.org/Lectures/GA177/English/RSP1993/19171007p01.html

12 https://physics.stackexchange.com/questions/478409/visible-light-as-fraction-of-the-em-spectrum

Chapter 3

13 https://www1.cbn.com/cbnnews/us/2020/april/new-barna-survey-more-americans-believe-in-satanthan-believe-in-god

14 https://newspunch.com/satanism-fastest-growing-religion/

15 https://pubmed.ncbi.nlm.nih.gov/7960286/

16 American Psychiatric Association, Diagnostic and Statistical Manual of Mental Disorders (5th ed.), Arlington: American Psychiatric Publishing, 2013

17 https://www.youtube.com/watch?v=taU3p8-Bbc4&ab_channel=StrangePlanet

18 https://www.dailymail.co.uk/news/article-8077785/Nazi-photo-album-HUMAN-SKIN-death-camp-victimdiscovered.html

Chapter 4

19 https://journeyfree.org/religious-trauma-syndrome-articles/

20 https://journeyfree.org/religious-trauma-syndrome-articles/

21 https://pubmed.ncbi.nlm.nih.gov/24029109/

Chapter 5

22 https://www.hopkinsmedicine.org/health/wellness-and-prevention/mental-health-disorder-statistics

23 https://www.cdc.gov/nchs/health_policy/adult_chronic_conditions.htm

24 https://drugabusestatistics.org/

25 https://www.cdc.gov/suicide/facts/index.html

26 https://www.aoasm.org/assets/docs/bodine.pdf

27 https://www.autismspeaks.org/autism-statistics-asd

28 https://anh-usa.org/half-of-all-children-will-be-autistic-by-2025-warns-senior-research-scientist-at-mit/

29 https://www.cnbc.com/2022/03/08/as-prices-rise-64-percent-of-americans-live-paycheck-to-paycheck.html

30 https://www.bloomberg.com/opinion/articles/2021-05-19/toilet-waste-to-tap-water-welcome-to-the-future-of-recycled-sewage

31 https://time.com/5942290/eat-insects-save-planet/

32 https://www.independentsentinel.com/celebrities-now-pushing-us-to-eat-bugs-no-no-and-nope/

33 https://www.nytimes.com/2022/07/23/style/cannibalism-tv-shows-movies-books.html

34 https://archive.ph/Funys

35 http://bitelabs.org/

36 https://www.weforum.org/agenda/2018/07/good-grub-why-we-might-be-eating-insects-soon/

37 https://www.nature.com/articles/ncomms11382

38 https://www.wbcsd.org/Overview/News-Insights/WBCSD-insights/An-exciting-future-for-positive-agriculture-at-a-global-scale

39 https://www.intelligence.senate.gov/sites/default/files/hearings/95mkultra.pdf

40 https://www.britannica.com/science/information-theory/Physiology

41 https://www.technologyreview.com/2009/08/25/210267/new-measure-of-human-brain-processing-speed/

42 Tanabe, Rosies, Rubin vase. New World Encyclopedia, July 2015

Chapter 6

43 From Aion: Phenomenology of the Self published in The Portable Jung, edited by Joseph Campbell, Penguin Books, 1976, p. 145

44 The substance sought by alchemists for its supposed ability to transform base metals into gold—ametaphor for the key to enlightenment and immortality.

45 http://sustainablelove.com

Chapter 7

46 https://age-of-the-sage.org/mysticism/world_religions_populations.html

47 Wallis, Paul, The Scars of Eden: Has humanity confused the idea of God with memories of ET contact?, 6TH Books, 2021

48 Erich von Däniken, Chariots of the Gods, Souvenir Press; New Ed edition (June 27, 2019)

49 Ibid.

50 Op. cit.

51 https://www.newsweek.com/donald-trump-aware-aliens-verge-disclosing-public-israeli-ex-space-chiefsays-1553354

52 https://evolutionnews.org/2012/08/a_big_bang_theo/#fn108

53 https://www.sciencedaily.com/releases/2005/01/050111165229.htm

54 Ibid.

55 https://en.wikipedia.org/wiki/Mitochondrial_Eve

56 http://www.sitchin.com/adam.htm

57 Genesis 1:26-27

58 https://newsrescue.com/ancient-200000bc-human-metropolis-found-in-africa/

Chapter 8

59 https://www.businessinsider.com/these-6-corporations-control-90-of-the-media-in-america-2012-6?op=1

60 https://childrenshealthdefense.org/defender/blackrock-vanguard-own-big-pharma-media/

61 https://www.frbsf.org/education/publications/doctor-econ/2003/september/private-public-corporation/

62 https://www.adn.com/voices/article/colonialism-wreaked-havoc-alaska-native-peoples/2009/02/05/

63 https://www.csun.edu/science/health/docs/tv&health.html

64 https://www.csun.edu/science/health/docs/tv&health.html

65 https://news.stanford.edu/news/2005/july13/med-tv-071305.html

66 https://www.webmd.com/parenting/news/20110503/survey-too-much-tv-time-at-day-care-centers

67 Robert F. Kennedy address to Vermont Town Hall. https://www.youtube.com/watch?v=j2UJ2oBeya0&t=387s

68 https://www.pewresearch.org/internet/2008/09/16/teens-video-games-and-civics/

69 https://www.center4research.org/violent-video-games-can-increase-aggression/

70 https://www.gamespot.com/articles/study-89-percent-of-parents-believe-game-violence-aproblem/1100-6402290/

71 https://www.pewresearch.org/internet/2020/07/28/parenting-children-in-the-age-of-screens/

72 J Abnorm Child Psychol. 2016 Jan; 44(1): 75–86.

73 https://www.nbcnews.com/think/opinion/iq-rates-are-dropping-many-developed-countries-doesn-tbode-ncna1008576

74 BMJ 2021;374:n203, “COVID-19: Children born during the pandemic score lower on cognitive tests, study finds” 4 iScience. 2021 Oct 12;24(11):103262. “Role of adipocyte Na,K-ATPase oxidant amplification loop incognitive decline and neurodegeneration”

75 Diabetes Metab Syndr Obes. 2019 Oct 24;12:2221-2236.
76 https://www.westonaprice.org/health-topics/nutrition-greats/weston-a-price-dds/
77 https://www.fao.org/news/story/en/item/1173588/icode/
78 JAMA. 2019;322(20):1996-2016. doi:10.1001/jama.2019.16932
79 https://www.cnn.com/2018/01/08/health/child-mortality-rates-by-country-study-intl/index.html
80 https://www.cnn.com/2018/01/08/health/child-mortality-rates-by-country-study-intl/index.html
81 https://www.hopkinsmedicine.org/health/wellness-and-prevention/mental-health-disorder-statistics
82 https://www.cdc.gov/nchs/health_policy/adult_chronic_conditions.htm
83 https://drugabusestatistics.org/
84 https://www.cdc.gov/suicide/facts/index.html
85 https://www.cdc.gov/suicide/facts/index.html
86 https://www.autismspeaks.org/autism-statistics-asd
87 https://anh-usa.org/half-of-all-children-will-be-autistic-by-2025-warns-senior-research-scientist-at-mit
88 https://pubmed.ncbi.nlm.nih.gov/25355584/
89 https://childrenshealthdefense.org/defender/blackrock-vanguard-own-big-pharma-media/
90 https://www.businesswire.com/news/home/20220208005226/en/Pfizer-Reports-Fourth-Quarter-and-Full-Year-2021-Results
91 https://www.pharmaceutical-technology.com/news/moderna-reports-revenue-2021/
92 https://www.psychologytoday.com/us/blog/dangerous-ideas/201910/psychology-s-dark-triad-and-the-billionaire-class
93 Ibid.
94 https://www.cbsnews.com/news/big-tobacco-kept-cancer-risk-in-cigarettes-secret-study/
95 https://www.bbc.com/news/business-35339475
96 https://www.ctvnews.ca/world/26-individuals-are-as-wealthy-as-half-of-all-humanity-combined-oxfamreport-1.4262012
97 https://www.youtube.com/watch?v=Alyi7PjZljI&ab_channel=Let%27sMakeCanadaGreatAgain%21
98 Ibid.
99 Ibid.
100 https://en.wikipedia.org/wiki/George_Soros
101 https://www.opensocietyfoundations.org/who-we-are
102 https://townhall.com/columnists/rachelmarsden/2016/08/17/leaked-soros-foundation-docs-revealmachiavellian-agenda-n2205931
103 https://www.youtube.com/watch?v=hL9uk4hKyg4&t=509s&ab_channel=WorldEconomicForum

104 https://www.youtube.com/watch?v=NV0CtZga7qM&ab_channel=IceAgeFarmerResources

105 https://www.gmc-limousines.com/News/world-economic-forum-2020-wef-in-davos-after-improvingthe-state-of-the-world-you-may-as-well-spend-an-extra-week-in-the-swiss-alpine.html

106 https://www.younggloballeaders.org/

107 https://www.dailymotion.com/video/x7y4pxt

Chapter 9

108 https://news.gallup.com/opinion/chairman/212045/world-brokenworkplace.aspx?g_source=position1&g_medium=related&g_campaign=tiles

109 https://www.bloomberg.com/graphics/2021-payday-loan-lenders/

110 https://www.sunshinebehavioralhealth.com/resources/mental-health-issues-facing-generation-z/

111 https://www.tlnt.com/hr-we-have-a-problem-up-to-80-of-employees-dont-trust-us/

112 https://www.nytimes.com/2000/04/02/us/vast-trade-in-forced-labor-portrayed-in-cia-report.html

113 https://www.ilo.org/global/about-the-ilo/newsroom/news/WCMS_574717/lang--en/index.htm

114 https://www.theroot.com/how-many-slaves-landed-in-the-us-1790873989

115 Vonderlehr, R.A., Clark, T., Wenger, O.C., Heller, J.R., Untreated Syphilis in the Male Negro, Journal of Venereal Disease Information. 17:260-265, (1936)

116 https://www.pbs.org/newshour/show/u-s-military-exposed-minority-soldiers-toxic-mustard-gas

117 https://themillenniumreport.com/2017/09/illegal-human-experimentation-conducted-by-the-c-i-a-in-the-united-states-abridged-list/

118 Behind the Fog: How the U.S. Cold War Radiological Weapons Program Exposed Innocent Americans, Lisa Martino-Taylor, Routledge press, 2018

119 https://www.atomicheritage.org/history/atomic-veterans-1946-1962

120 Toxicologic Assessment of the Army's Zinc Cadmium Sulfide Dispersion Tests: Answers to Commonly Asked Questions. https://www.ncbi.nlm.nih.gov/books/NBK233549/

121 https://bioethicsarchive.georgetown.edu/achre/

122 https://www.businessinsider.com/biological-agents-were-tested-on-the-new-york-city-subway-2015-11?op=1

123 https://en.wikipedia.org/wiki/Operation_Sea-Spray

124 https://www.dailymail.co.uk/news/article-2210415/Revealed-Army-scientists-secretly-sprayed-St-Louis-radioactive-particles-YEARS-test-chemical-warfare-technology.html

125 https://en.wikipedia.org/wiki/Project_ARTICHOKE

126 https://en.wikipedia.org/wiki/Project_MKUltra

127 https://www.intelligence.senate.gov/sites/default/files/hearings/95mkultra.pdf

128 https://www.nytimes.com/1975/06/11/archives/summary-of-rockefeller-panels-cia-report-the-fundamental-issues-a.html

129 https://en.wikipedia.org/wiki/Edward_Snowden

130 https://www.nvic.org/nvic-archives/newsletter/vaccinereactionjune1996.aspx

131 https://www.scirp.org/journal/paperinformation.aspx?paperid=81838

132 https://www.nytimes.com/2001/09/04/world/us-germ-warfare-research-pushes-treaty-limits.html

133 https://themillenniumreport.com/2017/09/illegal-human-experimentation-conducted-by-the-c-i-a-inthe-united-states-abridged-list/

134 Ibid.

135 https://www.newdawnmagazine.com/articles/the-secret-origins-of-aids-facts-fallacies-conspiracy-theories

136 Ibid.

137 https://www.cdc.gov/coronavirus/2019-ncov/hcp/planning-scenarios.html

138 https://www.cdc.gov/mmwr/volumes/70/wr/mm7008e3.htm?s_cid=mm7008e3_w

139 https://pubmed.ncbi.nlm.nih.gov/33342929/

140 "Ivermectin for Prevention and Treatment of COVID-19 Infection: A Systematic Review, Meta-analysis, and Trial Sequential Analysis to Inform Clinical Guidelines," American Journal of Therapeutics: July/August 2021 -Volume 28 - Issue 4 - p e434-e460

141 https://www.isglobal.org/en/healthisglobal/-/custom-blog-portlet/ivermectina-del-suelo-a-laslombrices-y-mas-alla/3098670/0

142 https://newsrescue.com/the-undeniable-ivermectin-miracle-indias-240m-populated-largest-state-uttar-pradesh-horowitz/

143 https://www.fda.gov/regulatory-information/search-fda-guidance-documents/emergency-use-authorization-medical-products-and-related-authorities#footnote6

144 https://www.forbes.com/sites/forbesdigitalcovers/2021/05/14/virus-book-excerpt-nina-burleigh-how-the-covid-19-vaccine-injected-billions-into-big-pharma-albert-bourla-moncef-slaoui/

145 https://expose-news.com/2022/05/09/confidential-pfizer-docs-90percent-pregnancies-miscarried/

146 https://www.medalerts.org/vaersdb/findfield.php?TABLE=ON&GROUP1=CAT&EVENTS=ON&VAX=COVID19

147 https://speedtheshift.wordpress.com/2016/02/18/it-is-estimated-that-only-1-10-of-all-vaccine-adverse-reactions-are-ever-reported-to-vaers/

148 https://www.ncbi.nlm.nih.gov/pmc/articles/PMC59524/

149 https://allenandabaray.com/duract/

150 https://papers.ssrn.com/sol3/papers.cfm?abstract_id=3949410

151 https://insulinresistance.org/index.php/jir/article/view/71/224

152 https://expose-news.com/2022/10/24/deaths-of-american-under-25s-is-soaring/

153 https://www.thepostemail.com/2022/06/20/the-latest-tragedy-sudden-adult-death-syndrome/

154 https://goodsciencing.com/covid/athletes-suffer-cardiac-arrest-die-after-covid-shot/

155 https://www.biznews.com/health/2022/10/13/pfizer-vaccine-transmission

156 https://www.kusi.com/bill-gates-says-Covid-is-kind-of-like-the-flu-and-that-the-vaccines-are-imperfect/

157 https://www.weforum.org/agenda/2021/02/covid-employment-global-job-loss/

158 https://www.pewresearch.org/fact-tank/2020/09/04/a-majority-of-young-adults-in-the-u-s-live-with-their-parents-for-the-first-time-since-the-great-depression/

159 https://www.cdc.gov/mmwr/volumes/69/wr/mm6932a1.htm

160 American Institute for Economic Research: https://www.aier.org/article/cost-of-us-lockdowns-a-preliminary-report/

161 https://www.weforum.org/agenda/2021/05/america-united-states-covid-small-businesses-economics/

162 https://nypost.com/2020/07/18/corporations-are-buying-houses-robbing-families-of-american-dream/

Chapter 10

163 https://www.weforum.org/about/the-fourth-industrial-revolution-by-klaus-schwab

164 https://www.youtube.com/watch?v=hL9uk4hKyg4&ab_channel=WorldEconomicForum

165 https://medicalxpress.com/news/2020-12-brain-implants-enable-simultaneously-prosthetic.html

166 Musk, E. (2017). *Elon Musk on AI and The New Future 2017.* Western Culture. Available online at: https://www.youtube.com/watch?v=SYqCbJ0AqR4

167 https://www.youtube.com/watch?v=eZuJ4WyJNGQ&ab_channel=WorldLeader

168 https://www.nanowerk.com/what_are_quantum_dots.php

169 https://pubmed.ncbi.nlm.nih.gov/35631579/

170 https://pubmed.ncbi.nlm.nih.gov/32531395/

171 https://pubmed.ncbi.nlm.nih.gov/19730421/

172 https://www.drrobertyoung.com/post/transmission-electron-microscopy-reveals-graphene-oxide-in-cov-19-vaccines

173 https://anamihalceamdphd.substack.com/p/self-assembly-nanostructures-in-c19

174 https://coronavirus.delaware.gov/wp-content/uploads/sites/177/2021/05/20210513-Vaccine-Component-and-Allergy-Information.pdf

175 Journal of Pharmacology and Experimental Therapeutics October 2019, 371 (1) 121-129;

176 Curr Med Chem. 2017;24(22):2359-2391.

177 J Pharm Pharmacol. 2015 Dec;67(12):1650-62.

178 www.CDC.gov/coronavirus/2019ncov/hcp/planning:scenarios.html; and https://www.cdc.gov/mmwr/volumes/70/wr/mm7008e3.htm?s_cid=mm7008e3_w

179 https://www.nytimes.com/interactive/2021/world/covid-vaccinations-tracker.html

180 https://www.theguardian.com/society/2021/jan/15/covid-vaccine-passports-what-are-they-and-do-they-pose-a-danger-to-privacy

181 https://www.ctvnews.ca/politics/banks-begin-unfreezing-accounts-of-freedom-convoy-supporters-finance-official-1.5791589

182 https://sfbayview.com/2012/12/electroshock-torture-handcuffs-now-patented-deliver-shocking-torture-gas-injections-and-chemical-restraints-to-prisoners-via-remote-control/

183 https://lynnemctaggart.com/the-leaf-intention-experiment/

184 https://Covid19criticalcare.com/

Chapter 11

185 https://www.biologicalmedicineinstitute.com/post/2019/09/20/schumann-resonances-and-their-effecton-human-bioregulation

186 https://pubmed.ncbi.nlm.nih.gov/30503683/

187 https://news.berkeley.edu/2018/07/12/awe-nature-ptsd/

188 https://www.ncbi.nlm.nih.gov/pmc/articles/PMC4997467/

Chapter 12

189 https://www.osho.com/osho-online-library/osho-talks/love-here-and-now-inner-being-4abe3b4e-3ea?p=481c4b4a8faf68baef89ea665dd23c4c

190 https://en.wikiquote.org/wiki/Albert_Einstein_and_politics

Chapter 13

191 "Thought and Consciousness"; http://etresoi.ch/krishnamurti/q/44.html

192 http://srinisargadattamaharaj.com/

193 Atria/Enliven Books, 2017

Chapter 14

194 https://www.oraclegirl.org/

About Cate Montana

Photo by Barbra Kates

A professional journalist specializing in alternative medicine and health, since her (surprise!) awakening in 2007, Cate Montana has written four extremely different books: a feminist memoir, *Unearthing Venus: My Search for the Woman Within* [Watkins 2013], an explanation of the ego and enlightenment, *The E Word, Ego Enlightenment & Other Essentials* [Atria 2017], and a spiritual novel, *Apollo & Me* [Rampant Feline Media 2019].

Her latest book, *Cracking the Matrix: 14 Keys to Individual & Global Freedom*, takes a deep dive into the nature of evil, global agendas and how to develop an individual pathway to freedom. She is co-author of *The Heart of the Matter* with Dr. Darren Weissman [Hay House 2013] and writes for the UK health magazine *What Doctors Don't Tell You*. www.wddty.com. She has a master's degree in psychology and lives on the island of Maui in Hawaii.

www.catemontana.com

Ingram Content Group UK Ltd.
Milton Keynes UK
UKHW020633120523
421641UK00014B/220

9 798218 093501